The
MOFFATT
NEW TESTAMENT COMMENTARY

Based on *The New Translation* by the
REV. PROFESSOR JAMES MOFFATT, D.D.
and under his Editorship

THE GOSPEL OF MARK

The Moffatt New Testament Commentary

MATTHEW
BY THEODORE H. ROBINSON, D.D.

MARK
BY B. HARVIE BRANSCOMB, PH.D.

LUKE
BY W. MANSON, D.D.

JOHN
BY G. H. C. MACGREGOR, D.D.

THE ACTS OF THE APOSTLES
BY F. J. FOAKES-JACKSON, D.D.

ROMANS
BY C. H. DODD, D.D.

I CORINTHIANS
BY JAMES MOFFATT, D.D.

II CORINTHIANS
BY R. H. STRACHAN, D.D.

GALATIANS
BY GEORGE S. DUNCAN, D.D.

PHILIPPIANS
BY J. H. MICHAEL, D.D.

COLOSSIANS, PHILEMON AND EPHESIANS
BY E. F. SCOTT, D.D.

HEBREWS
BY THEODORE H. ROBINSON, D.D.

THE GENERAL EPISTLES
BY JAMES MOFFATT, D.D.

THE PASTORAL EPISTLES
BY E. F. SCOTT, D.D.

THE JOHANNINE EPISTLES
BY C. H. DODD, D.D.

THESSALONIANS
BY WILLIAM NEIL, M.A., B.D., PH.D.

REVELATION
BY MARTIN KIDDLE, M.A.

THE GOSPEL OF MARK

BY
B. HARVIE BRANSCOMB
M.A. (Oxon.), Ph.D.
*Professor of New Testament, Duke University
Durham, North Carolina*

HARPER AND BROTHERS PUBLISHERS
NEW YORK

6-86

gift from J.H.

EDITOR'S PREFACE

MOFFATT'S NEW TESTAMENT COMMENTARY

THE aim of this commentary is to bring out the religious meaning and message of the New Testament writings. To do this, it is needful to explain what they originally meant for the communities to which they were addressed in the first century, and this involves literary and historical criticism; otherwise, our reading becomes unintelligent. But the New Testament was the literature of the early Church, written out of faith and for faith, and no study of it is intelligent unless this aim is kept in mind. It is literature written for a religious purpose. 'These are written that ye might believe that Jesus is the Christ, the Son of God.' This is the real object of the New Testament, that Christians might believe it better, in the light of contemporary life with its intellectual and moral problems. So with any commentary upon it. Everything ought to be subordinated to the aim of elucidating the religious content, of showing how the faith was held in such and such a way by the first Christians, and of making clear what that faith was and is.

The idea of the commentary arose from a repeated demand to have my New Testament translation explained; which accounts for the fact that this translation has been adopted as a convenient basis for the commentary. But the contributors have been left free to take their own way. If they interpret the text differently, they have been at liberty to say so. Only, as a translation is in itself a partial commentary, it has often saved space to print the commentary and start from it.

As everyman has not Greek, the commentary has been written, as far as possible, for the Greekless. But it is based upon a first-hand study of the Greek original, and readers may rest assured that it represents a close reproduction of the original writers' meaning, or at any rate of what we consider that to have been. Our common aim has been to enable everyman to-day to sit where these first Christians sat, to feel the impetus and inspiration of the Christian faith

EDITOR'S PREFACE

as it dawned upon the minds of the communities in the first century, and thereby to realize more vividly how new and lasting is the message which prompted these New Testament writings to take shape as they did. Sometimes people inside as well as outside the Church make mistakes about the New Testament. They think it means this or that, whereas its words frequently mean something very different from what traditional associations suggest. The saving thing is to let the New Testament speak for itself. This is our desire and plan in the present commentary, to place each writing or group of writings in its original setting, and allow their words to come home thus to the imagination and conscience of everyman to-day.

The general form of the commentary is to provide a running comment on the text, instead of one broken up into separate verses. But within these limits, each contributor has been left free. Thus, to comment on a gospel requires a method which is not precisely the same as that necessitated by commenting on an epistle. Still, the variety of treatment ought not to interfere with the uniformity of aim and form. Our principle has been that nothing mattered, so long as the reader could understand what he was reading in the text of the New Testament.

JAMES MOFFATT.

CONTENTS

INTRODUCTION

	PAGE
THE READERS FOR WHOM THE GOSPEL WAS INTENDED	xiv
WHERE THE GOSPEL WAS WRITTEN	xv
THE PURPOSE OF THE GOSPEL	xviii
THE SOURCES OF THE GOSPEL	xxii
THE ARRANGEMENT OF THE MATERIALS	xxvi
THE DATE OF THE GOSPEL	xxix
THE AUTHOR	xxxi

COMMENTARY

I. THE TITLE 3

II. THE BEGINNING OF THE GOSPEL (i. 1–13) . . 5
   i. 1–3 : 'As was Prophesied by Isaiah' . . . 5
   i. 4–8 : The Prophet in the Desert 10
   i. 9–11 : The Baptism of Jesus 16
   i. 12–13 : The Temptation 20

III. THE MINISTRY IN GALILEE (i. 14–viii. 26) . . 23
   i. 14–15 : Jesus Appears in Galilee 23
   i. 16–20 : The Call of Four Galilean Fishermen . . 26
   i. 21–22 : Jesus Teaches in the Synagogues . . 28
   i. 23–28 : Jesus Casts Out an Unclean Spirit . . 26
   i. 29–31 : Peter's Mother-in-Law is Healed . . 32
   i. 32–39 : Crowds of Sick People at the Door . . 34
   i. 40–45 : A Leper is Healed 36

CONTENTS

	PAGE
CONTROVERSIES WITH THE SCRIBES AND PHARISEES (ii. 1–iii. 6)	41
ii. 1–12 : The Healing of the Paralytic	41
ii. 13–17 : The Dinner in Levi's House	48
ii. 18–20 : Why Do Not Your Disciples Fast ? . . .	52
ii. 21–22 : Two Sayings on the Separation of the New from the Old	54
ii. 23–28 : The Disciples Pluck Grain on the Sabbath . .	55
iii. 1–6 : A Healing in the Synagogue on the Sabbath .	59
iii. 7–12 : Crowds Come From a Distance	62
iii. 13–19 : The Names of the Twelve	63
iii. 20–21 : Jesus' Family is at a Loss to Explain His Deeds	67
iii. 22–27 : ' By Beelzebub He Cast Out Demons ' . .	69
iii. 28–30 : Blasphemy Against the Holy Spirit is Unforgivable	73
iii. 31–35 : Who Are My Mother and My Brothers ? .	75
iv. 1–2a and 10–12 : Jesus' Use of Parables . . .	76
iv. 2b–9 and 13–20 : The Parable of the Sower . .	79
iv. 21–25 : Two Parables on the Revealing of Hidden Truth	81
iv. 26–29 : The Parable of the Seed which Grows of Itself .	82
iv. 30–34 : The Parable of the Mustard-Seed . . .	85
iv. 35–41 : Jesus Quiets a Storm on the Sea of Galilee .	86
v. 1–20 : The Possessed Man of Gergesa	88
v. 21–43 : The Healing of Jairus' Daughter and an Unnamed Woman	93
vi. 1–6 : The Rejection at Nazareth	96
vi. 7–13 : The Mission of the Twelve	101
vi. 14–16 : Popular Rumours about Jesus	105
vi. 17–29 : The Death of the Prophet John . . .	107
vi. 30–44 : The Feeding of the Five Thousand . . .	111
vi. 45–52 : Jesus Walks Upon the Water	116
vi. 53–56 : The Sick Crowd Around Jesus Wherever He Goes	118
vii. 1–16 : The Controversy over the Ritual Washing of Hands	119
vii. 17–23 : The Meaning of the Saying in vii. 15 . .	127
vii. 24–30 : A Syrophœnician Girl is Healed . . .	128
vii. 31–37 : ' He Makes the Deaf Hear and Dumb Speak ' .	133
viii. 1–10 : The Feeding of Four Thousand . . .	135
viii. 11–13 : The Demand for a Sign	137
viii. 14–21 : ' Beware of the Leaven of the Pharisees and of Herod '	139
viii. 22–26 : Jesus Restores the Sight of a Blind Man in Bethsaida	141

CONTENTS

	PAGE
IV. THE MESSIAH IN SECRET (viii. 27–xiii. 37)	143
viii. 27–33 : 'Thou Art the Christ!'	144
Did Jesus Regard Himself as the Messiah?	145
viii. 34–ix. 1 : Sayings on the Consequences of Discipleship or its Refusal	154
ix. 2–8 : Jesus is Transfigured Before His Disciples	159
ix. 9–13 : Jesus Forbids the Disciples to Tell What They Had Seen, and Explains the Prophecy of Elijah's Return	163
ix. 14–29 : The Healing of an Epileptic Boy	165
ix. 30–32 : The Second Prediction of the Passion and the Resurrection	167
ix. 33–37 : On True Greatness and On Service in the Name of Christ	168
ix. 38–41 : The Exorcist Who Was Not a Follower	170
ix. 42–50 : Sayings Concerning Hindrances	172
x. 1 : Jesus Enters Judæa and Peræa	175
x. 2–12 : The Question about Divorce	176
x. 13–16 : The Blessing of the Children	179
x. 17–27 : A Rich Man Asks what he Must Do to Gain the Life of the Kingdom	180
x. 28–31 : The Reward of Discipleship	184
x. 32–34 : The Third Prediction of the Passion	185
x. 35–40 : The Request of the Sons of Zebedæus	186
x. 41–45 : On True Greatness	189
x. 46–52 : The Healing of the Blind Son of Timæus	191
THE MINISTRY IN JERUSALEM (xi–xiii)	193
xi. 1–11 : The Entry into Jerusalem	195
xi. 12–14 : The Cursing of the Fig Tree	200
xi. 15–19 : The Cleansing of the Temple Courts	202
xi. 20–25 : Sayings on Faith and Prayer	206
xi. 27–33 : The Question Concerning Jesus' Authority	207
xii. 1–12 : The Parable of the Wicked Vinedressers	209
xii. 13–17 : Jesus is Asked as to His Attitude toward Paying Taxes to Cæsar	212
xii. 18–27 : The Question about the Resurrection	215
xii. 28–34 : The First Commandment	219
xii. 35–37 : The Messiah is not David's Son but David's Lord	222
xii. 38–40 : Jesus Warns Against the Scribes	225
xii. 41–44 : The Widow's Gift to the Temple	227
xiii. 1–2 : 'The Temple Will Be Destroyed'	228
THE APOCALYPTIC DISCOURSE (xiii. 3–37)	231
xiii. 3–5 : Introduction to the Apocalyptic Discourse	233
xiii. 6–13 : The Beginning of the End	234
xiii. 14–23 : The Appearance of the Antichrist	236
xiii. 24–37 : The Parousia of the Son of Man	238

CONTENTS

V. THE DEATH AND RESURRECTION OF JESUS (xiv. 1–xvi. 8) 241

    xiv. 1–2 : Priests and Scribes Plot to Secure Jesus' Execution before the Feast 242
    xiv. 3–9 : The Anointing in Bethany 243
    xiv. 10–11 : Judas Turns Traitor 247
    xiv. 12 : Was the Last Supper the Passover Meal ? . . 249
    xiv. 13–16 : The Preparations for the Last Meal of Jesus with His Disciples 255
    xiv. 17–21 : Announcement of Judas' Betrayal . . . 257
    xiv. 22–25 : The Last Supper 258
    xiv. 26–31 : Jesus Foretells the Disciples' Desertion of His Cause and His Resurrection Appearance in Galilee . . 264
    xiv. 32–42 : Gethsemane 266
    xiv. 43–52 : The Arrest 268
    xiv. 53–54 : Jesus is Delivered to the Jewish Authorities . 271
    xiv. 55–64 : The Examination Before the High Priest . 277
    xiv. 65 : Mockery and Blows from the High Priest's Attendants 280
    xiv. 66–72 : The Denial of Peter 281
    xv. 1–5 : The Trial before Pilate 283
    xv. 6–15 : ' Jesus or Barabbas ' 288
    xv. 16–20 : Mockery by Roman Soldiers 290
    xv. 21–32 : The Crucifixion 291
    xv. 33–39 : The Death of Jesus 295
    xv. 40–41 : The Women Watch from a Distance . . 299
    xv. 42–47 : The Burial 301
    xvi. 1–8 : ' He Has Risen ; He is not Here ' 304
    xvi. 9–20 : The Endings Which Have Been Added . . 311

INTRODUCTION

THE Gospel according to Mark, as the book with which this study is concerned is commonly known, was the first of the Gospels to be written. Not only is it thus the earliest extant record of the events of Jesus' life, but it is virtually the only record. For careful study has shown that it is Mark's life of Christ which underlies Matthew and Luke, while John, who also had read Mark, is interested rather in interpreting the familiar story. And yet in spite of the basic importance of this work in Christian history we know virtually nothing about it except what can be learned from its own pages. True, there is the oft-quoted passage from Papias, a bishop of Hierapolis in Asia Minor in the second century, which states that it was written by Mark, the interpreter of Peter. But the passage is too brief, too isolated, and too enigmatic in some of its phrases to be very helpful, even if it be accepted without question. We are therefore dependent upon a painstaking and repeated study of the Gospel itself for information concerning it.

Such study has been carried on for a full century. The Gospel which stands forth as the result is one of contrasts and antitheses. Written in Greek, it is yet the 'most Aramaic' of the Gospels. Though the story it narrates took place in Palestine, the Gospel comes from the Hellenistic world, quite probably from as far west as Rome. It records at the same time primitive traditions and reminiscences, and the developed convictions of the Church a generation or more after Christ's death. Though it relates a series of historical events, the author's interest is clearly not in history for its own sake but for its value to faith and practice. These and other antitheses, together with some questions to which no final answers are available, have produced a vast literature in which widely divergent views are represented. Yet out of the discussion and study certain basic conclusions are becoming generally accepted.

THE GOSPEL OF MARK

THE READERS FOR WHOM THE GOSPEL WAS INTENDED

The Gospel was certainly composed for Christian readers. For words, ideas, and personages which would not be familiar to non-Christians are introduced in the story without comment or explanation. Such terms as 'the Spirit,' 'baptism,' 'the gospel,' 'the Kingdom of God,' would have been meaningless to pagan readers. We read that 'John came baptizing in the wilderness,' that 'it was in those days that Jesus arrived from Nazareth,' that He called 'Simon and Andrew his brother,' without being told who these persons were. It is evident that the names were familiar to those who would read the book. That the stories are presented in virtually the form in which they circulated in the Christian communities indicates that no other audience was being addressed.

It is equally evident that these Christian readers were not Palestinians, but, to use a general term, were Hellenists. This is indicated in the first place by the fact that the Gospel is in Greek. In recent years efforts have been made to demonstrate that this was not the case, that not only Mark but all the Gospels were written in Aramaic, and that what we have are Greek translations. The argument thus far has not proved convincing. Parallels in Hellenistic Greek writings have been adduced for a great many of the alleged Aramaisms. Not only is there no trace of any Aramaic forms of the Gospel, but there is no patristic evidence that such ever existed. In addition, there are positive objections to the Aramaic hypothesis, some of them linguistic, some derived from the study of the Synoptic Problem. Mark is a Greek Gospel, though the material bears many signs of the Aramaic origin of constituent elements.

Other considerations support this indication of language. The greater number of the Old Testament quotations are cited from the Septuagint or Greek version. Those Aramaic words and phrases which are retained in the text are all translated into Greek. References to details of life in Palestine are frequently explained (vii. 2, xii. 18, xv. 42, etc.). The theological point of view of the Gospel, furthermore, is that

INTRODUCTION

of the Hellenistic Christian Churches of the first century. Such terms as the 'gospel' or 'good news' to designate the Christian message, 'Christ' as a proper name (see ix. 41), 'the Son of God' as a preferred title of Jesus, and such basic ideas as the abolition of the Jewish food laws, and the obligation of preaching the gospel to the whole world, show the background of experience and the mental affiliations of the writer.

Where the Gospel was Written

It is thus clear that the Gospel was written for one of the Christian centres of the Hellenistic world. An endeavour to determine its provenance more definitely is dependent upon a Christian tradition that it was written at Rome.

The earliest direct witness to this tradition is Clement of Alexandria at the close of the second century. Clement states that Mark, Peter's follower, wrote the book at the request of Peter's Roman hearers. The tradition, however, can be traced back earlier. Irenæus, in the third book of his work *Against Heresies*, written while Eleutherus was Bishop of Rome (A.D. 174-189), makes the following statement:

> 'Matthew published his Gospel among the Hebrews in their own language, while Peter and Paul were preaching and founding the Church in Rome. After their death, Mark, the disciple and interpreter of Peter, also transmitted to us in writing those things which Peter had preached; and Luke, an attendant of Paul, recorded in a book the gospel which Paul had declared. Afterward John . . . published his Gospel while staying in Ephesus in Asia.'

The reference to Rome here is quite pointless unless Irenæus means that Mark and Luke arose there. That he specifies carefully the localities in which Matthew and John were produced strengthens the impression that this is his meaning as regards the other two as well. His statement is valuable evidence as to the accepted beliefs in the West at the time. For Irenæus had resided in Rome and frequently appeals to the open tradition of the Roman Church.

Earlier than Irenæus there is only one statement which has been preserved concerning the origin of the Gospel. This is a famous passage which Eusebius quotes from Papias, bishop of Hierapolis in Asia Minor in the first half of the second century. Papias declared that he preferred the living voice to the things written in books and so inquired regularly of those who could tell him the words and deeds of the apostles. Among his informants was the Presbyter John, whom he describes as one of the 'disciples of the Lord.' His statement is so important for the origins of Mark that it may as well be quoted in full at this point:

> 'This also the Presbyter said: Mark having become the interpreter of Peter, wrote down accurately though not indeed in order whatsoever things he remembered of the things said or done by Christ. For he neither heard the Lord nor followed Him, but afterwards, as I said, he followed Peter who adapted his teaching to the needs [of the hearers] but with no intention of giving a connected account of the Lord's discourses. So that Mark committed no error in writing some things as he remembered them. For he was careful of one thing, not to omit any of the things which he had heard, and not to state any of them falsely.'
> (*Church History*, iii. 39.)

In this passage the tradition that the author of the Gospel had been connected with Peter is carried back to the Presbyter John—that is, to the end of the first or beginning of the second century. But nothing is said here of the origin of the Gospel at Rome. One might conclude that the earliest tradition of the Church knew nothing of this, the connection with Rome being a later development. But there is a final piece of evidence coming from a date as early as the Presbyter John which shows that this was not the case. In 1 Pet. v. 13 appears the greeting, 'The church that is in Babylon salutes you, and Mark my son.' The epistle is generally regarded as having been written after Peter's death, but it was probably by the end of the first century, and certainly by A.D. 115 when Polycarp quotes it. Babylon here is almost certainly a symbolic name for Rome, as in a number of the Jewish apoca-

INTRODUCTION

lypses. This presence of a salutation from the Roman Church and Mark, in an epistle written in Peter's name about the end of the century, indicates very definitely the existence of a tradition at the time which brought together Mark and Peter in Rome. Papias's statement which omits the reference to Rome appears, therefore, to preserve only in part the traditions concerning the Gospel current in the Church at the beginning of the second century. The belief of Irenæus and Clement of Alexandria that the Gospel was written in Rome can thus be traced back to the first century.

Is this part of the tradition dependable? There is no way by which it can be proven or disproven, but there is one piece of internal evidence which strongly supports it.

In the second century there existed a divergence between the practice of the Churches of Asia and a number of others led by the Church of Rome, as regards the date of the Easter celebration. It can be demonstrated that this divergence went back at least to the beginnings of that century. The Asiatic Churches celebrated Easter on Nisan 14th, the Jewish Passover, whatever day of the week this happened to be. The Roman Church celebrated the festival always on the Sunday of the resurrection, regarding the Asiatic custom as a Judaizing practice. The Roman Christians argued, as a fragment preserved from Apollinaris shows, that ' on the 14th the Lord ate the sheep with His disciples, but Himself suffered on the great day of unleavened bread '—that is, His death was subsequent to the Passover. The details of this controversy are given in the note on xiv. 12. The point to note here is that the dating of the Passion story in Mark is in agreement with the Roman contention. Furthermore, this is achieved by the definite assertion of a date in xiv. 12 which is at conflict with indications in the rest of the story. The evangelist, in other words, has modified his Passion story so as to make its dating of the Last Supper agree with what we know to have been the Roman view. This, of course, does not prove a Roman origin for the Gospel, since there were other Churches also which rejected the Asiatic practice. However, the Roman Church led the opposition, and this chronology, taken together with the Church tradition which has been cited, points strongly toward the capital city.

To these positive arguments must be added a negative one : there is no alternate tradition or claim concerning the Gospel's place of origin except a late suggestion that it was written in Egypt. This is refuted by the earlier testimony of Clement of Alexandria, and is derived obviously from the tradition that Mark was the first Bishop of Alexandria. The fact of Roman origin would explain, furthermore, the Gospel's ready acceptance and rapid dissemination. Rome was an ideal distributing centre, and the influence and prestige of that Church would have given the Gospel standing and authority, even though it was known that its author had neither seen nor heard the Lord. In the absence, therefore, of reasons to the contrary, it would seem reasonable to regard the early tradition that Mark was written in Rome as worthy of acceptance.

The Purpose of the Gospel

The Gospel, as already remarked, was intended for Christian readers. There are no indications that the writer had in mind appealing to pagans. The explanations and exhortations which one would expect in such a case are completely absent.

Its object or purpose is to be gleaned from its contents. These are the deeds and, to a limited extent, the sayings of Jesus. The only additional material consists of a few introductory sentences about John, the prophetic forerunner, and a popular version of his death at the hands of Herod of Galilee. The material concerning Jesus deals with a variety of themes : the beginning of His work, His conflicts with the religious leaders of the Jews, some of His parables, the names of His twelve chosen disciples, some of the wonderful works which He performed, His disciples' declaration that He was the Messiah, His teaching on some important subjects, the events which led up to His death. It would appear from this that the writer undertook to provide his readers with information about Jesus, in whose saving work he and they confidently believed. To put it simply, the members of the Christian community in the

INTRODUCTION

Hellenistic city in which Mark wrote wished to know more about Jesus, and the Gospel was produced to meet this need. But Mark's motive was not that of a modern historian. He had no thought, for example, of preserving a record for the use of future generations, for, like his Christian brethren, he believed that the present age would soon pass away. Nor did he write with the idea of explaining or making understandable the central figure of his book, as do modern biographers. All ancient biography was written from a different standpoint—that of holding up the deeds and accomplishments of a great individual for the admiration and emulation of less heroic persons. This was especially true of the evangelist, for the subject of his book was God's chosen and endowed representative, whose teachings and example were to be obeyed and whose life had brought to men a way of salvation. Mark is interested, therefore, not in material in which a modern biographer would be interested, but rather in religiously valuable information. This included teachings of Jesus on important subjects such as divorce, the resurrection, and the chief commandments. It also included the facts about the relation of Jesus and His followers to Judaism—a problem with many aspects—and also to the Roman authority. It included the story of the beginnings and the meaning of the most important Christian rites. Above all, it included the story of the causes and circumstances of Jesus' death, since it was very necessary that Christians be not misinformed on that subject. All this information was of practical religious value, and its importance to the Christian believers certainly determined its selection.

So impressed have scholars been with this religious interest and purpose on the evangelist's part that there has been a tendency more recently to describe Mark as a theologian rather than a historian, and his book as a theological tract. One writer, for example, calls the Gospel a 'theological pamphlet.' To a certain extent this point of view is correct, and one must be careful not to become involved in an argument over words. The real question is not whether the evangelist is interested in theological questions or even makes his own contribution to them, but whether that is the primary character of the Gospel and the conception of it which will enable one to understand it most fully and correctly. Though Mark is interested in theological beliefs, this conception of him and his work neglects and obscures other features of the Gospel in such a fashion as to be a very misleading description. In particular it tends to lead to two errors.

The first of these is the assumption that the Gospel was written to maintain certain specific doctrines or beliefs. Usually some one theme is made the key to the entire Gospel. The refutation of this is to be seen in the inadequacy of the various theological theses which have been postulated to explain the contents of the Gospel. Ropes, for example, assumes as the purpose of the Gospel the explanation of the paradox that the Messiah had suffered a criminal's death. This is obviously one of the writer's more important interests. But one must ask what, on this assumption, is the point of such material as the introduction about John, the stories of the call of the first disciples, the parables of the Kingdom, many of the miracle stories, and other data not directly connected with the problem of the Messiah's death? Other theological themes which have been proposed, such as the revelation of the secret Messiahship of Jesus, are similarly inadequate to account for the various episodes and sayings. Only by increasing the number of the theological interests so that they cover most aspects of the life of Jesus in which early Christians were interested can this point of view be maintained. For the Gospel supplies information on too many points to be reduced to a single theme. It can be understood only as the writer's answer to the desire of early Christians for information on many aspects of the life of Jesus.

The description of Mark primarily as a theologian is very likely to lead to a second error. This is the assumption that the theology to be found in the Gospel is Mark's theology. Here again the question is one of degree and of specific instances, for Mark has his convictions as to Jesus' work, and gives expression to them in his book. Yet a reading of the commentary will show that the theological beliefs which the

INTRODUCTION

Gospel stories convey are predominantly the work of the early Christian movement, not of the evangelist. Thus the doctrine of Jesus as the Son of Man had been embraced by the Church so long before Mark wrote as to have become an inseparable part of many of the stories preserved in the tradition, as, for example, the Transfiguration story, the saying about the Messiah being David's lord, the story of healing the paralytic, the account of the trial before the Sanhedrin and others. Nor was it Mark who formulated the story of Jesus' baptism, with its conviction that at that moment Jesus had been endowed with the Holy Spirit and declared to be God's son. It was the early Church which sought out the Old Testament passages which seemed to have points of connection with the events of Jesus' life and made them an inseparable part of the narrative of the events. What the evangelist does for the most part is to tell the story of Jesus' life as it was known and understood in Christian circles. Fact and theology had already been combined in this tradition, and what is often described as Mark's theology is really the early Christian belief as to the historical facts.

Mark was by no means indifferent to matters of belief, and he presents clearly his understanding of Jesus' work on a number of points. Probably the most important of these was the question of Jesus' Messiahship, which he conceives of in terms of the heavenly Son of Man. He is careful to bring this out, guarding against and correcting the idea that Jesus thought of Himself as a Messiah of a political sort. He also believes strongly that none of the Jewish food laws was binding any longer, that the followers of Jesus must suffer persecution as did their Leader, that the Kingdom of God will come before many years, that Jesus' contemporaries were unworthy of receiving the full revelation of His Messiahship and His teaching and therefore much was concealed from them. As he recounts the events of Jesus' life, these and other beliefs are clearly expressed.

The contrast of information and interpretation, or history and theology, is really a false antithesis. It has meaning only in terms of relative importance. All history is really interpretation. By selection, emphasis, and explanation the bare events of time are given unity and meaning. Of this, the Christian account of the life of Jesus is the supreme example. In the events of His life His followers saw the working out of a divine purpose for man's salvation. From the beginning the career and its interpretation became one. The routine and unimportant details were dropped out, while the significance and meaning of other events inevitably and unconsciously became a part of the narrative. Thus the theological interpretation of Jesus' life was an inseparable part of the Church's recollections of Him, even before the story was committed to writing. Mark takes over these elements in this tradition along with the rest and undoubtedly added to them. To ask whether the Gospel is a theological or historical work is thus to set up a false alternative. It is both. But dogma and doctrine seem plainly secondary with the evangelist to telling the Christian story as it was known and believed in the Churches of the Hellenistic world a generation after Jesus' death.

The Sources of the Gospel

Where did the author get the materials out of which his account is built ? Until recently the answer was based on the statement of Papias quoted above, and the Gospel was often described as the Memoirs of Peter. The last half century of study has definitely eliminated this comfortable and easy answer. For it has become increasingly apparent that instead of the simple, direct testimony of an eyewitness we have an account made up by piecing together materials of different origin and date. While Peter figures prominently in a number of the narratives, there is no impression of freshness and exactness of detail such as to suggest an immediate personal source. While some of the stories doubtless go back to Peter ultimately, they have had a considerable history before they were incorporated in the Gospel. In the face of these facts, the view that the Gospel contains Peter's reminiscences falls to the ground.

In the work itself one finds abundant evidence that the

INTRODUCTION

author has made use of a number of written sources. Unfortunately, none of these is extant, and we are therefore much in the dark as regards the extent and character of some of them. But of their existence and Mark's use of them there can be no doubt. Blocks of material dealing with a single theme and with a fitting conclusion standing in the midst of a narrative not topically arranged, connecting links, not due to the evangelist, between episodes which would have been independent of each other in a purely oral tradition, stylistic characteristics in certain sections different from the rest of the Gospel, all constitute positive evidence of documentary sources.

The extent to which Mark rests on these earlier writings has not been sufficiently recognized, due no doubt to the absorption of scholars in recent years with the study of the oral tradition. It is only necessary to enumerate the more certain of these sources to make it clear that the Gospel rests to a large extent on earlier writings :

1. The series of conflicts between Jesus and the Jewish religious leaders narrated in ii. 1–iii. 6 evidently came to the editor in written form. This is generally accepted. But the source from which this came also contributed some further material. For in xii. 13 there appears another conflict episode introduced by a reference to the combination of Pharisees and Herodians against Jesus with which iii. 6 closes. The Herodians as a party are not mentioned elsewhere in ancient literature. Nowhere else does Mark mention this combination of opponents, nor do the contents of either section suggest their names. It seems plain that there is a connection between the two passages, and the influence of a written source would seem to be the natural explanation. But how much more this document supplied, whether the one additional episode only, or the section from xii. 13 to xii. 34, cannot be said with assurance.

2. Chapter xiii. is also recognized as having existed in writing previous to the composition of the Gospel. The evangelist, however, may have inserted some additional verses. The reasons for regarding this section as an independent unit are stated in the commentary.

3. Chapter iv. contains a group of parables concerning the Kingdom of God, all of which bear upon the missionary endeavours of the early Church. The formula, ' He who has ears to hear, let him hear,' appears at the end of two of these parables and nowhere else in Mark. The section seems to rest upon a written source which, however, has been expanded, probably in part by the evangelist.

4. The Passion story certainly existed in written form. From xiv. 1 on we have a detailed account, with exact notes of place and time, such as is not to be found in the previous portion of the book. The distinctive character of this account can be explained only on the assumption that this part of the story had already been put into writing.

5. The names of the Twelve in iii. 16 ff. are taken from a written list. One notes the very awkward introductory words, the separation of Andrew from Peter in spite of the close association of the two in i. 16, and the absence of any mention of most of the names in the rest of the Gospel.

6. In view of the use by Matthew and Luke of some document or documents giving further information about John the Baptizer, it seems more than likely that the compact summary of the prophet's work in chapter i. has been abbreviated from some written account.

7. It has long been recognized that citations from the Scriptures in Mark, as in the other Synoptic Gospels, were taken from early Christian collections of proof texts, rather than from the Scriptures themselves.

8. In addition to these sources which stand out more or less clearly there are numerous indications of the use of other written records which are so obscured that they cannot be described with any definiteness. One can only be assured that they lie behind the present writing. One of the most important and intriguing of these sources is one which seems to have contained information about episodes which took place around the Sea of Galilee. Such a documentary source is indicated by the place names which are attached to a number of the episodes in the middle of the Gospel, as well as by some indications of connections between certain episodes. The

INTRODUCTION

topographical references in vi. 45 and 53 and in chapter viii., for example, are quite incidental and unnecessary. They do not clarify the account—which might make one attribute them to the evangelist—but rather confuse it. Nor does Mark habitually provide such data for his narratives. They cannot be attributed to an oral tradition, the drift of which would be quite away from such meaningless statements as the one in viii. 10. The only satisfactory explanation of these details would seem to be that Mark had available some document in which this data was preserved. We are quite in the dark, however, as to the extent or character of this document. Chapter v. has also been thought to have come from a written source, since the stories here differ strikingly in wealth of detail from similar narrations elsewhere in the Gospel, and seem to be connected with each other. The presence of an Aramaic phrase in the midst of the Greek of this chapter points in the same direction, since oral traditions are not usually in two languages. Outside these sections there are some indications of the use of written materials, but they are too scattered and indefinite to provide any clear idea of the sources from which they have been taken.

A review of this data, even granting that some of it may be misread, points to the conclusion that by far the greater part of the Gospel rests upon documentary sources.

These early documents of the Christian movement seem to have been short. As one would expect, they deal with subjects of vital interest to the Church—Jesus' interpretation of the Jewish law, the signs of the coming Kingdom, the obligation and fruitfulness of Christian preaching, the circumstances of the crucifixion. Some of them arose in Palestine certainly—the apocalyptic chapter, with its concern with the temple; the conflict stories dealing with Palestinian issues; the basic account of the Passion. But it is also apparent that these documents had been developed subsequently, and this in the direction of Hellenistic interests and ideas. The evidence for this as regards the conflict stories, the Passion narrative and probably the apocalyptic chapter will be found in the commentary. While one does not like to make sweeping generalizations on such a subject, yet so far as the evidence goes it indicates that the documents which Mark used had come to him through the medium of Christian circles in the great sea-coast towns of the Hellenistic world.

In addition to these documentary sources it is no doubt true, as is commonly assumed, that the evangelist made use of oral traditions. The existence of such traditions even as late as well into the second century is specifically attested by the statement of Papias that he preferred these to the written records. Narratives which seem independent of other sections in the Gospel may well have come to the writer by this means. The account of the healing of the leper in i. 40 ff. is attributed with plausibility to such a source. One might guess that the story of the execution of John the Baptizer rested also on popular oral tradition. Oral tradition would likewise have preserved its version of events narrated in the documents, and thus would have supplied details for the expansion or modification of stories which Mark takes from these sources. The oral tradition would also have supplied certain very general ideas as to the course of Jesus' life, which would have guided the evangelist in the arrangement of his materials. But this phase of its contribution will be discussed in the next section.

The Arrangement of the Materials

From the data surveyed in the preceding section it appears that the Gospel was based on a number of short written records supplemented by oral traditions. Unless one assumes that a number of these had already been strung into a consecutive story making a sort of pre-Marcan Gospel—a hypothesis which cannot be disproved, but for which there is no convincing evidence—it is clear that the evangelist's tasks would be primarily those of selection, emphasis, and arrangement. The first of these would be governed by his sense of what would be of most interest to, and value for, his readers. But how would he be guided when it came to the arrangement of the materials into a consecutive account?

INTRODUCTION

In recent years this question has received a good deal of attention, due to the study of the general character of the early Christian traditions. The more these are examined the more independent and unconnected the original stories and sayings appear to have been. By the time they were reduced to writing most of them had already lost all notes of chronology and topography. Nor were the first Christian scribes particularly interested in such matters. So long as one was concerned merely with a collection of incidents dealing with a single theme, such as Jesus' attitude toward the law, it did not matter at what point in the ministry the episode took place. The case was the same with a collection of Jesus' sayings. The Apocalyptic Discourse, for example, did not carry any indication of time or occasion. But when the Christian writer Mark undertook to gather a number of these records into a consecutive account, the question of their proper order had to be dealt with.

So impressed have scholars been with the disparate character of the oral and, consequently, the subsequent written tradition, that some have been inclined in recent years to deny any value whatever to the order in which Mark has arranged his materials. But this again is to overdo the case. Mark had some guidance for this part of his work. In particular three guiding principles should be mentioned:

(1) Although individual episodes and sayings tended to become timeless and placeless, there can be little doubt that the Church preserved in its oral tradition a general idea of the character of Jesus' public activity. Professor Dodd has pointed out that a skeleton outline of the ministry is preserved in more than one of the speeches in Acts. In Acts x. 37 ff. there is one of the fullest of these outlines. In his speech to Cornelius, Peter mentions that Jesus' home was Nazareth, that His work began with the preaching of John, that He ' went about doing good and healing all who were oppressed of the devil,' that He was first in Galilee and then in Judæa and Jerusalem, and that after His crucifixion He appeared alive to those witnesses whom God had chosen. Most of this outline is to be found also in Acts xiii. 23–31. Parts of it are echoed

in i. 22, ii. 22 f., iii. 13 ff. Even such general knowledge as that Jesus' work began with John's preaching, consisted first of an itinerant ministry in Galilee, and was concluded in Jerusalem, would be of very great assistance to an editor of the early Christian records. This general outline Mark follows consistently. He begins with the work of John, and Jesus' connection with him. Then follows the Galilean ministry. He has no information concerning Jesus' visits to Judæa previous to the last one, and all material which relates to the temple or belongs in Judæa—such as the question concerning the tax to Cæsar—he reserves for the latter part of his book. While this principle may not be accurate in each case, it is no doubt sound in the main.

(2) With this general outline in mind a second source of assistance would have been such topographical and chronological references as were preserved in the earlier writings. These, indeed, were not frequent, but there were some. Events placed at Capernaum, or at places around the Sea of Galilee, would naturally fall into place in the earlier part of the account. On the other hand, episodes connected with Jericho or Bethany are placed in the second half. A journey from Galilee to Jerusalem connects the two sections.

(3) A third guide for the organization of his material Mark finds in the tradition that toward the close of the Galilean ministry Jesus' disciples recognized Him as the Messiah. This tradition most probably came to him in one of his written sources. It provided a clue for the arrangement of the data. Material in which the Messiahship was involved is placed after this confession—the Transfiguration, the request of the sons of Zebedee, the parable of the vineyard, the saying that the Christ was not David's son, practically all sayings in which the title Son of Man appears. Whether this principle of arrangement is sound depends, of course, upon the historical accuracy of the tradition involved. Such a story as that of Cæsarea Philippi seems to the present writer not only likely, but almost necessary, to explain the subsequent events. If the tradition be granted, its use as a principle of arrangement is in general a sound procedure. Its value becomes immediately

INTRODUCTION

apparent from a comparison of Mark with the Fourth Gospel in which no such principle is maintained.

These principles which the evangelist had to guide him are no guarantee obviously of the correctness of Mark's arrangement throughout. His lack of exact and detailed information on many points is indicated by two facts. As regards chronology, one cannot tell from the Gospel how long Jesus' ministry lasted. As to location, Mark knows of no visits to Jerusalem other than the last one, a presentation unlikely in itself, and contradicted by the traditions of the Fourth Gospel. Only in its general lines can one regard the arrangement as dependable. A study of the psychological development of Jesus' ideas from Mark's account, for example, is quite out of the question. Nevertheless, Mark's major principles of arrangement seem sufficiently sound to regard his presentation of Jesus' work as, in general, a dependable and trustworthy picture.

The Date of the Gospel

There is no difficulty in defining the limits of a period of about fifteen or twenty years within which the Gospel was written.

The later limit is fixed by the use of Mark by the compilers of Matthew and Luke. Both of these Gospels were written before the close of the first century. Allowing a few years earlier for Mark would give a limit of about A.D. 85. On the other side we have the statement of Irenæus that Mark and Luke were written after the deaths of Peter and Paul. Since the tendency of the early Church was to carry the Gospels back as early as possible, this tradition which Irenæus repeats can no doubt be trusted. Peter and Paul were believed to have perished in the Neronian persecution in A.D. 64–65, which may be taken as the earlier limit. This would give the period from A.D. 64 to A.D. 85 as that in which the Gospel was composed.

With this general dating various internal indications are in agreement. Mark ix. 1, ' There are some of those standing here who will not taste death until they see the coming of God's reign with power,' implies a date when the greater number, but not all, of the first generation of Christians had passed away. The reference in xiii. 9 to standing before governors and kings seems to have in mind Paul's trials before the Roman procurators and at Cæsar's Court. The statements in xiii. 12 f. of individuals delivering up members of their own family ' to death,' and of being ' hated by all men,' are most naturally explained as referring to Nero's persecution of the Christians in Rome. All this would mean after A.D. 65. On the other hand, the words placed in Jesus' mouth in xiii. 30, ' I tell you truly, the present generation will not pass away till all this happens,' fix the end of the century as the outside limit. Some such a period of thirty-five or forty years from the death of Jesus is also suggested by the development of Christian theology which the Gospel reflects, as well as by the existence of the written records which it uses.

A more precise dating turns on the answer to the question whether the Gospel indicates a knowledge of the fall of Jerusalem and the destruction of the temple in A.D. 70. The evidence of chapter xiii. as a whole points strongly to a date after the destruction of the sacred city. For the writer is plainly anxious that his readers not be discouraged or confused by the delay of the Parousia. In apocalyptic thought the ' Messianic Woes ' always led up to the coming of the great reward, and the *Appalling Horror*, or ' Abomination of Desolation,' as the older translation gave it, was evidently the culmination of these Woes in the original form of this document. In its present form in Mark, however, there is a clear separation between the coming of the *Appalling Horror*, which is very vaguely worded (verses 14 ff.), and the appearance of Christ subsequently. Mark warns his readers that those who foretold the appearance of Christ during that trouble in Judæa were false prophets (verse 21). The coming of the Son of Man will only be ' when that misery is past ' (verse 24). This separation between the great calamity and the Parousia, and the warning against expecting the latter to follow immediately upon the former, is intelligible only on the assumption that

INTRODUCTION

Mark was written after the Judæan catastrophe. Jerusalem had fallen, but the New Age had not appeared. Mark distinguishes carefully between the two events. However, the coming of the Son of Man will not be long delayed after those events. It will be 'in those days' (verse 24), and will take place before the generation of Jesus' hearers have passed away (verse 30).

The apocalyptic chapter thus indicates a date a few years after the fall of Jerusalem and the destruction of the temple—that is, about A.D. 75.

THE AUTHOR

Here again one must begin with indications which the Gospel itself supplies rather than with traditional views. Although the book itself is completely anonymous, there is much information concerning its author which can be gleaned from its language, its special interests and point of view, and its familiarity or lack of familiarity with things Palestinian.

This internal evidence makes it virtually certain that the writer was a Christian Jew. Three general facts point to this conclusion. He knows the Jewish Scriptures, not only quoting from them, but using terms, phrases, and ideas which these Scriptures supplied. In the second place, it is obvious that he knows the Aramaic language, since he incorporates in his text a number of phrases in that language, and in x. 51 even leaves the Aramaic *rabboni* without translation. In the third place, the writer possesses a full knowledge of Jewish life and thought. He knows the general geographical divisions of Palestine, is acquainted with the different political conditions of Galilee and Judæa, speaks of the Pharisees, Sadducees, scribes, elders, chief priests, the synagogues, the temple, without any tendency to explain the terms, and uses with all naturalness phrases and ideas which come from Jewish religious thought. Of the latter one might mention ' the Kingdom of God,' ' the commandments,' ' the son of David,' ' eternal life,' and a number of others. The combined force of these several facts is such that it is highly improbable that the writer was a Gentile by birth and upbringing.

On the other hand, it is abundantly clear that this Christian Jew was one who held the convictions and point of view of the Hellenistic wing of the early Church. The Gentile mission is strongly endorsed. Jewish food laws are declared to be meaningless and futile. Strict Sabbath observance is disapproved. The cross of Christ dominates the story of Jesus' work. Terms and ideas characteristic of Hellenistic Christianity —' the gospel,' ' the Son of God,' ' because ye are Christ's,' etc.—are present throughout. The version of the Scriptures used was, as remarked, the Greek, not the Hebrew one.

When we pass beyond these two basic facts supplied by the internal evidence, the questions become more difficult to answer. Did the writer know Palestine? Here the data is conflicting. It is also difficult to evaluate. For since we know that the writer used a number of written sources, it is obvious that one cannot attribute all references and allusions to his own knowledge. Probably the most useful procedure will be to survey the more important indications of the writer's knowledge of the scene of his story, and also the indications which point in the contrary direction.

The first area in which one seeks an answer to this question is that of geography. That the writer is familiar with the larger geographical units of Palestine has been mentioned. Galilee, Judæa, ' the country across Jordan,' ' the regions of the Decapolis,' Idumæa, are mentioned with evident understanding. That this is so is strikingly demonstrated in viii. 27 and ix. 30. In the former of these passages Jesus and His disciples are at the villages of Cæsarea Philippi. The name distinguishes the town from the Cæsarea on the Mediterranean coast; but this distinction may have come to the editor in the source which he is using. But that he understands the general situation, that Cæsarea of Philip is outside Galilee, is shown by ix. 30. This is the next geographical reference. It reads: ' On leaving they passed through Galilee.' The author is well aware that when Jesus was at Cæsarea Philippi, he was outside Herod's domain.

Of a detailed knowledge of the Galilean region in which the first half of the Gospel is located, however, there is no

INTRODUCTION

indication. The statements of Jesus' movements are repeatedly vague and seem to be taken over from earlier sources. But in regard to Jerusalem the case is somewhat different, for several references suggest an acquaintance with the city and its environs. In xiii. 3, an undoubtedly editorial passage, the Mount of Olives is said to be 'over against the temple,' a strikingly descriptive phrase. That the author knew that it was near Jerusalem is also indicated by xiv. 26, which describes Jesus and His followers as repairing there after the last meal together. This, too, is in an introductory and probably editorial sentence. In xi. 1, another introductory sentence, Bethany and Bethphage are correctly described as near Jerusalem and 'at the Mount of Olives.' Familiarity with the location of Bethany is also suggested by xi. 11 and 12. Acquaintance with Jerusalem may be indicated also in xv. 16 and xv. 22.

Over against these suggestions of acquaintance with Palestine three geographical errors have been alleged. (1) In vii. 31 is an obscure statement, 'Passing from the borders of Tyre he came through Sidon to the Sea of Galilee, by way of the territory of the Decapolis.' There are several textual variants which show that early copyists were also puzzled by the expression. It is, however, just as likely that the obscurity of the statement is due to a lack of clarity in the data which Mark was using, as that it is due to ignorance of the geography involved. (2) In v. 1 we read that Jesus crossed the Sea of Galilee and came to the country of the Gerasenes, which, as the sequel shows, was on the shore. Gerasa, however, is far inland to the south. But here our text is most probably wrong. The reader is referred to the commentary for the discussion of the passage. (3) In xi. 1 cited above, Jesus is said to have travelled from Jericho toward Jerusalem, coming to Bethphagê and Bethany. Here the order in which the villages are mentioned is definitely wrong. Bethphagê was nearer Jerusalem, Bethany over the shoulder of the Mount of Olives. But here again it was very likely that our text has become corrupt. It is improbable that both names stood in the original writing, though scholars have differed as to which one should be read.

INTRODUCTION

impressed, however, with the accuracy of the general picture of Palestinian life which the Gospel presents. The synagogues are the centres of community life in Galilee, the temple in Jerusalem. The scribes are the social and religious authorities. The standard to which they appeal is the Mosaic law and the traditions of the fathers. The Pharisees are strict interpreters of the law and criticize and ostracize those who do not obey certain precepts which they stressed. The close relationship between scribes and Pharisees, and yet the distinction between them, is correctly reflected (see ii. 16). We do not meet with the Sadducean priests until the story reaches Jerusalem. Jesus is described as drawing crowds from all parts of the country, but in the list of sections represented Samaria is omitted (iii. 8). The people hope for God's reign to come, are concerned over how they are to gain eternal life. Among the subjects of current discussion were what was the chief commandment, what were the grounds for believing in the resurrection, whether one should wash one's hands before eating, whether taxes should be paid to Cæsar, and what were the signs of the establishment of God's reign. The faithfulness of this general picture is such as to suggest that the writer had some acquaintance with Jewish life in Palestine.

A writer who did not have such an acquaintance would no doubt betray himself by numerous errors. Only two or three have been cited in Mark. In x. 12 Jesus is said to have forbidden a wife to divorce her husband and marry another. Since Jewish law made no provision for divorce on the wife's initiative, the saying is inapplicable to Jesus' hearers, and the conclusion has been drawn that the writer was not familiar with the Jewish laws concerning divorce. This would no doubt mean that he was a Gentile. In the face of the indications to the contrary, however, it seems more likely that the saying in question represents the application of a Christian principle to the conditions of the Gentile world. Paul, who certainly was acquainted with the Jewish law, makes the same application in the name of the Lord in 1 Cor. vii. 10. A second error has been alleged in the language of xiv. 12, 'on the first day of unleavened bread, when they sacrifice the passover.'

INTRODUCTION

Could this writer have been John Mark of Jerusalem, as the early Church believed? What do we know definitely of this Mark? The following are the main facts: His mother occupied a house in Jerusalem which was evidently fairly commodious. How long the family had been there we do not know. His cousin was Barnabas, who was from Cyprus. In A.D. 44 Paul and Barnabas took Mark with them back to Antioch (xii. 25). The narrative suggests that he was then a young man. He went with Barnabas and Paul on their journey to Cyprus, and later, after criticism of him by Paul, travelled with Barnabas. He then drops out of the story. In the later letters of Paul (Col. iv. 10; Philem. 24; 2 Tim. iv. 11) we find the Apostle reconciled with Mark, and the latter described as his fellow worker in the Kingdom of God. 1 Pet. v. 13 speaks of Mark as Peter's 'son,' which relates itself to the Christian tradition that Mark served as Peter's 'interpreter.'

The date of the Gospel we have seen to be about A.D. 75. Assuming that Mark was twenty-five when Paul and Barnabas took him to Antioch, he would have been fifty-six at the time of its composition.

A comparison of what the Gospel tells us about its author and what we know of this John Mark shows that the indentification of the two is not only possible but is from several standpoints plausible. Mark had been in Jerusalem, had family connections with the Jews of the Dispersion and had spent his adult life—so far as we know—as a Christian missionary in the Hellenistic cities of the Roman Empire. He undoubtedly knew both Greek and Aramaic. He was associated with Paul, Barnabas, and other leaders of the movement which was rapidly breaking away from Judaism. His name is associated with that of the Church in Rome (the Babylon of 1 Peter). The objections to this identification are several assumptions, which, however, the facts themselves do not supply. The association of Mark with Peter has been interpreted to mean that the Gospel must then contain the reminiscences of the Apostle. But we know nothing about this association, when it took place, how long it lasted, or what its character was. It was evidently remembered

THE GOSPEL OF MARK

because it enabled the Church to claim apostolic authority for a Gospel which was admittedly by one who had not himself followed the Lord. It has also been felt that a Jew of Jerusalem would not have gone so far as to declare all meats clean, as Mark vii. 15 does. But Paul adopts the same position, Peter's vision of unclean meats carried the same implication, and Stephen's speech deprecated the temple worship. The radical tendencies in Hellenistic Judaism of the day were evidently stronger than used to be assumed. In the third place, our Gospel is so completely a Hellenistic product that one might hesitate to attribute it to a resident of Jerusalem. But we have no grounds for asserting that Mark, after he left the city in A.D. 44, kept up a closer connection with it than did, let us say, the Apostle Paul.

The tradition which attributes the Gospel to Mark is very early. It can be traced back, as we have seen, to the beginning of the second century at least, that is, to within twenty-five years of the writing of the book. The facts are such as to make it open to acceptance. Only one must be careful not to make assumptions concerning this Mark, and on the basis of these shut one's eyes to the facts of the Gospel.

. . . .

The commentary which follows, in conformity with the other volumes of the series, has been written primarily for the use of general readers and students. The avoidance of footnotes has prevented the acknowledgment of an indebtedness to other scholars which those who know the literature will recognize on practically every page. Of the commentaries on Mark most use has been made of those by Swete, Klostermann, Rawlinson, and Montefiore. Of other works special mention should be made of Schmidt, *Der Rahmen der Geschichte Jesu*; Dibelius, *Die Formgeschichte des Evangeliums*; Streeter, *The Four Gospels*; Jackson and Lake, *The Beginnings of Christianity*; and Goguel, *The Life of Jesus*. In the citation of rabbinic parallels and references I am indebted constantly to Billerbeck's great commentary which goes by the name of Strack and Billerbeck, *Kommentar zum Neuen Testament aus Talmud und Midrasch*.

COMMENTARY

I. THE TITLE

It must be kept in mind that the title to this book was not a part of the original document. In the extant Greek manuscripts, and even in the early printed text, the form varies considerably. In the oldest manuscripts it appears simply as two short Greek words best translated, 'according to Mark.' The word 'gospel' is implied in this earliest form and is added in later manuscripts.

The title comes from the period when the word 'gospel' was only known in the singular, and meant, not a book, but the Christian preaching of salvation, a preaching in which the story of Jesus' life, death, and resurrection played a primary role. The preposition 'according to' does not mean simply authorship—the Greek is not used in that sense until later—but has rather a distributive sense, and implies the existence of other records. Thus we have titles which mean, 'the gospel, as given by Matthew,' 'the gospel, as told by Mark,' or by Luke, or by John. In the second half of the second century the word 'gospel' comes to be used of these books, and so appears in a plural form. Our brief titles are earlier than this usage and belong to the period when the word 'gospel' occurs only in the singular and means the Christian proclamation. *Didache* viii. 2 provides an excellent illustration of this use of the word. The title to the Gospels may be dated from the first half of the second century.

II. THE BEGINNING OF THE GOSPEL
(i. 1–13)

i. 1–3: 'As Was Prophesied by Isaiah'

	i.
The beginning of the gospel of Jesus Christ the Son of God.	1
As it is written in the prophet Isaiah,	2

> *Here I send my messenger before your face*
> *to prepare the way for you :*
> *the voice of one who cries in the desert,*   3
> '*Make the way ready for the Lord,*
> *level the paths for him*'—

These words seem clear enough until one reflects upon them. Then they become a puzzle. What does the word **gospel** in this first sentence mean, and what is it that is the beginning of the gospel?

The first question is not so difficult to answer. As remarked above, the word ' gospel ' did not come to have the meaning of particular books until the time of Justin Martyr. Literally it meant ' good news,' and is used by Josephus in that sense. The term was adopted by Greek-speaking Christians, perhaps originally by Paul, to refer to the means of salvation which they proclaimed. 'I am not ashamed of the gospel,' writes Paul, ' for it is the power of God unto the salvation of every one who believes.' When Paul speaks of ' my gospel ' (Rom. ii. 16), it is ' the gospel preached by me ' (Gal. i. 8, 11). What this gospel was is best seen perhaps in 1 Cor. xv. 1 f., ' I make known to the brethren the gospel which I have preached among you ... by which you are saved ... that Christ died for our sins according to the Scriptures, and that He was buried and that He rose on the third day.' The phrase ' the gospel of Christ,' which appears often in the New Testament, does not mean the gospel preached by Jesus in Galilee, but the message about Him. That message, however, even from the beginning, included certain facts about Jesus' life, as Mark xiv. 9 clearly

THE GOSPEL OF MARK

shows. This element of the events in connection with Jesus' work became more and more important. By the middle of the second century the word ' gospel ' is used in this specialized sense of the story of Jesus' life and passion, though the basic meaning of the Christian way of salvation is not displaced. By the second half of the century it comes to be used of the four documents which stand first in the New Testament.

Now the opening sentence of our book was written long before this later development. **The gospel of Jesus Christ** here refers to the Christian message of salvation—not to this book, nor Christ's preaching in Galilee. Mark uses the word eight times, and it has this meaning regularly in his text (see i. 14, viii. 35, xiv. 9, etc.). But what, in that case, is **the beginning** of this gospel ? Two interpretations have been suggested. (1) Mark means to say that he proposes to give the story of Jesus' life and work, for this was the beginning of the Christian missionary activity and preaching. On this view, the beginning which is meant is the entire story of his book. The thought suggested is the same as that in Heb. ii. 3. (2) **The** beginning to which Mark refers was the work of John the Baptist. That this is the correct reading of the sentence is shown by several considerations : (*a*) verses 2 and 3, which refer to John's work, seem to go with the opening words, being a parenthetical expression before verse 4. (*b*) Early Christian thinking laid great stress on John's work as the beginning of the new movement. This is plainly stated in Acts i. 22, x. 37 ; Matt. xi. 10, and elsewhere. That Mark shared this view is shown by ix. 13 and by the long digression on the death of the Baptizer. (*c*) This was the interpretation of a number of the early fathers, who were accustomed to reading the unpunctuated Greek of the original manuscripts.

Thus we may restate Mark's opening words : The beginning of the proclamation of good news about Jesus as the Messiah and Son of God was John's preaching in the wilderness. This was slightly embarrassing to the early Christians, but they never denied the facts. They emphasized the connection, and developed a theological interpretation of John as the Elijah who was to prepare the way for the Messiah.

CHAPTER I, VERSES 1-3

Jesus Christ. The proper name **Jesus** is a Greek writing of the Hebrew name Jehoshua, or Joshua, being formed from the shortened form Jeshua, current after the Exile, with a Greek ending added. It was a common name, meaning, " he whose salvation is Jahwe " (Jehovah in the English Bible). Josephus in his writings mentions about twenty persons named Jesus. In the New Testament, aside from Jesus of Nazareth and the Joshua of the wilderness wanderings, we meet with two cases in which the name is unquestioned (Luke iii. 29, Col. iv. 11), and two other cases in which the name has dropped out of a large number of the manuscripts. Following the rise of the Christian Church, the name disappeared rapidly. Christians ceased to use it from a sense of reverence, and Jews from opposition. Only in Spanish countries is it still used as a Christian name. In Islam, however, neither piety nor prejudice prevented its use, and it is said to be still common. One effect of the canonization of the name is seen in the manuscripts of the New Testament. That Barabbas the robber should have had the name Jesus was intolerable to Christian scribes, and it was dropped from Matt. xxvii. 16, although Jesus Barabbas is almost certainly the original reading. A similar tendency was at work in the case of Bar-jesus the sorcerer in Acts xiii. 6.

The second term, **Christ,** was not a proper name, but a title. Strictly it should read ' the Christ.' The omission of the article reveals a significant development in early Christian thinking which the transfer of Christianity from Palestinian to Hellenistic soil occasioned.

The word ' Christ ' was a translation into Greek of the Hebrew word ' Messiah,' which meant ' anointed.' The word was used of the anointed priests, of the Hebrew kings who were anointed for their office, and of other divinely commissioned individuals or groups. Thus it was applied to the expected deliverer of the nation. The Hebrew word ' Messiah ' did not make the transfer to Greek usage. It does not occur in the Greek Old Testament, and, aside from two cases in the Fourth Gospel, never in the New Testament. Instead, the word was translated literally, i.e. ' the Christ,' the anointed one. But

Greek peoples did not anoint their kings, and the idea which the phrase, ' the one anointed with oil,' brought to Greek ears was more repulsive than honorific. It was not surprising, therefore, that a change took place very quickly in the vocabulary of Greek-speaking Christians. ' The Christ ' tends to drop out, and the word is used as a proper name, either alone or in the phrase ' Jesus Christ.' Two centuries later when the gospel made the transfer from Greek into Latin, the word *unctus*, the Latin translation of ' anointed,' never made its way, and the Greek term *Christos* was taken over, virtually as a proper name, whence our term Christ.

This opening phrase **Jesus Christ** is thus the terminology of Hellenistic and not Palestinian Christianity. Mark, however, is not consistent ; he writes Christ both as a name (ix. 41) and in its proper form, with the article, as a title (viii. 29). The Gospel thus represents the stage of transition.

The words **Son of God,** while characteristic of Mark's thought and expression, are omitted by a number of important manuscripts, and are, therefore, doubtful.

The first endeavour of Christian leaders, however, was not to create a new theology, but to seek to find in the history and literature of the Hebrew people the ground and foreshadowing of their faith. There was a practical reason for this, since the Roman authorities were suspicious of new religions, and toleration could be gained by convincing them that the ' gospel ' was simply the fulfilment of the ancient and officially recognized religion of the Jews. But deeper than the apologetic motive was the sincere conviction of the Church that it was the true Israel of faith. It held to the Jewish Scriptures, found in the law and the prophets prophecies which it believed to have been fulfilled in its own day, and regarded itself as a fulfilment of, and heir to, the promises and teachings of the past. Some half-century after the time when Mark was written there came a reaction against this tendency, and certain leaders, the most notable of whom was Marcion, attempted to repudiate the entire Jewish connection and inheritance. By that time it was too late. The religious and moral achievements of Judaism had already become the

CHAPTER I, VERSES 1-3

permanent possession of the Church. Though many of the references to sacrifice, high priest, and the like, and many of the Old Testament citations to be found in early Christian literature, seem tedious and even fanciful to-day, nevertheless they are the visible landmarks of a process that was deeply significant. Jewish monotheism, the Jewish Scriptures, Jewish ethical ideals, and that vital sense of historical continuity which saved the early Church from the sea of gnostic speculation, were thus preserved in the new movement.

The passage before us is one of the many results of this basic Christian belief. John the Baptist, whose preaching was the beginning of the gospel, they identified with the ' voice crying in the wilderness ' of the Greek version of Isaiah's prophecy, and with ' the messenger ' of Jehovah, whose coming Malachi had foretold. This identification had become axiomatic in early Christian thought. We meet with it also in Matt. xi. 10 ; Luke vii. 27 ; and John i. 23.

It is an open question, however, whether Mark wrote the quotation in its present form, certain curious facts rather suggesting that he did not. (*a*) The quotation is said to be from Isaiah, which is true only of the second half. (*b*) It is very noticeable that Matthew and Luke, both of whom used Mark as a literary source, omit the first half of the quotation. (*c*) Mark generally quotes Scripture passages from the Septuagint (Greek) version in quite faithful form. The quotation of verse 2 differs in this respect from other quotations which he makes, being either an independent translation of the Hebrew text or a conflation of two passages Exod. xxiii. 20 and Mal. iii. 1. (*d*) Lastly, one notes that the quotation occurs in practically identical form in Matt. xi. 10 and Luke vii. 27, and seems to be derived there from the source often called ' Q ' rather than from Mark. On the whole, it seems more likely that it was introduced into Mark's text from the latter passages by some early copyist, than that Matthew and Luke both independently struck out the first half of Mark's quotation because they knew what was coming later on in their own works. The point is of importance only as being one of several instances which show that our text of Mark has suffered from slight editing in the process of its early transmission.

i. 4–8 : THE PROPHET IN THE DESERT

4 John appeared baptizing in the desert and preaching a baptism
5 of repentance for the remission of sins ; and the whole of Judæa and all the people of Jerusalem went out to him and got baptized by him in the Jordan river, confessing
6 their sins. John was dressed in camel's hair, with a leather girdle round his loins, and he ate locusts and wild
7 honey. He announced,
'After me one who is mightier will come,
and I am not fit to stoop and untie the string of his sandals :
8 I have baptized you with water,
but he will baptize you with the holy Spirit.'

Early Christian tradition was so interested in interpreting John's work in relation to that of Jesus that it has obscured the fact that John was an outstanding figure in his own right. This is clear from a number of pieces of evidence. Josephus, writing two generations after John's death, knows of his great following and tragic end, and recalls that the populace regarded a defeat of Herod's army as a divine punishment for the execution of John. The Gospels, which are somewhat nearer in time to John, refer repeatedly to his influence. 'All the people regarded John as a prophet' (Mark xi. 32, Mt. xxi. 26). When Jesus began to attract the multitudes about Him, it was rumoured that He was John raised again from the dead, a conjecture to which even Herod gave credence (Mark viii. 28 and vi. 14). It was because Herod feared John that he put him to death—a fact which speaks loudly of his influence. He left a following which continued for many years after his death (Acts xviii. 25 and xix. 3), and we hear of disciples of John in the writings of Justin Martyr in the middle of the second century. Some of the passages in the Fourth Gospel imply that possibly certain of these followers regarded their late master as the expected Messiah. Thus it is plain that our Gospels in their account of John give only part of the picture. The important place which John occupies in the New Testament—it has been pointed out that he is mentioned more often than any person except Jesus, Paul, and Peter—is due first of all to his intrinsic importance to the Christian movement; secondly, no doubt, to the apologetic task created by the existence of the rival Johannine movement; and thirdly, to the elaboration of the thesis that the events of the gospel story were in fulfilment of words of prophecy.

John was a prophet. That was the view of him which the nation had, and it is clear from his raiment that it was also his own conception of himself (note 2 Kings i. 8 and Zech. xiii. 4). The characteristic thing about a prophet is that the message which he delivers he believes to be from God. It is not taught him by any man. In the Judaism of the century preceding John the tendency had been in another direction. Those who would lead Israel in the right way were taught not to lean upon their own understanding. The proper course was to attend upon the instruction of a recognized teacher and to take to oneself an associate in study—in a word, to become one of the scribes. The system of guidance and control by the scribes had not in the first century become a rigid one. On the contrary, the Pharisaic theory and scribal organization were only just being felt in all parts of the nation. We may assume that John's appearance represents a reaction in favour of the older, freer type of religious leadership. There is no indication, however, of any conscious opposition to the scribes on the part of John. Matt. iii. 7 is an editorial touch, as is shown by the parallel passage in Luke.

John's work was in the desert. **He ate locusts and wild honey,** i.e. the food of the wilderness. Jesus spoke of the fact that John came ' neither eating nor drinking.' In other words, John was an ascetic. In this respect he was not unique in the Judaism of the first century. The hopeless national outlook in the world of politics had deepened and intensified religious hopes and aspirations. One effect of this which is discernible is the appearance of ascetic tendencies in the sect of the Essenes and in many pious individuals. Josephus, for example, describes one of his teachers, a man named Banus, as remaining in the wilderness, eating the wild food of the place, wearing clothing provided by nature, and bathing often in cold water for the sake of religious purity (*Life*, ii). This Banus may have been an Essene, and attempts have been made to regard John as a member of that body. Certain of the most characteristic features, however, are lacking, notably the frequent ritual cleansings, the white garments, and the creation of a separate community life on the basis of ritual practices. John more probably was influenced by the same general spirit which affected the Essenes and other pious individuals (Hasids), rather than directly by the Essenes.

Mark speaks only of John's preaching of repentance, baptism, and the coming of a Mighty One after him. Matthew and Luke, however, supply further details of a ' coming wrath,' of the ' axe already laid at the root of the tree,' and of how every unfruitful tree shall be ' cut down and cast into the fire.' We also learn that the Mighty One who comes will separate good from bad, gathering His grain into His barns and burning the chaff with unquenchable fire. It is clear that John was a prophet whose message was formulated in terms of the apocalyptic hopes which had been current in Judaism for more than a century. The present order of things was at an end, and the Great Judgment would soon be accomplished. These were John's basic thoughts. And it may be that this is why John went out into the desert to preach. For it was a common idea that the Messianic deliverance would take place in the desert, as had been the case in that first deliverance under the leadership of Moses. We know that there were various Messianic pretenders who endeavoured to capitalize this idea in the first century (see Josephus, *War*, ii, 13, 4). Against the background of this impending judgment John flung his demand for repentance and good works.

The part of John's work which seems to have most impressed his contemporaries was his **baptism of repentance**. For it **was**

CHAPTER I, VERSES 4-8

this rite that gave him his title. How shall we understand this rite? It was not simply a part of the Jewish system of ceremonial lustrations nor of the Essenic ritual cleansing, for these were repeated as often as occasion required, while John's baptism was once and for all. Some have thought that John took the rite from the baptism which in his day was being required of proselytes when they were admitted into Judaism; for this is the only single act of baptism which, so far as we know, was practised in Judaism at this time. The words in Matt. iii. 9 and Luke iii. 8 lend some support to this view. But the baptism of the proselyte was not one of repentance, and no confession of sin accompanied it. Furthermore, neither John, nor Jesus after him, seems to have been particularly concerned with the problem of the relation of Jew and Gentile, though both repudiated the complacent confidence of the Jews in their physical descent. Thus we must seek elsewhere for the dominating idea of John's baptism. The explanation is probably to be found in John's eschatological expectations and preaching. His baptism was a preparation for entrance into the new order which would be established soon. Immediately there come to mind a number of passages of the Old Testament which speak of a divine cleansing of the nation in the Messianic time, the figure of cleansing by water being used often. See, for example, Ezek. xxxvi. 25; Isa. xliv. 3; Zech. xii. 10; Joel ii. 28. The rabbis also found in the law proof that the forefathers had been baptized in the wilderness before entering the Promised Land, an idea found in 1 Cor. x. 2. The analogy of the first salvation to the one to come is often expressed. It seems most likely that it was these ideas which ay behind John's demand that his hearers come to a baptism of water which would represent that new cleansing essential for admission into the coming rule of God.

Jewish thought, however, is insistent on one point: apart from **repentance** there could be no forgiveness of sins. Hence John demanded that his hearers must repent, confessing their sins, the latter being the normal accompaniment of repentance in Jewish practice. This confession was general and in public, in no way resembling the Catholic confessional. Repentance thus preceded John's baptism most certainly. Josephus' description of John's baptism insists most carefully on this point. He says that this baptism ' was acceptable to God ... provided that the soul had been thoroughly purified beforehand by righteousness ' (*Ant*. xviii. 5. 2). He adds that the baptism itself was ' for the purification of the body.' It is quite likely that John included ritual or bodily purification in his thought, but it is probable that he did not make so sharp a distinction between the cleansing of the soul and the purification of the body as Josephus suggests.

The manner of John's baptism cannot be asserted with certainty, but probably was a self-immersion in the presence of the prophet. All Jewish ceremonial lustrations were performed by the individual for himself, and John's baptism probably conformed to this Jewish mode. The language of several passages in the New Testament bears this out. In what appears to have been the original text of Luke iii. 7 one reads of crowds who were baptized ' before ' John. Acts xxii. 16, speaking of the Christian baptism, reads, ' Rise up, baptize yourself, and wash away your sins.' It is also worth mentioning that the earliest pictorial representations of Jesus' baptism show the Baptist standing on the bank beside the stream. The baptism by John would mean, then, under his influence and in his presence.

John's announcement of the coming Messiah is stated here in the briefest terms : **After me one who is mightier will come.** So stated, the text would convey to an early Christian reader the impression that John prophesied the appearance and work of Jesus. The longer record of John's preaching which Matthew and Luke have taken from their common source, however, makes it very probable that John expected a different type of figure. According to the records in Matthew and Luke, John expected that this Coming One would inaugurate the great judgment. ' He will gather His wheat into the granary, but the straw He will burn with unquenchable fire.' The figure John expected thus seems to have been a supernatural one, the delineation of which is to be found in the Jewish

CHAPTER I, VERSES 4–8

apocalyptic books. To untie, or put on, **the sandals** was the work of a slave, and John emphasized by this figure the majesty and might of the Coming One.

The saying, **I have baptized you with water, but he will baptize you with the holy Spirit**, was widely quoted in the early Church. Matthew and Luke both have it, having taken it, not from Mark, but from the 'Q' source. It appears in John i. 26, 33, though the two halves of the saying are separated. Twice in Acts i. 5 and xi. 16—it is attributed to the Lord, though in all the Gospel passages it is said to have been an utterance of John. The tendency to transfer to Jesus all striking sayings which were remembered in the Church is familiar to students of the Gospels. In the light of this tendency, and of the congruity of the ideas of the saying to John's expectations, we need not hesitate to conclude the correctness of the Gospel tradition on this point.

This logion was evidently of great importance in early Christian circles. Its contrast between John's baptism by water and the Christian baptism of the Spirit obviously had point. It is weighty evidence, which is supplemented by the entire Gospel story, that Jesus did not baptize with water as did John. One can go even further. The appearance of the saying six times in the Gospels and Acts points to a period in the history of the Church when baptism by water had not yet become a Christian rite. Once the Church had adopted baptism, the saying, or at least its first half, ceased to have any point. In the preservation of the saying we have a relic of the earliest stage of Christian practice.

It was a commonplace of Jewish apocalyptic thought that the Holy Spirit would be poured out on those who attained the Messianic Age, endowing them with special powers and grace. The saying thus emphasizes again the apocalyptic character of John's preaching. But it was not only apocalyptic. Hand in hand with his announcement that the great event was near went his programme of preparing men for the new age by an inner cleansing which should have fruit in works of justice, mercy, and peace.

THE GOSPEL OF MARK

i. 9–11: THE BAPTISM OF JESUS

9 Now it was in those days that Jesus arrived from Nazaret in Galilee and got baptized in the Jordan by John.
10 And the moment he rose from the water he saw the heavens cleft and the Spirit coming down upon him like a dove;
11 then said a voice from heaven,
'Thou art my Son, the Beloved,
in thee is my delight.'

Up to this point we have been dealing with the introduction to the story. Now we come to the actual beginning. For, in addition to the evidence of the Gospel accounts, there are two statements in Acts which specifically state that the 'good news' began with the baptism of Jesus by John (i. 22 and x. 37). There can be no doubt that the event actually took place. That the Greater should have been baptized by the Lesser, and particularly that He should have accepted a baptism of repentance, created a grave difficulty for early apologists, and we may be sure that the episode was not invented by them.

As the first act with which the drama of salvation began, it was natural that the baptism should loom large in Christian thought. Until that moment Jesus had lived quietly in His native village. Following it, He became the 'prophet like unto Moses' (Acts iii. 22), the performer of mighty works, the destined head of the New Age that was about to dawn. The birth stories of Matthew and Luke, which told that Jesus had been different from other men from His birth, were not yet in circulation, and the first Christology was constructed on the basis of this contrast between what preceded and what followed the baptism. This primitive Christology affirmed that at the time of the baptism Jesus was appointed to be God's Messiah and the Holy Spirit was made to descend upon Him. By means of this endowment He had wrought the 'miracles, wonders, and signs' by which God had accredited Him to the nation (Acts ii. 22). This belief was no doubt strengthened by the fact that the early Church came to hold

CHAPTER I, VERSES 9–11

that the Spirit was bestowed upon believers at the time of their baptism (Acts ii. 28). At any rate, it is clear that this is the meaning of the account both for Mark and his first readers.

The Christian tradition recalled that Jesus' home had been in **Nazaret in Galilee**. The existence of this town has been questioned, on the grounds that it is mentioned neither in the Old Testament in Josephus' writings, nor in the Talmud, and the name has been explained as referring originally to the religious sect of the Nazarites, but later erroneously regarded as a place name. Josephus, however, states that in his day there were 204 towns in Galilee, and only a small number of these are mentioned in any of our sources. Since a Galilean origin was contrary to the conventional equipment of the Messiah (see John vii. 41), scepticism as to the tradition on which it was based seems unwarranted.

Reports concerning the preaching of the prophet John had evidently spread as far as Galilee, and Jesus was one of the many who came to hear him. Traditions which indicate that He remained for some time in the entourage of John are preserved in the Fourth Gospel ; Mark's account is condensed, and interested only in the central facts. Early Christian writers were troubled by the statement that Jesus underwent a baptism of repentance, since it seemed to imply some fault on His part. Matthew explains that John was reluctant to administer the rite to Jesus, while the early *Gospel According to the Hebrews* has Jesus explain that He could only repent of sins due to ignorance. Jesus' act was a natural, instinctive one, quite in accord with His later refusal to accept the title ' good teacher,' with His condemnation of the pride and self-righteousness of some of the Pharisees, and with His frequent praise of the modest and humble spirit. As already remarked, it is probable that the baptism was self-bestowed.

The narrative of the central experience is noticeably restrained as compared with the story in the other Gospels. We are told that Jesus saw the dove, while the voice speaks in the second person to Jesus only. In Matthew this is changed to the third person, which means that the evangelist thinks that the crowd was addressed. Luke adds that the Spirit descended ' in bodily form,' while in John i. 33 it is said that the descent of the dove was a sign by which the Baptizer recognized the Messiah. This is not to say that Mark thinks of the experience as subjective on Jesus' part. He would scarcely have raised such a question concerning the story. The difference is due simply to the fact that in Mark we are further up-stream in a constantly flowing and enlarging tradition. Utterances by **a voice from heaven** are frequent in Jewish literature of the period. It was one of the devices by which use of the name of God was avoided. The heavenly voice delivers in each case the divine judgment.

A great deal has been written concerning the words of this heavenly voice. The utterance is a composite one. The first half comes from Ps. ii. 7, which the Christians interpreted Messianically, and from which they quoted many times in the New Testament. The second half is from Isa. xlii. 1. To avoid being entangled in lengthy technical discussions it will be necessary to set down almost arbitrarily the answers to the more important of the questions which these words raise:

(1) The word translated **Beloved** grammatically may be taken as an adjective, i.e. ' My beloved son.' Dr. Moffatt's choice of translation, however, seems thoroughly justified. The word represents the term of address with which the passage from Isaiah—that is, the second half of the utterance of the heavenly voice—begins.

(2) In Jewish usage the phrase, **Thou art my son,** would normally connote only divine approval. This was because, on the one hand, Jewish monotheism did not permit a conception of divine sonship in any literal sense, and, on the other, because of the common Semitic idiom by which ' son of ' was used to indicate a quality or a likeness of character. As a result, ' the son of God ' never became in Jewish usage a title or description of the Messiah exclusively. It did, however, in Christianity— another evidence of Hellenistic influence in the development of early Christian theology. The words of Ps. ii. 7, ' Jehovah said unto me, Thou art my son; this day have I begotten thee,' were regularly applied to the Messiah by early Christian

writers. It is noteworthy that the verse is quoted in full four times in the New Testament alone, besides the partial quotation of the verse here and in the parallel in Matthew (Luke iii. 22, Western text ; Acts xiii. 33 ; Heb. i. 5 and v. 5).

These facts in themselves would make it highly probable that Mark understands the words, **Thou art my Son,** to mean, ' Thou art the Christ.' But this is made abundantly clear by examining his Gospel elsewhere. The phrase ' the Son of God ' or ' the Son,' in the sense of ' the Messiah,' appears in iii. 11, v. 7, ix. 7, xiii. 32, and xiv. 61. One cannot doubt, therefore, that this is its meaning here.

(3) The remainder of the utterance comes, as has been said, from Isa. xlii. 1, with slight modifications. The Hebrew text —the Greek here being quite different—reads : ' My chosen, in whom My soul delighteth. I have put My spirit upon Him and He shall bring forth judgment to the Gentiles.' This verse is quoted in full in Matt. xii. 18. It is evident that the appropriateness of the words attributed to the heavenly voice depends on the rest of the verse in Isaiah, namely, on the reference to the pouring out of the Spirit on the Chosen One. This suggests that the utterance has had a considerable history before it reached its present form in Mark. The part quoted here, however, does carry out the meaning of the first half of the utterance. **The Beloved** is the substitute for the Hebrew ' My Chosen One '—the two ideas of divine love and divine choice for a task being close together in Jewish thought. The thought of a divine act of choice is present also in the verb **in thee is my delight.** For this verb is in aorist tense, and should be taken as expressive of a definite act of approval rather than of a continuous state of mind.

(4) Thus the meaning of the words from heaven are clear. When Jesus was baptized, He was declared to be God's chosen representative, His Messiah, and endowed with the Spirit. The analysis of the passage also makes it evident that the story in its present form is a construction of the Christian tradition. The words from heaven are a composite of pertinent Scriptural passages. The theme of the whole vision is theological, a definition of Jesus' office and a statement of His

equipment for His work. It does not represent so much an inner experience of Jesus as what Christians came to think about Him.

It is often thought that we can get behind the scene as it is here described to the original experience of Jesus. The most reasonable way of doing this is to assume that the words, **Thou art my Son,** are those which Jesus actually heard, but that they are to be interpreted in the Jewish sense, as a declaration of the divine approval of Jesus' character, rather than as an appointment to an office. One can reasonably assume that Jesus did have a deep inner experience at the time of His baptism. But the experience—if we may judge by the activity which followed from it—must have been similar to the call of the Old Testament prophets to undertake a specific task, rather than a declaration about Himself, such as these words give. The story of the baptism, as we now have it, seems an attempt of the early Christians to pierce the mystery of the forces that lay behind Jesus' decision to begin His proclamation of the coming Kingdom of God. We can see the dim outlines of what took place, but no more than they can we trace it in detail.

i. 12–13 : The Temptation

12 Then the Spirit drove him immediately into the desert, and in
13 the desert he remained for forty days, while Satan tempted him; he was in the company of wild beasts, but angels ministered to him.

Jesus, now led by the Spirit, is directed into the solitary wilderness, where He is tempted by Satan, the Prince of Evil. Two thoughts underlie the narrative. On the one hand, it was a familiar Jewish conception that God tries or tests the righteous. Abraham, whom God proved (Gen. xxii. 1), and Job, whom He tested, were the most conspicuous examples of this principle. God does not test the wicked, for they cannot endure it, but the righteous ; their faithfulness redounds to the glory of God. Jesus had just been declared the Beloved Son, and is immediately put to the test. A second thought is expressed in the story. Jesus has been designated as the divine agent for the overthrow of Satan and all his powers. The Prince of Evil immediately endeavours to conquer and destroy Him. Jesus does not yield. He faces the Devil and defeats him. This victory is the prelude to the power which Jesus was to show over all evil spirits and demons.

These two ideas seem to be the meaning of the narrative for the first Christians. As in the case of the baptism, the account is given in symbolic language. **Forty days** is a conventional period, and comes from the Old Testament. Moses was in the Mount forty days and nights; Elijah fasted forty days; Goliath challenged Israel forty days, etc. The mention of **wild beasts** may be simply to accentuate the desolation of the place of temptation. More likely, it is an echo of the thought which is several times expressed in Jewish literature that wild beasts are subject to the righteous man and do him no harm (see Job v. 22 f.; Test. Napht. viii. 4, 6; Test. Benj. v. 2). The average reader usually assumes that the **angels who ministered to him** came after the temptation was over, being unconsciously influenced by the statements in the Matthew-Luke account that Jesus fasted during the temptation. There is no suggestion of this, however, in the narrative before us, and Mark's thought probably is that during the stay in the desert Jesus was, like Elijah of old, fed by angels. Moffatt's translation brings out admirably this contrast of Satan and the wild beasts on the one hand, and the ministering angels on the other. The whole story is illustrated by a remarkable passage in the Testament of Naphtali viii. 4: ' If ye do good, my children, both men and angels shall bless you, and the Devil shall flee from you and the wild beasts shall fear you, and the Lord shall love you.'

The above facts show that the stories of the baptism and temptation owe their present form to certain ideas of the early Christians. As they now read, they can scarcely go back to Jesus Himself. One would not be warranted, however, in asserting that no real experience of Jesus lies behind them. That Jesus was baptized by John is one of the certain facts

THE GOSPEL OF MARK

about the beginnings of Jesus' work. That an inner experience of deep significance occurred in connection with the event is evidenced by the fact that shortly afterwards He began His work. That such a break with His accustomed life involved temptation and testing was inevitable. But the details of those inner experiences probably were not divulged. What we have are the reverent speculations of members of the early Christian community.

III. THE MINISTRY IN GALILEE
(i. 14–viii. 26)

i. 14–15 : JESUS APPEARS IN GALILEE

After John had been arrested, Jesus went to Galilee preaching 14
the gospel of God; he said, 'The time has now come. God's 15
reign is near ; repent and believe the gospel.'

The prologue is over. The hour has struck, and the work of Jesus begins. Mark, as other early Christian writers, felt keenly the lack of some appropriate opening event. Luke provided this by shifting the story of the appearance in Nazareth to the beginning of the ministry, and making it the occasion of a public announcement of Jesus concerning His work. Mark has to content himself with a formal statement of the beginning of Jesus' public activity, dating it, and summarizing the contents of His preaching.

The dating—**after John had been arrested**—raises a problem of some importance. How much time has elapsed since the baptism, in which episode we see John actively at work in the midst of a great throng of repentant or curious pilgrims? What has Jesus been doing in the interval? Is the statement that Jesus' public work began after John's arrest indeed correct, for a quite different picture is presented in the Fourth Gospel?

The latter account seems, indeed, to supplement and possibly to correct Mark's story at this point. There is evidently a gap of a certain interval of time between the events of the baptism and the beginning of Jesus' public work. The Fourth Gospel gives a number of indications that, following his baptism, Jesus remained for a limited time in John's *entourage* (see John i. 29, 35), near John, but apparently independent of him (see John iii. 22 f. and iv. 1 f.) In other words, a brief Judæan ministry preceded the Galilean one. Of this, however, Mark has no knowledge. Matthew also knows nothing of it, and implies that the reason why Jesus took up

His work of preaching was that He had heard that John was cast into prison (Matt. iv, 12). The Fourth Gospel, however, pointedly denies the Synoptic statement (see John iii. 24), and goes on to say that Jesus withdrew into Galilee to avoid competition with John (John iv. 1–2). This presentation in the Fourth Gospel of Jesus' work near the Baptizer in Judæa has all the marks of verisimilitude, and, while the details are obscure, the main fact may be accepted. Jesus worked at first in connection with, and near to, John. That is no doubt why His teachings and those of the prophet of the wilderness are so similar. Quite probably His separation from John was due to His maturing conviction of His own programme and work. Jesus was too original and too independent to remain long merely as one of John's assistants. There are some reasons for thinking that a difference of view as to baptism was one phase of this developing independence. Whatever the factors were, there was no quarrel, for Jesus later speaks of John in the very highest terms.

If this be the correct view of the facts, Mark's statement, **after John had been arrested**, must be explained as the general public opinion concerning the relation of the two men. Even though there may have been some short period before John's arrest when Jesus worked in Galilee, it could not have been long, for later we find both Herod and the populace believing that Jesus was John raised from the dead (Mark vi. 14 f., viii. 28 f.). Quite evidently there was no overlapping of the public careers of the two; scarcely had one been removed than the other appeared. Mark shares this general view of the chronology of the two. Viewing John the Baptist as the forerunner, it appeared most reasonable that he should disappear before the Mighty One Himself appeared. That this brief overlapping of the work of Jesus and the Baptizer was an embarrassment to the evangelist of the Fourth Gospel is shown by the explanations in John iii. 28, 30.

The summary of Jesus' activity which follows is instructive. Though Mark contains fewer of the sayings of Jesus than either of the other Synoptic Gospels, he is well aware that Jesus' **active work consisted largely in teaching.** The summary of

CHAPTER I, VERSES 14-15

the work in Galilee here given should be compared with the plain statement in Mark i. 38 and with such passages as i. 39, ii. 13, etc. It must have been true that some collection of the sayings of Jesus was in circulation when Mark wrote, so that the evangelist did not feel it necessary to include in his work any extensive collection of the teachings.

Mark says that Jesus came preaching **the gospel of God**. The word gospel, as has been remarked, meant at this stage of Christian history the good news of salvation proclaimed by the Christian missionaries. The full phrase means the gospel of which God was the author. It quite probably goes back to Paul[1] (see 1 Thess. ii. 2, 8, 9 ; Rom. i. 1, xv. 16, etc.).

Instead of a lengthy collection of Jesus' sayings such as Matthew places at the beginning of the public ministry, Mark summarizes the message. It is the glad announcement that God's long-awaited reign over all men and nations is at hand. The time of waiting is ended, and the Kingdom which pious Jews had dreamed of for so many centuries is about to appear. The day of God's decision between good and evil is near. In this crucial hour men must do two things—**repent and believe the gospel.**

The wording of this summary is obviously the evangelist's. To **believe the gospel** is distinctly a later Christian summary of what men must do to be saved. **The time is now come** reminds one of Paul's statement, ' When the fulness of time came, God sent forth His son ' (Gal. iv. 4), and of the similar phrase in Eph. i. 10. But, even though the ideas of developing Christianity are to be seen in the wording, there can be no doubt that the main thought which Mark presents is true to the facts. Jesus, like John His predecessor, believed that the day of the divine visitation was at hand. His parables enjoining readiness, His sayings concerning judgment, His

[1] It is possible that the original text here read ' the gospel of the Kingdom of God,' though the manuscript evidence for this reading is distinctly inferior to the shorter one. The fact that Mark nowhere else writes ' the Gospel of God,' that the words which follow in verse 15 deal with the Kingdom, and that in Mark this is regularly the theme of Jesus' teaching, make this longer reading an attractive conjecture. Turner, in *J. T. S.*, Vol. xxviii., p. 153, points out that the twelve letters additional in the longer phrase is the average length of the lines in the earliest papyri. The omission of one line by an early copyist would have been responsible for the change.

declaration that many kings and prophets had desired to see the things being fulfilled (Luke x. 23 f.), His insistence on the urgency of the hour (Matt. viii. 22 and elsewhere), His sense of power over evil spirits and declaration of the fall of Satan (Luke x. 18), His anticipation of the coming Kingdom even in the words at the Last Supper (Mark xiv. 25), all taken in connection with the unquestioned belief of the early Church, make this one of the dependable facts of the record of Jesus. The eschatological belief which had come into influence in Palestine toward the beginning of the first century formed the framework of His teaching. By means of it He gave vivid expression to His sense of the immediacy and imperativeness of the ethical ideal which He proclaimed.

The preaching of Jesus, then, in broad outline was similar to that of the Baptist. Both proclaimed the coming of the day of judgment and the necessity of repentance. But even in Mark's brief summary a different note already appears. The Christian word gospel (good news) was not a distortion of Jesus' teachings. Throughout His sayings there runs a note of confidence and trust in God which is absent from the recorded sayings of the prophet of the wilderness. With John the central thought is that of judgment. With Jesus an equal if not greater emphasis falls on the blessedness of life in harmony with the will of God, and on the desire of the heavenly Father that not one of these little ones should perish.

i. 16–20 : THE CALL OF FOUR GALILEAN FISHERMEN

16 Now as he passed along the sea of Galilee he saw Simon and Simon's brother Andrew netting fish in the sea—for they
17 were fishermen ; so Jesus said to them, ' Come, follow
18 me and I will make you fish for men.' At once they
19 dropped their nets and went after him. Going on a little further he saw James the son of Zebedæus and his brother John ; they too were in their boat, mending their
20 nets ; he called them at once, and they left their father Zebedæus in the boat with the crew, and went to follow him.

CHAPTER I, VERSES 16–20

The previous summary gave no indication of the exact locality nor of the method of Jesus' work. In this first episode of the ministry we find Him beside the Sea of Galilee in the neighbourhood of Capernaum (i. 21). Why He did not begin in the region of Nazareth is not stated. Perhaps it was because the populous region around the sea offered a more promising field; perhaps it was due to a natural reluctance to begin His preaching of the Kingdom where He had been known only as a youth and a carpenter; possibly it was because there was from the very first that opposition to His work in His own family which we learn of later (see Mark iii. 21). It is implied by the phrasing of the passage that His preaching was itinerant, and this is stated in i. 39 and in vi. 6. That He began His work of preaching before He called any disciple is evident, although we do not know how long He had been engaged in His public activity.

It was not at all unusual for religious teachers and leaders to have disciples who accompanied them wherever they went. Josephus tells of having lived for three years with Banus, an ascetic religious teacher, and the Talmud has numerous references to rabbis with pupils who ' came after them.' This was because they would study the Torah not only by hearing the words of the rabbi, but also by observing the practical applications of his knowledge. The phrase in Mark, **Come, follow me**, is the usual one, and means, ' Be my disciple.' But, while it was customary for rabbis to have disciples about them, there is a new note in the rest of Jesus' call as here stated. The primary function of the scribes was to study the Torah, to teach it, and to ' raise up many disciples,' who would learn and practise it. Jesus seems to have had a different objective. The task to which He calls is to **fish for men**. His primary work was not to study, nor even to teach, but to save men, to bring them into the Kingdom. Teaching was only a means toward that end. Thus, while Jesus appeared in many respects as a travelling teacher of the Torah, and adopted certain of their modes of activity, His purpose and spirit were never imitative, but free and even unconventional.

As Mark gives the story, the call to these four was peremptory and without preparation. It is unlikely that this was the case. In fact, there is evidence of a previous acquaintance with Jesus on the part of Andrew and Simon. According to the Fourth Gospel (i. 40 ff.), they had been together in their attendance on the preaching of John. In any case, they would have known something about the teacher or prophet before leaving their daily work to become His disciples. These earlier contacts have dropped out of the tradition. Only the dramatic episodes remain. Whether we should regard the call of James and John as occurring simultaneously with that of Simon and Andrew is also uncertain. The **at once** of verse 18 is purely stylistic on Mark's part, and occurs repeatedly where it cannot be taken literally. Some have thought that these two stories of the call of fishermen to become fishers of men are double accounts of the same episode, but there is nothing unlikely in the assumption that four of the disciples came from the fishing circles among whom Jesus began his Galilean ministry.

Simon is the same individual elsewhere called Peter, or Cephas (its Aramaic equivalent). (See Mark iii. 16 and John i. 42.) This episode is commonly called ' The Call of the First Disciples,' but there is no indication in the account itself that they were necessarily the first ones.

i. 21-22: JESUS TEACHES IN THE SYNAGOGUES

21 **They then entered Capharnahum. As soon as the sabbath came, he at once began to teach in the synagogue ; and**
22 **people were astounded at his teaching, for he taught them like an authority, not like the scribes.**

Capharnahum (commonly called Capernaum) on the northwest shore of the Sea of Galilee, in the midst of the remarkably fertile coast strip described by Josephus, is now definitely identified with the site Tell Hum, rather than further south. It was thus a border town of Herod Antipas' territory, and, since it lay on the trade route from the east which came north of the Sea of Galilee, it was probably one of the important tollstations of the region.

CHAPTER I, VERSES 21-22

The synagogue was the centre of Jewish life. Services were held on the Sabbath morning and afternoon, on festival days and on certain week-days. These consisted of the recitation of the 'Shema,' certain prayers and benedictions, readings from the law and the prophets, an exposition of the former if a suitable person was present, and a final blessing. There was no official Jewish clergy, and any male Israelite might read or expound, though priests or trained scribes naturally were preferred. Thus through the synagogue Jesus found ready to hand a means by which He could carry His message to the great body of Jews.

It is evident that His preaching made a deep impression, not only by its content, but also by the manner in which He spoke. That **he taught them like an authority, not like the scribes,** refers no doubt to Jesus' conviction of His prophetic commission and His ability to declare God's will and purpose. The scribes were learned men, versed in the Scriptures and the tradition. The statement often made that in their preaching they constantly cited the ancestral authorities, is probably overdone, for the synagogal expositions were supposed to be edifying and popular rather than juridical—that is, haggadic rather than halachic. Nevertheless, it was evident to the people that this new teacher belonged in a different category. He was a prophet, like one of the old prophets who in the long past had proclaimed a message from God. Mark does not give any examples at this point of His authoritative teaching. He seems to assume that his readers are familiar with it.

i. 23-28 : JESUS CASTS OUT AN UNCLEAN SPIRIT

There, in their synagogue, was a man with an unclean spirit, 23 who at once shrieked out, 'Jesus of Nazaret, what business 24 have you with us ? Have you come to destroy us ? We know who you are, you are God's holy One!' But Jesus 25 checked it ; 'Be quiet,' he said, 'come out of him.' And 26 after convulsing him the unclean spirit did come out of him, with a loud cry. They were all so amazed that 27 they discussed it together, saying, 'Whatever is this ? '

28 'It's new teaching with authority behind it!' 'He orders even unclean spirits!' 'Yes, and they obey him!' So his fame at once spread in all directions through the whole of the surrounding country of Galilee.

According to the views of the ancient Jews, and of other peoples of the Hellenistic area as well, the world was filled with myriads of disembodied spirits or demons, all under the leadership of a Prince of Evil (cf. Eph. ii. 2; 1 Cor. v. 5; John xii. 31, etc.). There were several explanations current concerning the origin of these spirits, but as to their constant presence and malicious activity there was general agreement. The development of this demonology is a marked feature of Jewish thought just before and after the beginning of the Christian era, and shows without doubt Persian influence. Satan, formerly one of God's angels and ' the adversary ' of men in the divine court, became more and more the embodiment of all evil and the opponent of God. Jewish thought never fully adopted dualism; God was still supreme. But for reasons which could be only dimly understood He had permitted Satan and his allies to possess the earth and to carry on for the time being their perverse activities. In the New Age the demons were to be banished, bound in the ' abyss,' and punished for their sins.

These demons were unbelievably numerous—seven and a half million, says one authority. They flew over the world. Though they were invisible, they could assume visible forms, which, however, would not cast shadows. They lived mostly in the wilderness, where their howling at times could be heard —around ruined structures or in unclean places like cemeteries. They could enter into human bodies and work all sorts of harm. They caused plagues and calamities, caused diseases and accidents, and tempted men to sin. Prayer, reciting the Shema, reading the Torah, and obedience to the commandments—as well as various charms—protected one from the demons.

This belief in demons was not the only explanation of disease and calamity, for the older explanation—the view expressed

CHAPTER I, VERSES 23-28

in the Old Testament, that suffering was a punishment sent by God for sin—was still maintained. In the first century this seems still to have been the basic teaching of the rabbis. The belief in the demons was harmonized with this older view by the doctrine that God permits the demons to carry out His punishments. Such attempts to co-ordinate the older and newer views on the problem of evil belonged, however, to the realm of theology; in the popular mind the demons did not confine themselves to inflicting deserved punishments, but did whatever their malicious natures suggested.

As superstitious as this belief in demons was, it should not be overlooked that from one standpoint it was an improvement on the older way of thinking. The conception of evil spirits which came into men from without, often through no fault of the individual, was the nearest approach possible in that unscientific age to the modern attitude toward disease. The conception directed the attention in the wrong direction as far as the cure was concerned, but at least it made it possible to view sickness as an accident rather than a punishment, and to regard people who were suffering with sympathy rather than with reproach. It made suffering due, in part, to factors in our universe which God has permitted to exist, rather than attributed it in each instance to His direct decree.

The 'possessed' individual in the story before us shows symptoms which would probably be diagnosed to-day as one of the several forms of hysteria. Under the influence of Jesus' personality and of the mass psychology of the crowd in the synagogue he cried out, acclaiming Jesus as **God's holy One** who had **come to destroy** all evil spirits. That Mark means this to be a Messianic acclaim, due to the supernatural knowledge of the demon, is evident from verse 34 and iii. 11. According to these passages the demons always recognized Him.

That Jesus did cure cases of possession is one of the best supported facts of the history. Not only do we have various narratives of, and references to, such exorcisms, but the explanation of His opponents, that He did this by Beelzebub, has been preserved (iii. 22). In *Sanh.* 107a the Talmud also states that Jesus practised magic, which means the same thing.

In addition, we have several of Jesus' answers to this charge: His query, ' How then do your sons cast them out ? ' and His —or the early Church's—indignant denial of the use of magic (Mark iii. 23). The scepticism of some of the recent exponents of the ' Formgeschichte School ' seems in this instance to be certainly without justification.

These exorcisms were apparently very significant to Jesus' mind. Though he refused to work ' signs ' for display, nevertheless He charged His disciples to cast out demons (vi. 7), and it is the one ' work of power ' to which He appealed as proof of the divine character of His mission (Matt. xii. 28 and Luke xi. 20). When the disciples reported that the demons were subject to them, He exultingly exclaimed, ' I saw Satan falling like lightning from heaven.' In the coming age the demons were to be cast into the abyss, and in the power of Himself and His disciples over them Jesus saw evidence that the establishment of God's universal reign was beginning.

i. 29–31 : Peter's Mother-in-Law is Healed

29 **On leaving the synagogue they went straight to the house of Simon and Andrew, accompanied by James and John.**
30 **Simon's mother-in-law was in bed with fever, so they told**
31 **him at once about her, he went up to her and taking her hand made her rise; the fever left her at once, and she ministered to them.**

A second illustration of Jesus' wonder-working power is given, this time over a more ordinary case of fever. There seems to be a genuine reminiscence back of the account. If so, the ultimate origin of the story was no doubt Peter. Schmidt thinks that the account of these events on one day in Capharnahum came to Mark in a connected account, for it is not the evangelist's usual method to group episodes in a day-to-day record. The house of Peter was quite likely Jesus' headquarters in this section of Galilee. It is probably mentioned again in ii. 1 and ix. 33. The mention of Andrew, James, and John in verse 29 is probably an early gloss on the text,

CHAPTER I, VERSES 29–31

due to the influence of the story in i. 16 ff. They are not mentioned in the parallel accounts in Matthew and Luke, and the singular form of the verb and participle in the opening words of verse 29 seems clearly to be preferred.

On entering the house, Jesus is told of the illness of **Simon's mother-in-law** either by way of apology or, as Luke understands it, as an inquiry concerning her case. The cure is described in brief and conventional terms. Jesus takes her by the hand and makes her rise. This is the same procedure recorded of healings by various rabbis in the Talmudic literature. The phrase ' to make to rise ' seems, indeed, to be the conventional Talmudic expression meaning to cure or heal.

This story raises the whole question of the healing miracles of Jesus. Fortunately the problem stands in a much clearer light than a generation ago. The growing body of accurate knowledge with reference to the close relation between mental and bodily states and the power of individual and mass suggestion has eliminated much of the scepticism which narrations of wonderful healings once aroused. In a day when medical knowledge had scarcely begun, when in popular circles diseases were ascribed in many, if not all, cases to possession by evil spirits, and when prophets and religious teachers were expected to have the power to do marvels, modern inhibitions were largely absent and psychic suggestion and influence could work more effectively. When one remembers the deep impression which Jesus made on all who came in contact with Him, foes as well as friends, one has little inclination to doubt that mental and even bodily effects could have been produced by His words and personal influence.

This, of course, was not the way in which these experiences were explained by the first Christians. To them they were proofs of His supernatural power, and the accounts were accepted and retold in an uncritical spirit. The cycle of stories of healings became a major item in the Christian apologetic.

The presence of similar stories in other cults of the day —the stories about Pythagoras, Apollonius of Tyana, the temple of Æsculapius at Epidauros, and even about certain rabbis—would have served both as a stimulus and a formative force in this development. It will not be surprising, therefore, if one meets with an enhancement of the miraculous element in some of the stories, and with generalizations which leave, no doubt, a false impression of the frequency of such cures. At the same time one can see, oft-times by details which seem genuinely reminiscent, or which are in conflict with the apologetic purpose, indications of an authentic basis for the narratives. Careful study of the stories in Mark suggests that most of the authentic cures were of people suffering from hysteria, the varied physical effects of which are now well known. But no one can speak with confidence as to the full limits of this therapeutic power of personal influence and suggestion.

The healing of Simon's mother illustrates some of these difficulties. She had **fever,** the cause or nature of which we do not know. The healing is recorded, but, as already remarked, in conventional language, which gives no indication of the mode by which it was effected. Luke adds the point—probably a deduction on his part—that Jesus 'rebuked the fever,' which evidently means that he regarded it as due to possession by a demon. That the woman when restored **ministered to them** is probably a touch to emphasize the completeness of the cure. Stories of healings commonly ended with some such indication (cf. ii. 12 and v. 15).

i. 32–39: Crowds of Sick People at the Door

32 **When evening came, when the sun set, they brought him**
33 **all who were ill or possessed by dæmons**—indeed the whole
34 town was gathered at the door—**and he cured many who were ill with various diseases and cast out many dæmons ; but as the dæmons knew him he would not let them say**
35 **anything.** In the early morning, long before daylight,
36 he got up and went away out to a lonely spot. He was
37 praying there when Simon and his companions hunted him out and discovered him ; they told him, 'Every-
38 body is looking for you,' but he said to them, 'Let us go

somewhere else, to the adjoining country-towns, so that
I may preach there as well ; that is why I came out here.'
And he went preaching in their synagogues throughout 39
the whole of Galilee, casting out dæmons.

As a sequel to these two miraculous healings of the day we
have the statement that at evening the whole town was
gathered at the door, having brought all who were sick or
possessed of demons. The story is told with considerable
vividness in popular, hyperbolic fashion. Mark says that Jesus
cured many. Commentators have called attention to the
implication that there were some whom He could not heal.
This implication, while true, is no doubt unintentional, the
language **many who were ill with various diseases** and **many
dæmons** being intended certainly to bring out the magnitude
of His healings rather than the opposite. Matthew and Luke
both see the difficulty and change the wording. The delay until
sundown was because of the Sabbath law of work, which
forbade carrying the sick to Jesus' door, and also His healing
of them unless life itself was endangered.

The meaning of verse 34*b* is that the demons, through
their supernatural knowledge, recognized Jesus as the Messiah, just as had the demon which possessed the man in the
synagogue (verse· 24). Jesus forbids them to reveal this
knowledge, as also in iii. 12. After the confession of Peter at
Cæsarea Philippi, the same injunction to silence is imposed
on the disciples (see viii. 30 and ix. 9). Whatever conclusion
one may come to hold concerning Jesus' view of His office
and work, one fact is quite clear from these passages : the
evangelist—or the tradition before him—is aware that during
His ministry Jesus made no public claim to be the Messiah.
The presentation of the Fourth Gospel in this respect, therefore, must be corrected. Mark's view is that Jesus was aware
of His Messiahship from the time of His baptism, and that the
words from heaven were constantly confirmed by His mighty
works. But Mark knows that Jesus did not publicly announce
this. There is, therefore, in his thought a conflict of ideas :
Jesus knew of His office and demonstrated His power, but

refused to accept the title. The result is his theory of the
'Messianic secret.' It was not yet to be revealed. Whether
Mark's view of the facts is the correct one will be discussed
later. It may be questioned even at this point, however,
whether Jesus regarded Himself as the Messiah in the early
stages of His ministry.

The episode which follows is often called 'the flight from
Capharnahum,' and it is assumed that Jesus fled to escape the
crowds of sick who had thronged around Him the evening
before. In its present setting this is the impression which the
story makes, and it is probable that this setting or connection
is earlier than the Gospel. The sequence of events, however,
is artificial. It does not seem likely that Jesus came to
Capharnahum and remained only one day. Nor would one
have expected the whole town to bring their sick to His door
at the close of His first day there. This scene, if historical,
would seem to belong rather to a period after His reputation
had been made. In Jesus' reply to Peter, also, the thought
deals rather with a larger issue than escaping from the sick
of the town. It is whether He shall remain in Capharnahum
or continue an itinerant ministry. It seems plain that we
have here a story which rests on some recollection, and one
would naturally assume that recollection to have been Peter's.
But it would seem also that several different issues have been
confused in its re-telling. The main point seems to be Jesus'
refusal of Peter's urging that He remain in Capharnahum.

i. 40–45 : A Leper is Healed

40 A leper came to him, beseeching him on bended knee, saying,
41   'If you only choose, you can cleanse me'; so he stretched
      his hand out in pity and touched him saying, 'I do choose,
42   be cleansed.' As he spoke, the leprosy at once left the man
43   and he was cleansed. Then he sent him off at once, with the
44   stern charge, 'See, you are not to say a word to anybody ;
      away and show yourself to the priest and offer what Moses
45   prescribed for your cleansing, to notify men.' But he went
      off and proceeded to proclaim it aloud and spread news of

CHAPTER I, VERSES 40–45

the affair both far and wide. The result was that Jesus could no longer enter any town openly ; he stayed outside in lonely places, and people came to him from every quarter.

The leprosy of the Bible was a different disease from modern leprosy. The former is described in detail in Lev. xiii. and xiv., and regulations are given concerning pronouncements of recovery from it by the priests at Jerusalem. These regulations deal with a chronic skin disease, or diseases, characterized by ulcerous eruptions. Modern leprosy has features not mentioned in the biblical account—discoloured excrescences on the body, swelling of the features of the face, degeneration of nerves, and loss of fingers and toes. The Hebrew disease, also, was evidently subject to fairly rapid changes, the change at the end of a week's time being one of the points to which the priest was to pay attention. In so short a period modern leprosy would show no change. Lastly, the ancient disease evidently was curable, while the recoveries from leprosy proper previous to the medical discoveries of the last few years were very rare.

According to the Jewish law, the leper was ritually unclean. This was not on sanitary grounds, for the disease was not considered contagious (see *Jewish Ency.* viii. 10a), but rather because of the ritual uncleanness of a person with ulcerous sores. The leper was supposed to separate himself from the community, to avoid defiling others by his touch, and to give warning of his condition when others approached him. There is evidence, however, that this separation was not as strictly enforced as the regulations of Leviticus and the statements of Josephus would lead one to believe. They were permitted, for example, to attend the synagogue in booths built especially for them, and the exclusion from the towns was only applied to the walled cities of the land.

The story is told without any indication of place or time. These had been lost before it reached Mark. The leper may have met Jesus on a journey ; for him to have entered a house where Jesus was would have been against the law. According to the account Jesus **touched him saying, 'I do choose, be cleansed.'** This touching, if an authentic detail, while not contrary to the law, would have brought ritual defilement upon Jesus. Montefiore, the distinguished Jewish scholar, has a fine note on this touch. ' Here we begin to catch the new note in the ministry of Jesus; his intense compassion for the outcast, the sufferer, who by his sin or by his suffering, which was too often regarded as the result of sin, had put himself outside respectable Jewish society, who found himself rejected and despised by men, and believed himself rejected and despised by God. Here was a new and lofty note, a new and exquisite manifestation of the very pity and love which the prophets had demanded ' (*The Synoptic Gospels* i., p. 39). Quite apart from the act of touching the leper, which is such a regular feature of Mark's narratives of cures as perhaps to awaken some question (cf. i. 31, iii. 10, vi. 5), it should be noted that there is no suggestion in the story of the rabbinic view that leprosy was a visitation from God for the worst sins.

The law required that those who had recovered from leprosy should go to Jerusalem, be examined by the priest, make certain offerings, and be formally pronounced clean and re-admitted to the company of the people. This injunction, Jesus enforces, just as He does in the only other narrative in the Gospels of the healing of lepers (Luke xvii. 12 ff.). A comparison of the account in Mark with that story in Luke also suggests a solution for the difficult problem occasioned by the present story. Even though the disease from which the man was suffering was not modern leprosy, yet the statement that the ulcerous sores of the disease disappeared immediately when Jesus touched him is difficult to accept. Now in the Lucan story Jesus' method was different. The lepers were sent to Jerusalem to show themselves to the priest, ' and as they went away, they were healed ' (Luke xvii. 14). The almost identical wording of the command in the two stories suggests that perhaps this is what occurred here as well. Jesus sent the leper to Jerusalem, and as he journeyed on his way he was healed. That the leprosy disappeared immediately

CHAPTER I, VERSES 40-45

on Jesus' touch would be a natural development of the story in its retelling.

In verse 44 one notes again the strict charge to silence, this time to one who had been healed. The same injunction occurs in subsequent healings (v. 43, vii. 36, viii. 26), except where these were performed in public and the command would have had no meaning. These commands, like the ones to the possessed, are part of the pattern in which Mark sees the facts of Jesus' work. Yet, nevertheless, the editor may have had some actual tradition on which this part of his scheme is based. Jesus repeatedly refused to give a sign to those who requested it. That He wished to avoid the crowds of sick and the role of worker of marvels seems entirely reasonable. This part of the 'Messianic secret,' therefore, may have had some basis in the tradition. See, further, the note on iii. 22-27. But Mark is aware that the injunction to silence was not obeyed, and that the fame of the mighty works of the Galilean prophet spread far and wide. Verse 45 is editorial. It depicts in general terms the success which attended Jesus' work in Galilee, rather than the result of this one episode. The leper would have proceeded to Jerusalem, where, according to the law, he would have remained eight days.

There is a question of the text in verse 41 which raises an interesting point. Instead of **he stretched out his hand in pity** a number of manuscripts read 'in anger.' On the general principle that the more difficult reading is more likely to be the original, this reading has claim to acceptance. The explanation of the difficult reading may be only a linguistic confusion between two similar Aramaic words. But if this be not the explanation, it is probable that it should be sought in the thought world of the first century, a world in which human illness and misery were attributed to the agency of evil spirits or to their chief, Satan. The indignation of Jesus, aroused by the pitiable condition of the leper kneeling before Him and seeking help, would have been directed at those unseen powers of evil. Edwyn Bevan has recently illustrated this point of view. 'Suppose we were to read in a life of Lord Shaftesbury,' he writes, 'that on some occasion when he was visiting a manufacturing town a child was brought to him in a state of extreme emaciation, and suppose the author went on to say, " Lord Shaftesbury expressed the liveliest indignation and took steps to have the child removed from its present surroundings," we should not be in a moment's perplexity, although the writer did not state against whom he was indignant ' (*J.T.S.*, Vol. xxxiii., p. 186).

CONTROVERSIES WITH THE SCRIBES AND PHARISEES

(ii. 1–iii. 6)

WITH ii. 1 a section begins in which a series of conflicts between Jesus and the religious authorities are recorded. In all of these episodes the scribes and Pharisees are ready at hand to criticize and oppose, without any explanation of their presence having been given. It has already been indicated in the Introduction that this section in all probability was in written form before Mark wrote. The chief reason for thinking this is the stereotyped character of the narratives, all dealing with the same theme, appearing in a document in which the material elsewhere is not topically arranged. Certain small items point in the same direction. In iii. 6 we are told that the Pharisees and Herodians formed a plot to put Jesus to death. This is out of place so early in the Gospel. Nor do the Herodians play any active part in the rest of the story. The verse is most easily explained as a note in a written document which Mark was following. In ii. 14 Levi, the son of Alphæus, is mentioned. In the list of the apostles one meets with James, the son of Alphæus. Had the author been composing freely, one would expect some explanation of the relationship of these individuals. In ii. 18 the disciples of John are mentioned, but nothing has been said earlier about John having a body of disciples, and the phrase appears very abruptly. The indications thus leave little room for doubt that we have before us an earlier document of the Church. But the section is integral to the plan of the Gospel. It is the foil to the story of the great crowds and wonderful deeds, and it also prepares the way for the final tragedy.

ii. 1–12 : THE HEALING OF THE PARALYTIC

ii.
When he entered Capharnahum again, after some days, it was 1
reported that he was at home, and a large number at once 2

gathered, till there was no more room for them, not even at the door. He was speaking the word to them, when a paralytic was brought to him; four men carried him, and as they could not get near Jesus on account of the crowd they tore up the roof under which he stood and through the opening they lowered the pallet on which the paralytic lay. When Jesus saw their faith, he said to the paralytic, 'My son, your sins are forgiven.' Now there were some scribes sitting there who argued in their hearts, 'What does the man mean by talking like this? It is blasphemy! Who can forgive sins, who but God alone?' Conscious at once that they were arguing to themselves in this way Jesus asked them, 'Why do you argue thus in your hearts? Which is the easier thing, to tell the paralytic, "Your sins are forgiven," or to tell him, "Rise, lift your pallet, and go away"? But to let you see the Son of man has power on earth to forgive sins '—he said to the paralytic 'Rise, I tell you, lift your pallet, and go home.' And he rose, lifted his pallet at once, and went off before them all; at this they were all amazed and they glorified God saying, 'We never saw the like of it!'

It is probable that the statement **When he entered Capharnahum again** has been prefixed to the section by the editor of the Gospel. One notes that none of the episodes which follow have any indication of place or time. The location of this episode at Capharnahum may have been due to the mention of a house, which suggested the house of Peter (i. 29). Or it may have been due simply to the idea that Capharnahum was the centre of the work in Galilee. There is a trace of this in nearly all of our sources (see Matt. xi. 23; Luke vii. 1 f. and John ii. 12).

The story gives a vivid picture of Jesus' popular success. The crowds fill the house and even the door. The friends of the sick man, fearing that they could not get in by any other means, showed great persistence. They went up by the outside stairway, took off part of the flat roofing, and so were able to lower their friend or relative directly in front of the

CHAPTER II, VERSES 1-12

teacher. Thus far the story appears to be an account of a miracle of healing, but at this point a new note is introduced, and we have instead a dispute over the question of Jesus' right to forgive sins.

This part of the narrative is one of the most difficult in the Gospel. In particular, there are four difficulties : (1) In no other passage in Mark previous to the acclaim by Peter at Cæsarea Philippi (one dubious instance being excepted) does Jesus make or admit a claim to Messianic or apocalyptic honours. In the episode here He uses of Himself the title ' Son of Man,' which seems to refer definitely to the descriptions of an apocalyptic figure in Daniel and Enoch. (2) In no other passage in the Synoptic Gospels (except again for one dubious exception in Luke) does Jesus claim the power to forgive sins by His own fiat. Constantly He urges men to repent in order that God may forgive them, or, more specifically, He demands that their repentance shall take the form of forgiving their brothers in order that God may forgive them. (3) These claims and prerogatives are supported or proved by the performance of a miracle. Elsewhere in the tradition it is recorded that Jesus refused to give signs to authenticate His claims, and Mark presents Jesus as endeavouring to avoid the notoriety of a marvellous healer. (4) Finally, one notes that in this episode Jesus seems to assume it as self-evident that the man's illness was due to sin, so that forgiveness of the latter is equivalent to healing the former. Aside from this passage, there is no indication that Jesus actively embraced this belief and that it governed His attitude toward those who were sick.

These difficulties all inhere in the section verses 5-10. To meet them it has often been proposed to regard the phrase ' Son of Man ' as being in this case a literal and mistaken rendering of an Aramaic idiom, which should in this instance be translated more correctly as simply ' man.' Verse 10 would then read, ' " But to let you see that man has power on earth to forgive sins "—He said to the paralytic.' The linguistic possibility of this is undeniable, but, even if the phrase be read as meaning simply ' man,' we are still left in confusion. Apart from the famous but questionable words to Peter about binding and loosing on earth and the similar phrasing in Matt. xviii. 18, there is no evidence that Jesus conceived of men as having this power. It seems best, therefore, to take the phrase ' Son of Man ' as Mark clearly intends it, namely, as referring to Jesus Himself, and to face up to the difficulties involved.

As the story stands it reflects very accurately the beliefs of the first Christians. The early Church did believe that Jesus was the coming ' Son of Man,' and it applied that title to Him without any sense of restraint. The proof of this last statement is the freedom with which Matthew and Luke insert the title into the narrative of their Marcan source. The Church did believe also that forgiveness of sins was accomplished by means of, or through Jesus (see Acts xiii. 38 and numerous other passages). The Church did regard the miracles as proof of Jesus' high office and the authentication of its claims for Him (see Acts ii. 22 and elsewhere). And, whatever criticisms were or were not levelled at Jesus during His lifetime, we may be confident that there were scribes who said as they listened to early Christian preaching, ' It is blasphemy ! Who can forgive sins but God alone ? '

The section thus reflects quite clearly the beliefs of the primitive Christian brotherhood, and contradicts what we can reconstruct of the beliefs and methods of Jesus of Nazareth. The conclusion seems incontrovertible, therefore, that the wording of the debate between Jesus and the scribes had its origin in the beliefs of the early Church.

The usual interpretation of the episode by writers like Bultmann, Klostermann, and others is that we have before us a typical story of a wonderful cure into which the later addition, verses 5 to 11, has been inserted. So simple and easy a statement of the case, however, is not entirely satisfactory. We are left with several questions on our hands. Why did the development take place in the case of this particular story and not in the case of any other miracle of healing ? One can think of other narratives which gave a better base for the presentation of the beliefs concerning Jesus' forgiveness of sin than this story of the healing of a paralytic. Would not, for example, the story of Zacchæus have been a better occasion? The latter was a publican, and practically confessed his rascality; and a pronouncement of forgiveness by Jesus, followed by a controversy with the scribes over the point, would have been more natural there than in this instance. If one replies that the Church preferred a miracle of healing to authenticate the declaration of forgiveness, one wonders why it was not added to one of the stories of the healing of lepers, for the presence of leprosy was regarded as proof positive of some of the worst sins. The presence of the debate in connection with this story thus calls for some explanation. Finally, it is obvious that the break in the narrative is not, as is usually maintained, with verse 5 (**When Jesus saw their faith, he said to the paralytic, ' My son, your sins are forgiven '**), but with verse 6, which introduces scribes who have not previously been mentioned and presents Jesus' answer to some of their unuttered thoughts. Whatever enlargement of the story has taken place seems plainly to have begun with verse 6.

One is led to ask, therefore, whether there may not have been some element in the original episode which underlies verse 5, and which suggested and stimulated the development which the story received in the course of its transmission. Was there any occasion of controversy between Jesus and the scribes which might have involved something about the forgiveness of sins in connection with a healing?

Once the question is stated in these general terms, an affirmative answer comes immediately to the mind. There was a difference of opinion in Jewish thought of the first century as to the cause and cure of disease, which has already been mentioned. The older view was that it was due to sin, a view which finds repeated expression in the Jewish Scriptures, and particularly in the Book of Job. It is most likely that the great majority of the scribes of Jesus' day held to this view, and used it for homiletic ends. If one became ill one should examine his ways, repent of his wrongdoing, and seek divine forgiveness. But, beside this view, there had grown up a widespread belief in evil spirits as the cause of the varied ills of mankind. This view was not necessarily incompatible with the older view: the evil spirits, where their activity was detected, could be regarded as carrying out the divine punishment. Paul, who had been trained as a scribe, combined the two views in this fashion (1 Cor. v. 5). But, though these ideas about demons had invaded scribal circles, the practical attitude of the scribes seems to have been dictated by the Scriptural teaching.

In the case of Jesus the facts are just the reverse. The evidence of His exorcisms and healings in which a demonic factor seems to have been assumed, taken together with the instructions which He gave the Twelve when He sent them on their mission, shows that He believed strongly that much of the suffering and evil of the present world order was due to evil spirits, who could by God's help be driven out. But it is unlikely that He denied completely the older Scriptural view that suffering was due to sin. A primary element in His preaching was that all men needed to repent. The ills men were heir to might be due to the nefarious activity of demons, but there is no reason to doubt that Jesus would have granted that the unrepentant hardness of men's hearts was an underlying reason for this. But if He did grant, or would have granted, this, it was only as a general conditioning factor. In individual cases He demanded specifically faith in God rather than repentance of sin. Perhaps He assumed the latter where the former was present. He saw in the case of those who came to Him for healing an opportunity for an immediate demonstration of the power of God, if they had faith, rather than an opportunity for moral instruction and edification. We must never forget that Jesus was a prophet more than He was a teacher. It is quite plain that the mind of Jesus and those of the scribes moved in different spheres in this particular. The rabbis insisted on the certainty of sin where sickness was present, and even worked out in time a schedule of particular sins for particular ills, though we must not take this too literally. Jesus insisted rather on the fact that men need not wait passively in the hope of divine favour, but could by faith be healed immediately of their complaints. To the

CHAPTER II, VERSES 1–12

scribes it must have seemed that He ignored the moral factor in sickness and neglected the opportunities it afforded for moral education. To their minds His cures must have had in them more of magic than of religion. We know from another passage that they explained His exorcisms in that way.

Such a conflict of attitude and emphasis with reference to illness did, then, exist, and it would seem to be this conflict which lies behind the story of the healing of the paralytic. If so, the original criticism of Jesus would not have been that He blasphemed, but that He had said nothing about the man's evident sins and the necessity of his securing divine forgiveness before he could expect a cure from God. That one finds exactly this contention expressed in the Talmud—'No one gets up from his sick-bed until all his sins are forgiven' (*Ned.* 41a)—shows that the reconstruction of the scribal attitude in the case is not fanciful. Jesus' reply seems to have been that the man's sins were already forgiven, a forgiveness which a man of repentant faith could assume. It is more likely that such a colloquy would have taken place after rather than during the course of the healing. The deposit which this episode left in the earliest Christian tradition was the recollection that Jesus healed a paralytic and pronounced his sins forgiven. This became the point of departure for a development in which the Christian soteriological system is formulated and declared to have been confirmed by the miracle.

If this interpretation is sound, the story throws light on the formation of the Gospel tradition. The controversy, as presented, had its starting-point in authentic words of Jesus, but the subject of the controversy has been unconsciously modified to make it conform more exactly to the needs and issues which the Church faced. The story also throws light on the personality and career of Jesus. Probably it would be more correct to say that it brings to light another of those contrasts of mental outlook between Jesus and the scribes. For the difference between them was not so much a difference of beliefs as a contrast of attitude and spirit. The point of view of the scribes was that of a logical and practical group who were under no delusions as to the moral accomplishments which could be expected from the people. Jesus, on the other hand, was one so passionately devoted to what He felt were the implications of God's rule, and so convinced that God was now ready to accomplish all that the prophets had dreamed of, that He ignored all ordinary considerations in an endeavour to make actual in His day the perfect rule of God.

ii. 13–17 : THE DINNER IN LEVI'S HOUSE

13 Then he went out again by the seaside, and all the crowd came to him and he taught them. As he passed along he saw
14 Levi the son of Alphæus sitting at the tax-office ; he said
15 to him, 'Follow me,' and he rose and followed him. Now Levi was at table in his own house, and he had many taxgatherers and sinners as guests along with Jesus and his disciples—for there were many of them among his
16 followers. So when some scribes of the Pharisees saw that he was eating with sinners and taxgatherers they said to his disciples, 'Why does he eat and drink with taxgatherers
17 and sinners ? ' On hearing this, Jesus said to them,
'Those who are strong have no need of a doctor, but those who are ill :
I have not come to call just men but sinners.'

This second of the stories of controversy contains two episodes—the call of Levi and the dinner which he gave. In spite of similarities in the wording to the account of the call of Simon and Andrew in i. 16 ff., which have suggested that the first part was due to the Gospel writer, the two episodes can scarcely be separated. The name **Levi son of Alphæus** raises too obvious a problem, when compared with 'James the son of Alphæus' in iii. 18, to have been put in by the evangelist without some further comment or explanation.

The name of the publican in this story has caused much trouble. Some manuscripts read here 'James the son of Alphæus,' and it has been argued that one whose personal call was narrated must have been one of the Twelve. But Luke supports the reading **Levi**, and the other readings seem secondary. Some copyists identified this individual with the member of the Twelve who was called ' the son of Alphæus,' while the author of the First Gospel identified him with the member of the Twelve who was known to be a publican, namely Matthew. As to the relationship between Levi and James, both described as ' son of Alphæus,' it is probable that Mark was as ignorant as we are. Both names came to him in his sources, and all he can do is to reproduce them.

Galilee was ruled by Herod Antipas, and Levi was no doubt one of his collectors. Though the story has no geographical indications except the vague and possibly editorial mention of **the seaside**, one tends to locate it near Capharnahum. As already remarked, there would have been a toll-house somewhere between the town and the Jordan river, which marked the borders of Herod's territory.

The customs during the Roman period were farmed out to some individual who took them over for a stated time and endeavoured to make a profit on the deal. It is evident that there was a good deal of looseness in the rates and amounts to be collected, and the taxgatherers, or publicans, were universally denounced and hated by the native population. ' Publicans and robbers ' is the phrase which appears in rabbinic literature in place of the New Testament ' publicans and sinners.' One publican in the Gospel story, Zacchæus, virtually confesses to having practised fraud. Besides being in most cases extortioners, their occupation brought them into contact with Gentiles of all sorts, with the result that they were notoriously negligent of the ritual requirements on which the Pharisees laid such stress. They and their families, therefore, were held in contempt by pious as well as by patriotic Jews. That Jesus had among His intimate disciples one or more of those who were tax-collectors throws into sharp relief the unorthodox and unconventional character of His movement.

The story of the dinner which Levi gave is one of the most illuminating which we possess from the Galilean period. In it we have a picture of the social life of the people, and one of Jesus in His hours of relaxation. At the table are **taxgatherers** and people who are designated simply as **sinners**. The term is clearly the Greek equivalent of the Hebrew 'people of the land,' which was the regular rabbinic phrase to describe those who were known to be indifferent concerning the requirements of the Torah. There are no grounds for insisting that those at the dinner were merely people who had violated the ritual or ceremonial commandments. Jesus did not avoid contact with those who were morally reprehensible as well. Besides the taxgatherers, there is a story of an anointing of Him by a woman who was a notorious sinner. With such individuals, the whole class of those who stood outside the pale of Jewish respectability, Jesus mingled freely and sympathetically. He lodged with Zacchæus, another publican, on His own initiative. One of the constant criticisms aimed at Him was that He was 'the friend of publicans and sinners' (Matt. xi. 19; Luke vii. 34 and xv. 2).

The Pharisees, mentioned here for the first time in the Gospel, were lay religionists who, under scribal leadership, had formed themselves into local associations or clubs. The members of these associations pledged themselves in general to keep the law, and in particular to obey certain requirements about which it was felt that there existed a deplorable laxity. Among these latter were the exact payment of the agricultural tithes and the observance of rules of ceremonial purity. The name of the organization or party, 'the Pharisees' or 'separatists,' probably referred to this separation from all that would defile and make unclean. Indeed, it was necessary that renewed emphasis be placed on these biblical rules about ceremonial purity if they were to survive at all, for the older motivation—fear lest one enter into the temple in a state of ceremonial impurity—was for Jews outside Jerusalem operative only at rare intervals. But this programme of strict law observance and separation from uncleanness which Pharisaism had undertaken involved also separation from those individuals who were known to be neglectful of the law. The motive for avoiding them as much as possible was twofold.

CHAPTER II, VERSES 13-17

To eat in their houses might entail the consumption of food on which the tithes had not been paid, or which had been improperly killed, prepared, or served. It would probably involve also personal defilement through contact with garments, dishes, or furniture that were unclean. In the second place, the association with such people might lead one to adopt their manner of life. Hence those who joined the Pharisaic movement pledged themselves not to be a guest in the home of such a person, nor to entertain one, unless he left his outer garment outside the house. Pharisaism thus was endeavouring to separate law-observant Jews from those who were neglectful of the commandments, just as the same spirit had, centuries earlier, separated Jews from pagan Gentiles. In Jesus' day this Pharisaic movement was rapidly becoming the dominant force in orthodox Judaism.

The **scribes of the Pharisees,** meaning scribes who belonged to the Pharisaic party, mentioned only at the close of the story, were not at the dinner. Of that we may be sure, for it was against the rules of their society to accept an invitation in such a house. The criticisms they expressed, therefore, were not made at the dinner, but in their houses and on the street corners. No doubt their strictures were sincere. They could not understand how a great religious leader could do such a thing. He seemed utterly indifferent to the fact that the scriptural laws concerning foods, dishes, and ritual cleanness were no doubt violated many times at such a dinner.

By eating with the 'people of the land,' or sinners, Jesus ran the risk of violating the precepts of the law in respect to these matters. But His answer to the criticisms shows His conception of the kind of obedience which God desires. Quoting first a familiar proverb, He adds, **I have not come to call just men but sinners.** He conceived it to be His duty to save those who were not ready for the coming of the Kingdom, even at the risk of violating certain of the laws. Obedience to the Torah was an active, positive endeavour to help those in need. He also threw **the** weight of His personal influence and example against the programme of social and religious ostracism which Pharisaism had initiated.

ii. 18–20 : WHY DO NOT YOUR DISCIPLES FAST?

18 As the disciples of John and of the Pharisees were observing a fast, people came and asked him, ' Why do John's disciples and the disciples of the Pharisees fast, and your disciples
19 do not fast ? ' Jesus said to them,
  ' Can friends at a wedding fast, while the bridegroom is beside them ?
  As long as they have the bridegroom beside them they cannot fast.
20 A time will come when the bridegroom is taken from them ; then they will fast, on that day.'

As in the case of the previous story, there can be little doubt as to the historicity of the controversy which is here recorded. We know from the extremely valuable saying preserved in Matt. xi. 18 and Luke vii. 33 that John was known as an ascetic, and that Jesus was notorious for His lack of any ascetic interests or practices.

Judaism as a whole was non-ascetic. There was the national fast on the Day of Atonement which everyone practised, and fasts were called for in times of severe drought or other national crisis. Aside from these, fasting was an individual and a voluntary matter. It was practised as a sign of mourning, and could be used as a special religious exercise for the atonement of sins, to secure an answer to a prayer, or simply as a practice meritorious in the sight of God. A tendency in the direction of the last-named practice was growing up in the first century among those individuals who aspired to a superior piety. While a fast could come on any day of the week, the custom arose of fasting on two special days of the week, Mondays and Thursdays. In Luke xviii. 12 there is mention of one of the Pharisees who followed this pious custom.

The fast mentioned in the text is not likely to have been the great national fast on the Day of Atonement, for all Jews observed this fast. It may have been a fast at a time of drought, but, in view of the ascetic outlook of John, it is more

CHAPTER II, VERSES 18-20

likely that what is referred to is the practice of fasting regularly as an act of piety.

Matthew and Luke both take over this story from Mark, but it is noticeable that both omit the opening words, beginning their accounts with the question addressed to Jesus. They would scarcely omit all mention of a specific event which was the occasion of the controversy had it stood before them in the text they were using. It appears quite likely, therefore, that these opening words have been added to Mark's text, their content being derived from the sense of the story. Some have thought that the original episode had to do with a question concerning John's disciples only, because of the awkwardness and inaccuracy of the phrase, ' disciples of the Pharisees.' For Pharisaism was a party, and, while it had its probationers—at least a little later—these were neither disciples of the Pharisees in general nor were they notable for fasting. On the basis of this argument it is proposed to view the fast as one by John's disciples in mourning over the death of their master, a suggestion which is based also on the wording of Jesus' answer. This is, of course, possible, but less likely than the view suggested above, for two reasons. In the first place, we know for a fact that Jesus' non-ascetic type of religion was the subject of criticism, in contrast in this respect to that of John on the one hand and that of the Pharisees on the other. (' Behold a drunkard and a glutton.') It would seem to be a sounder method to interpret the episode before us in the light of the known rather than to refer it to a hypothetical incident. In the second place, there was no real reason why Jesus and His disciples should have fasted because of the death of the Baptizer. J sus had begun an independent movement of His own, and the distinction between His disciples and John's was recognized. The importance of the point is that it affects the interpretation of Jesus' answer to the criticism.

The reply attributed to Jesus can scarcely be original. Jesus certainly did not speak openly of His death, nor even privately until after the close of the Galilean ministry. Nor would He, if we may judge by the other stories which have been preserved, have defended His disciples by an argument such as we have in verses 19 and 20. He does not elsewhere exempt His disciples from the requirements of the Torah, or the practices of pietists, on the grounds of His presence among them, but instead carries each issue back to the question of what is the true will of God.

The disciples during Jesus' lifetime did not practise fasting in the publicly recognized manner; by the time the Gospels were written the Church had come to do so. By the time of the *Didache*, in the second century, it had even re-adopted the Pharisaic custom of two set days per week for fasting. The saying before us does not answer the original question in verse 18, but rather the one, Why was it that the disciples did not fast during Jesus' lifetime, but later did? The answer here given was a satisfactory one for the early Church, and, I think one may say, the true one. Ascetic practices did not flourish in Jesus' presence; when He was taken away, they began to reappear.

Why do we not have the answer of Jesus to the question which was asked? For the reason that it no doubt contradicted the later Church practice. Not understanding it, the early Church dropped it out. We may surmise that in some vivid and characteristic saying he turned his questioners back to what he felt was the essence of God's command, and insisted that all fasting, like prayer, be known to God alone (see Matt. vi. 16 f.). We would give a great deal for that answer.

ii. 21–22 : Two Sayings on the Separation of the New from the Old

21 ' No one stitches a piece of undressed cloth on an old coat,
    otherwise the patch breaks away, the new from the old,
    and the tear is made worse :
22 no one pours fresh wine into old wineskins,
    otherwise the wine will burst the wineskins,
    and both wine and wineskins are ruined.'*

* Omitting ἀλλὰ οἶνονὰ νέον εἰς ἀσκοὺς καινούς, a harmonistic addition from the parallel passage in Luke v. 38 and Matthew ix. 17.

CHAPTER II, VERSES 21-22

Here we have a double parable added to the above discussion, and giving a broader answer to the question about fasting. Double parables are a feature of Jesus' style. One is reminded of the parables of the treasure hid in the field and the pearl of great worth ; of the leaven in the dough and the mustard seed ; of the tares in the field and the net cast into the sea. The thought in these parables is of the incompatibility of the new and the old. On an old garment one does not sew a patch of new unshrunken cloth, which will tear or pull the old cloth as soon as it gets wet, nor does one put new wine into old and brittle wineskins, which, when it ferments, will burst the skins. This second figure appears several times in ancient literature and evidently was proverbial. The point of these parables seems rather to be the damage which the new does to the old than the opposite. When Jesus uttered these short parables cannot be said. They can scarcely be made to fit the question about fasting. Jesus contrasted the new day that He affirmed was dawning with the old order, but He did not speak of His message as a new religion to be contrasted with the old. He declared rather that He was teaching the truth which God had given in the law and the prophets. We do not know the original occasion of the words ; the meaning they came to convey to the early Christian is clear. The new wine of the Christian message and belief could not be pressed into the older wineskins of Jewish ceremonial practice. The general thought of the parables is clear enough in themselves. But their specific reference and meaning has been given them by the use to which they were put by the courageous Church of the first century:

ii. 23-28 : THE DISCIPLES PLUCK GRAIN ON THE SABBATH

Now it happened that he was passing through the cornfields 23 on the sabbath, and as the disciples made their way through, they began to pull the ears of corn. The Pharisees 24 said to him, ' Look at what they are doing on the sabbath ! That is not allowed.' He said to them, ' Have you never 25

26   read what David did when he was in need and hungry, he and his men ? He went into the house of God (Abiathar was high priest then) and ate *the loaves of the Presence*, which no one except the priests is allowed to eat, and also
27   shared them with his followers.' And he said to them, ' The sabbath was made for man, not man for the
28   sabbath : so that the Son of man is Lord even over the sabbath.'

    This episode, like the others in this conflict section, is given without any statement of time or place. The disciples plucked the ripe grain, husked it by rubbing it in their hands, and ate it. There was no objection to this act in itself ; indeed, it is expressly permitted in Deut. xxiii. 25, being part of the humanitarian legislation which characterizes that book. The censure passed on the act was because it was done upon the Sabbath. Plucking the grain came under the head of reaping, which, as one of the thirty-nine primary acts of labour, was prohibited on the Sabbath. Rubbing the grain out of the husk would also come under criticism as being threshing, which was also prohibited. There is no doubt that, according to the scribal definition of ' work,' the deed of the disciples violated the fourth commandment. Incidentally, it is worth noting how frequently it is an act of the disciples, rather than of Jesus Himself, which called forth criticism. It was their failure to fast, their act of plucking the grain on the Sabbath, and their failure to wash the hands before eating, which brought forth objections. Taking the group as a whole, it is obvious that Jesus' disciples were members of the ' people of the land,' people who did not keep the laws with exactness, a fact which throws light on the early history of the Church. Jesus in each case, however, defends their behaviour. While the episode is not dated, the fact that the grain was ripe enables us to identify it as having occurred about the time of the Passover. This supplies some data for the chronology of the life of Jesus. One year at least lies between this incident and the final days in Jerusalem.

    In answer to the criticism, Jesus turned to an incident in

CHAPTER II, VERSES 23-28

the life of David—the story of how he came to Nob fleeing from Saul, and ate the holy bread which only the priests were allowed to eat. The reference to **Abiathar** may be a textual corruption. Although Matthew and Luke both follow Mark's wording closely for this story, neither has the words stating the name of the priest. In any case Abiathar is an error. The priest's name was Ahimelech (1 Sam. xxi. 1-7). It is notable that Jesus thus raises no protest against the definition of His disciples' deed as work. He accepts the fact that the Sabbath law had been technically violated, but appeals to an episode in the life of David to prove that such violations under certain circumstances were justifiable.

This incident in the Scriptures had not been unnoticed by the scribes, and two passages in which it is discussed have been preserved in Jewish literature. In both these the point is stressed that David's hunger had reached the point of necessity, a fact not specifically mentioned in 1 Samuel, and the danger to life thus justified his violation of the law about the shewbread. For rabbinic teaching was clear on this point—danger to life justified the suspension of the laws of the Torah, which were given ' that men might live by them, and not die by them.' Jesus perhaps understood the story in the same way, for He speaks of **what David did when he was in need and hungry.** The difference between the rabbinic treatment of the story and that of Jesus is the moral that is drawn. In the rabbinic passages it is made clear that it is only an actual danger to life which induced David to violate the law ; Jesus cites His example as justifying the disciples in satisfying their hunger, though obviously they were in no danger of death. Jesus thus was familiar with the rabbinic teaching in this respect, and probably even with their use of this particular passage from the Scriptures. He drew from it a far wider deduction—ritual laws were subordinate to human needs. His view was in line with rabbinic teaching, but went much further—so much further, indeed, as to become a quite new and independent teaching.

A further point requires notice. Jesus appealed to David's violation of the law of the shewbread and applied the incident to a violation of the Sabbath law of work. It is true that one of the Midrashic discussions of the incident states that David arrived at Nob on a Sabbath, and this may have suggested the reference, but nevertheless it was the law of the shewbread that David broke. The application of this to the Sabbath law is obviously only one of many uses to which the principle could be put. It would seem that Jesus had clearly stated to Himself the principle that service of men and women was commanded by God as a primary duty, and that all laws of ritual were secondary to this chief commandment.

To this defence by citation of David's example there is added two further verses. One notices that there is a break in the continuity of the passage, the introductory phrase **And he said to them** being repeated. It would appear that these verses originally were independent of the above discussion, and represent a different answer current in the Church to criticisms of Jesus' freedom as regards the Sabbath. Verse 27 was a familiar saying in the synagogue, virtually the identical saying being attributed to two rabbinic authorities. It seems to have been cited repeatedly in connection with the principle that the saving of life on the Sabbath was permissible. The words are not found in either Matthew or Luke, nor is there any suggestion of them. Furthermore, the verse is missing from a number of the early manuscripts. It appears thus to be a ' Western non-interpolation,' to use the language of Westcott and Hort—that is, a passage in which the Western family of manuscripts preserves the original, non-interpolated reading. The verse reflects exactly the attitude of Jesus toward the Sabbath, and may very likely have been uttered by Him on some occasion, but we are scarcely justified in regarding it as part of Mark's original account.

The interpretation of verse 28 turns on the meaning which one attaches to the phrase **the Son of man**. Scholarship for the last quarter of a century has been almost unanimous in regarding the phrase in this passage as a mistranslation of the Aramaic idiom which meant ' man,' but which through its use in Daniel and Enoch had come also to be a title for a heavenly figure. If one substitutes for the phrase **Son of man**

CHAPTER II, VERSES 23-28

simply the word 'man,' the meaning of the verse is brought into line with the thought of the preceding words about David —so that man is Lord even over the Sabbath. This avoids also the difficulty otherwise created that in this instance only Jesus claimed a special personal authority over the Sabbath. Unless the verse be rejected as a later Christian creation, this seems the view which should be adopted.

iii. 1-6: A Healing in the Synagogue on the Sabbath

iii

He next entered the synagogue. Now a man was there whose 1 hand was withered, and they watched to see if he would 2 heal him on the sabbath, so as to get a charge against him. He said to the man with the withered hand, 'Rise 3 and come forward': then he asked them, 'Is it right 4 to help or to hurt on the sabbath, to save life or to kill?' They were silent. Then glancing round him in anger and 5 vexation at their obstinacy, he told the man, 'Stretch out your hand.' He stretched it out and his hand was quite restored. On this the Pharisees withdrew and at once 6 joined the Herodians in a plot against him, to destroy him.

This is the fifth and last of the series of conflict episodes in this series. Like the others, it is quite without indications of place or date, and is related to the preceding stories only by its subject-matter.

In this incident the indignation of the Pharisees was aroused by Jesus' healing on the Sabbath. Healing was legally classified as work, and was therefore prohibited on the Sabbath, except where necessary for the preservation of life. There were apparently a number of these cases of healing on the Sabbath by Jesus, for Luke records two others (Luke xiii. 10 f. and xiv. 1 f.).

According to the older law, the violation of the Sabbath called for a penalty of death, as one may see from Exod. xxxi. 14, xxxv. 2, and the Book of Jubilees. In the Mishna (*Sanh.* vii. 8) it is said that one who defiles the Sabbath shall be liable ' to extermination.' The word used, however, means ' being cut off by heaven '—that is, the offenders were left to the punishment of heaven. Just how the matter stood in Jesus' day—a date half way between Jubilees and the writing of the Mishna—cannot be said definitely. Before A.D. 70 the School of Shammai was in the ascendancy, and their interpretation of the laws was stricter and harsher on most points than that which the School of Hillel established later. It is possible that the Pharisees in this story were prepared to cite the older law and make their accusation, trusting that the authorities would do something about so flagrant a violation in the presence of so many witnesses. If so, nothing came of it, for it was not on a charge of Sabbath violation that Jesus was arrested and tried. On the other hand, His critics may have desired merely specific proof that the Galilean teacher was a false prophet and a beguiler of the people, a charge which would have been adequately established by proving His indifference to the requirements of the Torah. In a definition of the false prophet, it is said specifically, ' He who prophesies in order to abrogate anything of what is written in the Law is guilty ' (*Sanh.*, *Tos.* xiv. 13).

The individual in the synagogue who wished to be healed had a **withered hand**. It is best to explain the cure, if one accept it as historical, as another instance of the power of Jesus' faith and confidence in God's help to throw off hysterical inhibitions. In the text the discussion concerning whether the act should be performed precedes the cure. In the two cases of Sabbath healing in Luke the defence of the deed by Jesus follows the cure. The latter seems the more natural, but on such details one would not expect literal accuracy.

It is important to note the defence which Jesus makes. He does not debate whether or not healing is ' work,' and is therefore within the meaning of the Sabbath law. He accepts the Pharisaic challenge. He merely raises in reply the larger issue : Is it right or wrong to do a good deed on the Sabbath ? To this question the Pharisees would have made a ready answer. They would have said that, while the law permitted work on the Sabbath to save life, it did not permit acts of work

CHAPTER III, VERSES 1-6

which might be good deeds, but which were unnecessary. In the case in question they would have urged that the man could wait until the morrow for his hand to be healed. Jesus, on the other hand, seems to have taken the proposition, ' to save life,' as a general principle rather than as a literal definition. In other words, He went further in the direction in which the scribes had gone in their ruling that danger to life abrogated the Sabbath law, declaring it to be God's will that deeds of healing should supersede the Sabbath law as well. In the story in Luke xiv. 1 He defends this position by appealing to the oral law that permitted one to pull up on the Sabbath an ox which had fallen into a ditch or well. One might ask whether this broadening of the principle to include not only acts of healing but all deeds of service to humanity may not have been the work of the early Church. In the light of the parallel story of Jesus' defence of His disciples in satisfying their hunger on the Sabbath, it would seem that Jesus Himself, in practice at any rate, made the wider application.

Verse 6 gives a conclusion not only to this episode but also to the whole series of conflict narratives in ii. 1–iii. 6. The **Pharisees** and the **Herodians** formed a plot to destroy Him. Who these Herodians were is uncertain, for they are not mentioned in any other extant document except Mark, and then only here and in xii. 13. That the introduction of them here is not due to Mark is clear from the fact that he does not mention them in his account of the Passion. By the time the Gospel was written the significance of this combination of Jesus' enemies had been lost, though earlier, to the Palestinian Christians, the question of the specific groups which had opposed Jesus was of primary importance. Nevertheless, the Gospels preserved a further recollection of Herodian opposition to Jesus, for the Herodians were evidently supporters of the Herodian royal family. Luke xiii. 31 states that Herod desired to kill Jesus, and in Mark viii. 15 we find Jesus warning His disciples against ' the leaven of the Pharisees and the leaven of Herod.' Evidently the religious leaders, desiring to get rid of a popular leader who was challenging the whole system of Jewish religious and social control, joined hands

THE GOSPEL OF MARK

with the political forces which wished no disturbance of the peace. Such a conjunction of forces, however, would have been much later in the career of Jesus than this point in the Gospel story.

iii. 7-12 : Crowds Come from a Distance

7 Jesus retired with his disciples to the sea, and a large number of people from Galilee followed him ; also a large number
8 came to him from Judæa, Jerusalem, Idumæa, the other side of the Jordan, and the neighbourhood of Tyre and
9 Sidon, as they had heard of his doings. So he told his disciples to have a small boat ready ; it was to prevent
10 him being crushed by the crowd, for he healed so many that all who had complaints were pressing on him to get
11 a touch of him. And when unclean spirits saw him, they fell down before him, screaming, 'You are the Son of
12 God!' But he charged them strictly and severely not to make him known.

In contrast to the preceding sections, each of which contained a separate and distinct episode which bore every mark of having been part of an oft-repeated primitive tradition, the present section is evidently an editorial summary. Similar *résumés* have appeared in i. 14 f., i. 28, i. 39, and i. 45. That the present one is from the pen of the compiler of the Gospel rather than from some source document seems clear for two reasons. The facts in this section all appear elsewhere in the Gospel—the great attention Jesus attracted in all parts of Palestine, His miracles of healing, His exorcism of demons and their recognition of Him. Even the mention of the boat —here without any point—would seem to be drawn from iv. 1. In the second place, the two chief themes of the section, the great popularity of Jesus and the recognition of Him as the Messiah by the demons, are favourites of the evangelist. The former has been stressed in the preceding editorial comments and the latter is mentioned in i. 24 and i. 34.

The purpose of the summary seems to be twofold. On the one hand, this emphasis upon the great popularity of Jesus sets off by contrast the stories of opposition which have been given, and particularly the statement just made of the plot to destroy Jesus. The section also looks forward. It prepares the way for another story of scribal criticism which begins in verse 20, in which the charge is made that it was by Beelzebub that Jesus cast out demons. In this section, therefore, we see the evangelist himself at work, throwing into contrast the popularity of Jesus and the opposition to Him, describing His great success and preparing the way for His next episode by emphasizing His power over the evil spirits.

The place-names merely enumerate all sections of Palestine in which Jews were to be found. That Samaria is omitted is evidence of the writer's familiarity with the inner conditions of the country. Only one new point appears in the section— the statement that Jesus charged the demons not to make Him known. This, however, is implied in i. 25 and 34. It is one of the clearest instances of the evangelist's belief that Jesus wished to keep secret His Messiahship.

iii. 13-19 : THE NAMES OF THE TWELVE

Then he went up the hillside and summoned the men he 13
wanted, and they went to him. He appointed twelve to be 14
with him, also that he might despatch them to preach, with 15
the power of casting out dæmons ; there was Simon, 16
whom he surnamed Peter, James the son of Zebedæus and 17
John the brother of James (he surnamed them Boanerges,
or ' Sons of thunder '), Andrew, Philip, Bartholomew, 18
Matthew, Thomas, James the son of Alphæus, Thaddæus,
Simon the zealot, and Judas Iscariot, who betrayed him. 19

At the head of the Church in the earliest period stood a group of individuals known as ' The Twelve.' They are mentioned in the early chapters of Acts (vi. 2), Paul knew of them (1 Cor. xv. 5), and, if our list of names be correct, knew some of them personally (Gal. ii. 9). Sometimes they are called ' apostles.' Thus in Acts i. 21 ff. Matthias is chosen to be numbered with ' the eleven apostles,' and in Rev. xxi. 14 it is said that the wall of the heavenly Jerusalem was inscribed with the names of the 'twelve apostles of the Lamb.' Outside the Gospels, however, these are the only references to 'twelve apostles,' and it is clear that the term began to be used very early in a more inclusive sense—one that embraced Paul (Rom. i. 1), Barnabas (Acts iv. 36), and others known to the Church of the Gentile mission. In Rom. xvi. 7 Paul even speaks of Andronicus and Junias as 'of note among the apostles.'

In view of this scanty reference to 'The Twelve,' doubts have been raised as to whether there was any such body appointed by Jesus. It has been suggested that this is an idealizing of the earlier events, the thought being suggested by the belief in Jesus' Messianic office. The testimony of Paul plus the evidence of the lists in the Gospels seems conclusive, however, that we are dealing with a fact of history. No later theological or typological development would ever have included in the list of the select group the name of Judas, the traitor. Nor, on the other hand, is it likely that such a name as that of James, the Lord's brother, who became the head of the Church in Jerusalem, would have been omitted.

The number twelve cannot be accidental, and is of real significance. Since these disciples were appointed **that he might despatch them to preach,** the number would seem to indicate the idea of a national mission. The stories preserved in the Gospels might suggest that Jesus worked only in certain portions of Galilee, and that it was only at the end of His life that He began to think in other than local and provincial terms. We shall return to this point in connection with the sending out of the Twelve recorded in vi. 7, but it may be remarked in anticipation that the selection of this number indicates strongly an active programme which was national in scope.

The phrases introducing the list of names are awkwardly related to each other. Moffatt has smoothed this over in his translation. The explanation is probably that Mark has incorporated the list from a written source. The setting for the names seems an artificial one. No actual details are known. Apart from the mention of the **hillside,** which is conventional (see vi. 46) and merely serves the purpose of removing Jesus from the crowds of the preceding sentences, only vague and general statements are made. We know nothing of the designation of the Twelve. It is possible that there was no single act of appointment, but rather the selection of individuals until the number twelve was reached. Had there been any formal investment into the office, one would expect some details of so important an event to have been preserved.

The names of the Twelve are preserved four times, once in each of the Synoptic Gospels and once in Acts. Some of the second-century Christian documents have names of the Eleven, but they are based on no new information. Sometimes in these Peter and Cephas appear as different individuals and sometimes Nathanael's name is listed. The canonical lists all agree except for one name. The tenth name in Mark's list seems to have been Thaddæus, but many manuscripts both of Mark and Matthew substitute the name Lebbæus. This may be a Græcized form of Levi, the disciple mentioned in ii. 14, or a different person. Some manuscripts identify the two—'Lebbæus who is called Thaddæus'—the harmonizing character of which appears clear. In the Lucan writings one finds, instead of Thaddæus, 'Judas son of James.' Since these names cannot all refer to the same individual, one must assume that the personnel of the Twelve changed during the ministry, or, more likely, that the full list had been forgotten before it was put into writing. In any case, the Twelve played no great part in the spread of Christianity. Except for Peter, James, and John, nothing is known of them, and no dependence can be placed on the legends which endeavour to supply the data, the lack of which was so painful to the later Church.

The names themselves are of much interest. In form they point back plainly to the Aramaic period. This evidently was the language which Jesus and His disciples spoke. The surname of **Simon** is given, and from this point on Mark calls him **Peter.** The Greek word and its Aramaic equivalent, Cephas, both mean rock or stone. Why Jesus conferred this name upon him, Mark does not tell us. Two traditions about it are preserved, one in Matt. xvi. 18 and one in John i. 41 f., but both are late and contradict each other. From what is known of Peter, however, it may be conjectured that the name was to designate him as in some sense a first or foundation-stone rather than to refer to any unshakableness of character. The case seems different with the two sons of Zebedee. Here it appears that **Sons of thunder** may be accepted as a correct translation of **Boanerges**, though possibly a free one—the experts are not agreed on the point. If so, one thinks naturally of their impetuous character as revealed in the stories in Mark ix. 38 and Luke ix. 54. **Thomas** is a particularly interesting name. It is the Aramaic word for ' twin.' This is recognized in the Fourth Gospel, when he is called Thomas the Twin (see the margin to John xi. 16 in the Revised Version). Whose twin he was, cannot now be said. The old Syriac tradition said he was Jude, the Lord's brother. Can it be possible that we have here a brother of Jesus, one of a pair of twins, who was therefore known simply as ' the Twin ' ? In the absence of any information, such questions must remain unanswered.

The name **Simon** in the Greek text, both here and in Matthew, is accompanied by the adjective, the Kananean. In Luke and Acts one finds ' Simon the zealot.' Kananean, however, when put back into Aramaic, is probably the word ' zealot,' though here again the experts disagree. The Zealots were the political radicals among the Jews, who were eager to bring in by force of arms the Kingdom of God. The Pharisees were opposed to this movement, realizing the futility of all attempts to rebel against Rome. That one of these Zealots became a member of the Twelve gives another indication of the popular and unconventional character of Jesus' movement.

The last name on the list is that of **Judas Iscariot**, the traitor. The meaning of Iscariot is uncertain. It is usually taken as a place-name—in Hebrew, is(h)-cariot, ' man of Kerioth.' Such surnames are not unknown. An alternative view has recently been put forward that it is a ' mongrel word formed with Greek suffix from the standing Aramaic epithet of Judas,' meaning ' the traitor.' In any case, the surname or

CHAPTER III, VERSES 13-19

epithet gives no information which can help to explain Judas' career.

iii. 20-21 : JESUS' FAMILY IS AT A LOSS TO EXPLAIN HIS DEEDS

Then they went indoors, but the crowd gathered again, so that 20 it was impossible even to have a meal. And when his 21 family heard this, they set out to get hold of him, for men were saying, 'He is out of his mind.'

Against the background of the great popularity and widening activity of Jesus, Mark introduces a story of the refusal of His own family to accept Him, and an account of the way in which the religious authorities explained His successful cures and exorcisms. Verse 20 seems to be an editorial connecting-link. One should compare it with ii. 2, ii. 13, and iii. 7 to see plainly the evangelist's method of work. He had at his disposal separate episodes and sayings, and these he must connect and weave into a continuous narrative as best he can. The phrase translated **they went indoors** may mean 'they came home,' as the same expression in viii. 3 is translated. In this case the reference would be to Capharnahum, no doubt to Peter's house. Mark's idea of Capharnahum as the headquarters of the Galilean ministry—aside from Nazareth it is the only Galilean town mentioned in his narrative—suggests that this was his thought. The editorial character of the sentence, however, makes the point scarcely worth arguing.

Over the meaning of verse 21 there exists a considerable body of controversial literature. Was it the family of Jesus that said that He was out of His mind ? Or did others say this ? The Greek text can be read either way, the words being taken in the one case to be an impersonal plural meaning, 'people were saying,' just as in English we have the expression 'they say.' Such an impersonal plural is used by Mark certainly in ii. 18 and perhaps in several other instances. Some writers, who on theological grounds object to the usual interpretation, adopt this view, and explain the story as meaning that Jesus' family, hearing rumours that were in circulation, came out to take Him away from the multitudes in order to give Him a much-needed rest.

But this interpretation is most certainly not Mark's meaning. (1) The story states that the common view of Jesus was that He was a great prophet, so much so that the crowds pressed on Him constantly—not that He was a madman. (2) No suggestion of such an attitude toward Him by the general public is suggested anywhere else in the Gospel. In viii. 27, for example, a quite different opinion is stated. (3) The sequel deals with what Jesus' family did : they came out to take Him. (4) John vii. 5 says that Jesus' brothers did not believe in Him. (5) The story in Mark vi. 1 ff. of Jesus' visit to Nazareth, while silent as to the views of Jesus' family, leaves the impression of an absence of any support or belief on their part. (6) In Mark's list of the women at the cross and at the tomb the mother of Jesus is not mentioned. (7) In Mark vi. 4 is the saying, ' A prophet is not without honour except in his native place and among his kinsfolk and in his home.'

Thus, according to Mark's account, and with some support from the other Gospels, the family of Jesus never accepted Him during His lifetime, and explained His activity—particularly, we may imagine, His independence of, and opposition to, the scribal authorities—as a mental aberration. In the light of this, one cannot but recall some of the vivid sayings of Jesus on the necessity of subordinating the claims of one's relations to higher duties. ' If anyone comes to Me without hating his father and mother and wife and children and brothers and sisters . . . he cannot be My disciple ' (Luke xiv. 26) ; ' He that loveth father or mother more than Me is not worthy of Me ' (Matt. x. 37). No doubt these sayings, and several others on the same theme, reflect the division of families which early Christianity caused, but it is evidently true also that one of the warnings of Jesus was against a loyalty to one's family that was above that of the Kingdom of God. Capharnahum was the Galilean centre, not Nazareth. While we are largely in the dark as to Jesus' relations with His family, such evidence as there is points toward His ministry as having caused a break with His own relations.

CHAPTER III, VERSES 22-27

iii. 22-27 : 'By Beelzebub He Casts out Demons'

But the scribes who had come down from Jerusalem said, ' He 22
has Beelzebul,' and ' It is by the prince of dæmons that he
casts out dæmons.' So he called them and said to them 23
by way of parable, ' How can Satan cast out Satan ?
    If a realm is divided against itself,   24
      that realm cannot stand :
    if a household is divided against itself,   25
      that household cannot stand :
    and if Satan has risen against himself and is divided,   26
      he cannot stand, he comes to an end.
No one can enter the strong man's house and plunder his goods 27
unless first of all he binds the strong man ; then he can
plunder his house.'

In verse 21 it is said that Jesus' family set out to take Him, but their arrival at the place of His activity is not announced until verse 31. In between is this account of the scribes' explanation of Jesus' success. The arrangement is purely stylistic, not actually chronological. Similar insertions of an episode in an interval between two parts of a story are to be seen in v. 21-43, vi. 7-30, and xi. 12-25.

That the opponents of Jesus accused Him of accomplishing His exorcisms, and no doubt also His cures, by the power of Satan is well attested. There are repeated references to Jesus as a sorcerer in the rabbinic writings. Certain early Fathers also state that this was the explanation which the Jews offered. It is, of course, the stock reply of religious authorities to the success of a heretic—he is expert in the black arts.

The charge in this instance was made by **scribes who had come from Jerusalem.** In vii. 1 a delegation from the capital is mentioned again. In spite of the fact that Galilee was under a different political power, religious matters would have been directed by the council of scribes which met in the ' Hall of Hewn Stones ' on the temple mount, ' whence the law went out to all Israel.' Whether these scribes were a committee sent by some official authority, or a voluntary group who were interested in the work of this Galilean prophet, is not said. It is probable that the relations of Jesus with the capital were more significant than a superficial reading of the Gospels might suggest. The movement of repentance which he endeavoured to create was national in scope, and it is not surprising that we find references to scribes from Jerusalem who were sufficiently interested to attend upon His teaching.

The origin of the name Beelzebul is uncertain, but it was obviously a name for **the prince of dæmons**, or, as we would say, of Satan. The attitude of these scribes can best be illustrated by a story which is told of a certain Rabbi Eliezer ben Hyrcanus. This rabbi taught contrary to the accepted decisions, but he worked miracles and called down a voice from heaven to authenticate his teachings. The scribes refused to heed such proofs, quoting a verse from Exodus, ' According to the majority [of the scribes] thou shalt regulate thyself ' (*Baba Mesia*, 59*b*). The scribal judgment, in other words, disregarded or explained in other ways the mighty deeds which a teacher might perform, if his teaching was contrary to the accepted interpretation of the law.

The answer of Jesus consists of two parts. In the first place, Satan would not cast out his own agents (verses 23–26). In the second place, the exorcism of the demons by Jesus proves that one stronger than Satan has bound him, and so **plunders his goods** (verse 27). The important question is whether this second half is an original part of Jesus' answer. It could easily be viewed as a Christian expansion of the first part, especially since the figure of plundering the goods of the strong man appears in Isa. xlix. 24 and again in the *Psalms of Solomon* v. 4. Evidently the expression was more or less proverbial. But two other sayings of Jesus express the same thought so clearly that there seems no good reason to deny that verse 27 in something approximating its present form goes back to Jesus. One of these is in the account of the same controversy in Matthew and Luke. The special features of this account are due to the non-Marcan common source. Among these is the following saying : ' If I by the finger [or spirit] of God cast out demons, then has the Kingdom of God come upon you.'

CHAPTER III, VERSES 22-27

(Luke xi. 20 ; cf. Matt. xii. 28.) The second saying was on the occasion of the return of the seventy disciples, and their announcement that evil spirits were subject to them. Jesus exclaimed, ' I saw Satan fallen like lightning from heaven ' (Luke x. 18). These sayings taken together indicate that Jesus regarded the power of Himself and His disciples over evil spirits as proof that ' the strong one ' was now bound and his power broken. Mark's account would suggest that the one who had bound the strong one was Jesus. But the fact that His disciples also had this power, that the ' Q ' saying quoted above emphasizes that demons were cast out by the ' finger of God,' and that Jesus' cures were dependent upon the faith of the sufferers (v. 36, vi. 6, ix. 29, etc.), points toward the view that it was God whom Jesus thought had bound the strong one. This is the belief involved in the proclamation, ' The Reign of God is near,' and in the other indications that Jesus held the apocalyptic belief of His day. For one of the basic elements of that conception was the belief that, when God's universal rule was established, then, as the *Assumption of Moses* expresses it, ' Satan would be no more and sorrow should depart with him ' (x. 1).

Before passing to the next verse, attention should be called to the fact that there are two conflicting attitudes taken in the Gospels toward the ' mighty works ' of Jesus. According to one, Jesus wished to keep these from being known, commanding those cured to keep the matter quiet (see v. 43, vii. 36, and viii. 26). These commands to silence might be attributed to the story-teller's art. They are chiefly editorial in character, and various Hellenistic stories of wonderful cures have been shown to exhibit the same detail. But supporting this strand in the tradition is a saying in Mark viii. 12 and in the ' Q ' saying, Matthew xii. 38 and Luke xi. 29, according to which Jesus refused to give a sign to those who requested it. This saying is certainly authentic, as the notes on viii. 12 will show. The other view is that Jesus saw in these wonderful works an authentication of His mission and an indication that the reign of evil was at an end. The evidence for the view consists of the passages quoted above in the discussion, and the ' woes ' pronounced on Capharnahum, Chorazin and Bethsaida for not repenting in the presence of works such as never had been done in Tyre and Sidon (Matt. xi. 21 and Luke x. 13). One also notes that in one case, at least, an individual who had been cured is told to go and tell his people what had been done for him (Mark v. 19).

There are two ways in which these conflicting strands in the tradition can be reconciled. One would be a radical one. The injunctions to silence are attributed to the editor of the Gospel, but the refusal of Jesus to give a sign is accepted as the clue to the whole problem of the miraculous cures. This saying shows that there were no such cures in actual fact. Perhaps some possessed people believed themselves to be cured by Jesus, but there was nothing in the history sufficiently notable to serve as the answer to the demand for a sign. The deductions, then, from these wonderful works that the 'strong one' had been bound, the use of them as proof that the Realm of God was coming upon men, and the 'woes' on the Galilean cities, are regarded as developments of the Church's theology—early, but not original with Jesus. The difficulty with this interpretation is that it requires sweeping into the discard too much in the Gospels which plainly belongs to the earliest tradition, not only the sayings here enumerated, but the many stories of cures, some of which are evidently very early, the explanations by the Pharisees and Herod as to the source of Jesus' remarkable power, and the reference to the 'mighty works and wonders and signs' in such early material as Acts ii. 22.

A second means of reconciling the data seems to be necessary. This would be to assume that, though the wonderful occurrences have been greatly magnified in the Christian tradition, there were nevertheless a sufficient number of these to have been significant evidence to Jesus of the dawning of God's power, and also to account for the Gospel tradition. But Jesus was aware that He could not produce these at will; they were dependent upon the individual's faith and God's answer to prayer. Thus He refused to attempt to give signs on request, particularly 'signs from heaven' (Mark viii. 11).

It is even possible that He endeavoured to avoid the constant role of healer of the sick. Yet these evidences of power were continually happening, and He saw in them, especially in the exorcism of the demons, signs of the breaking down of the rule of Satan and his emissaries. (See further the discussion on viii. 11.)

iii. 28–30 : BLASPHEMY AGAINST THE HOLY SPIRIT IS UNFORGIVABLE

'I tell you truly, 28
    the sons of men shall be forgiven all their sins,
    and all the blasphemies they may utter,
    but whoever blasphemes against the holy Spirit, he never is 29
      forgiven,
    he is guilty of an eternal sin.'
(This was because they said, 'He has an unclean spirit.') 30

To the above answer to the charge that Jesus was inspired by Beelzebul is appended a saying to the effect that blasphemy against the Holy Spirit is an unforgivable sin. This saying circulated in different forms, and its presence in Luke xii. 10 in a different context shows that it was independent of the Beelzebul controversy. In Mark it is presented with a new introductory formula, 'And I say unto you,' which usually indicates that the editor is combining units not previously connected in the tradition.

There are a number of rabbinic statements which can be cited to illustrate the thought of special sins which would bar one from the world to come. For example, in *Sanh.* x. 1 it is said, 'These are those who have no part in the future world : he who says, "There is no resurrection of the dead"; he who says, "The Torah is not from God," and the heretics.' But such sayings are to be viewed as a warning against a too great trust in God's mercy rather than as a fixed limitation of the divine grace. The warning in verses 28 and 29 in the Aramaic discourse of Jesus and His disciples would have carried the same idea, namely, that blasphemy against the Holy Spirit was one of the worst sins, and would receive God's full condemnation. Atonement by none of the usual methods —the sacrifices, suffering, or even death—could be hoped for. It is improbable that it would have been understood as conveying a doctrine of eternal punishment. For the emphasis falls, not on the punishment and its duration, but on the heinousness of the sin.

If this saying was uttered by Jesus, the placing of it here by the Gospel editor was entirely appropriate—that is, in answer to the charge that He was inspired by an unclean spirit. For, whatever else may be said about Jesus' conception of Himself, He certainly regarded Himself as a prophet. And the Spirit was in all cases the possession of the prophets; indeed, it is frequently called the Spirit of prophecy. He may, therefore, have uttered some such indignant warning to those who charged that He was inspired by Beelzebul.

But there are good reasons for suspecting that the saying is a product of the apostolic age. Belief in the possession of the Holy Spirit was a cardinal thought of the early Christian movement, as virtually every page of the Book of Acts will show. On the other hand, there is a notable lack of references to the Spirit in the recorded sayings of Jesus. Aside from the present saying and a conventional reference to the Psalms as spoken through the Holy Spirit, there are only one or two references to the Spirit. In comparison with this scanty list are the many expressions of God's knowledge of, and direct aid of, His children. All this gives the impression that Jesus' concept of the Spirit was conventional, and that He thought of God as working with Him directly in His campaign against the demons. It seems unlikely that He should think of blasphemy against the Spirit as the most serious of all sins.

But the early Church was absorbed with the conception of the Spirit both in its own life and as the controlling power in the career of Jesus. Matt. x. 25 shows, furthermore, that criticisms were levelled at them also that they were inspired by an evil spirit: ' If men have called the head of the house Beelzebul, how much more will they say such things of his servants.' It appears more likely, then, that we have Jesus' answer to the attacks on Him in verses 24–27, and in verses 28

CHAPTER III, VERSES 28–30

and 29 the answer which the apostolic age made to the same charge and repetitions of it levelled against themselves.

iii. 31–35 : WHO ARE MY MOTHER AND MY BROTHERS?

Then came his brothers and his mother, and standing outside 31 **they sent to call him ; there was a crowd sitting round** 32 **him, and he was told, ' Here are your mother and brothers and sisters wanting you outside.' He replied,** 33 **' Who are my mother and my brothers ? ' And glancing** 34 **at those who were sitting round him in a circle he said, ' There are my mother and my brothers ! Whoever does** 35 **the will of God, that is my brother and sister and mother.'**

The story which was begun in verse 21 is now completed. One notes that Joseph is not mentioned, an omission most easily explained by the assumption that Joseph was dead. It is to be noted that Joseph is not mentioned by the villagers of Nazareth in the story in vi. 1 ff. Jesus' sisters are also not mentioned, since they would scarcely have made the trip. His relatives find Him in the midst of a crowd, apparently inside a house. Mark probably assumes here unconsciously the setting which He gave in verse 20. We are not told that Jesus refused to see His relations, though there is no doubt that the story gives the impression that Jesus had separated from His family (see the remarks above on verse 21).

The saying, **Whoever does the will of God, that is My brother and sister and mother,** gives us a glimpse of the personal aspects of Jesus' conception of the reign of God. It was to be constituted by a number of people whose spirit of mutual service and fellowship would make it a social body with the ethical quality and value of a family group. The early Church grew naturally out of this conception. The reign of God was not in Jesus' mind an abstract concept or a theological necessity, but a personal fellowship with men and women who would do the will of God.

THE GOSPEL OF MARK

iv. 1–2a and 10–12 : Jesus' Use of Parables

iv.
1 Once more he proceeded to teach by the seaside ; a crowd gathered round him greater than ever, so he entered a boat on the sea and sat down, while all the crowd stayed on shore.
2a He gave them many lessons in parables, . . .
10 When he was by himself, his adherents and the twelve asked
11 him about the parable, and he said to them : ' The open secret of the Realm of God is granted to you, but these outsiders get everything by way of parables, so that
12 *for all their seeing they may not perceive,*
and for all their hearing they may not understand,
lest they turn and be forgiven.'

The evangelist now provides a collection of typical parables of Jesus. The word **parable** in Semitic speech is a term that includes illustrative stories, similes, metaphors, proverbs, and even allegories and riddles. Christian tradition remembered that Jesus' speech was full of such modes of expression, and the sayings which have been preserved bear this out. There are stories of human interest, like that of the Prodigal Son ; short illustrations like that of the treasure in the field or the lost sheep ; similes and metaphors such as, ' I saw Satan fallen like lightning from heaven,' and ' Cast not your pearls before swine ' ; proverbs like, ' A prophet is without honour only in his own home,' and other forms of figure and illustration. When, in addition to this characteristic, one observes that Jesus had the gift of summing up His thought in brief, vivid forms, that His teaching was by no means without humour, that much of it is definitely poetic in its rhythm and parallelism, it is evident that He was a literary genius of high order. It is interesting to note that the Jewish scholar Klausner, who cannot accept Jesus' religious teaching and depreciates His contribution in comparison with that of the best scribes of His day, interprets His influence as being due chiefly to His literary ability.

These **parables** of Jesus evidently made a deep impression on

CHAPTER IV, VERSES 1–2a and 10–12

the early Church, and collections of them were made either independently or in connection with other forms of His teaching. Thus there were parables in the common source or sources of Matthew and Luke, and both writers had independent access to additional collections. As the Introduction states, the group which Mark gives here was probably in existence in some form before the Gospel was written. The absence of any separate settings or introductions for the several parables, the repetition of the formula, **Anyone who has ears to hear, let him hear,** certain inner incongruities or contradictions in the material, and the absence of any evidence elsewhere in the Gospel that the editor was interested in organizing Jesus' teaching in accordance with its form, all point in this direction.

Whatever the original writing was, it seems plainly to have been expanded, either by Mark or by someone earlier, or perhaps by both, for the explanation of the parable of the sower is certainly an addition to the original writing. It is the only one of the parables which is interpreted, and requires Jesus being alone with the disciples, quite in conflict with the situation described in verses 1–3. Subsequent to this addition was the insertion of verses 11–12, which break into the question about the parable of the sower and necessitate the repetition of it in verse 13. Whether the short parables of verses 21–25 belonged to the original collection, or were added along with the interpretation of the parable of the sower—as is suggested by their contents—cannot be definitely said. A clear evidence of this process of accretion is furnished by the incongruity between verses 33 and 34. The former of these speaks of Jesus' use of parables as being limited by the ability of His hearers to understand, while verse 34 harks back to the explanation of parables in verse 11 f. as a conscious veiling of truth. It looks as if verse 33 was the original ending and verse 34 has been added, perhaps by Mark.

The picture of Jesus sitting in a boat and addressing the crowds on the shore, which serves as a setting for the whole collection, is a striking one, and has been depicted many times by the great painters. These opening sentences appear to be editorial ones similar to others which have been noted. Mark has a predilection for describing Jesus as preaching on the seashore—he refers to this in ii. 13, iii. 7–9, iv. 1, and v. 21. In both iii. 9 and iv. 1 this preaching is from a boat. Did the evangelist get this touch from his source document here and extend the picture elsewhere? Or did he know of such a scene from some oral source, and, being much impressed by the picture, put it into his story whenever he could? One cannot be sure, but the fact that the conclusion to the collection in verse 33 speaks of the hearers of the parables suggests that there was some introduction or setting at the beginning of the collection as well.

The explanation advanced in verse 11 as to why Jesus spoke in parables is an incredible one, and has troubled many Christian readers. A parable, no matter in what form it be, is to illustrate and make clear the thought, and Jesus' parables do this to a remarkable degree. Had Jesus not wished outsiders to understand certain teachings, the most obvious method would have been not to have dealt with those particular topics in public discourse. Furthermore, the explanation advanced totally misrepresents Jesus' attitude toward the common people. In contrast with other teachers, He appealed to the publicans and sinners, went to the multitudes with His message, and thanked God that it was understood even by 'the babes.' It is plain that we have to do with a theological explanation which the early Church created.

There seem two notions behind this idea that Jesus taught in parables to conceal His thought. On the one hand it was always a problem to the early Church why Jesus' immediate contemporaries for the most part rejected His message. The difficulty was met in general by the Christian doctrine of election, which declared that some were called to heed the message and others were not. God hardened the hearts of Israel in part, says Paul in Romans xi. 25. Thus the explanation was advanced that Jesus' hearers failed to accept Him because it was divinely intended that they should not do so. Once this idea had taken root, it could be easily applied to Jesus' use of parables. A second source of the idea was

CHAPTER IV, VERSES 1-2a and 10-12

supplied by the Hellenistic religions of the day. The thought of hidden, esoteric knowledge which those outside the religion could not know was so familiar that these popular religions of the time are, indeed, known as the 'Mystery Religions.' To reveal the secret mysteries of the cult to an outsider was one of the most heinous of all offences. The idea of a Christian mystery paralleling those of these various cults is to be found in several New Testament writings. It is presented plainly here. Verse 11 might be translated, ' To you it is granted to know the mystery of the Kingdom of God—but not to outsiders.' The idea is so exactly that of the Hellenistic religious world that its influence in the formation of the saying can scarcely be denied. The passage thus suggests the idea that to the inner circles of disciples and Christians there were truths and mysteries which others could not guess. This became an increasingly popular idea with Christian writers as the apologetic and literary programme developed. It gave Christian writers, for example, an obvious advantage over their critics and opponents.

iv. 2b-9 and 13-20 : The Parable of the Sower

and said to them in the course of his teaching ; ' Listen, a 2b, 3
sower went out to sow, and as he sowed it chanced that 4
some seed fell on the road, and the birds came and ate it 5
up ; some other seed fell on stony soil where it had not 6
much earth, and it shot up at once because it had no depth
of earth, but when the sun rose it was scorched and withered
away, because it had no root ; some other seed fell among 7
thorns, and the thorns sprang up and choked it, so it bore
no crop ; some other seed fell on good soil and bore a crop 8
that sprang up and grew, yielding at the rate of thirty,
sixty, and a hundredfold.' He added, ' Anyone who has 9
ears to hear, let him listen to this.' . . .
And He said to them, ' You do not understand this parable ? 13
Then how are you to understand the other parables ? The 14
sower sows the word. As for those " on the road," when 15
the seed is sown there—as soon as they hear it, Satan at

16
17
18
19
20

once comes and carries off the word sown within them. Similarly those who are sown "on stony soil" are the people who on hearing the word accept it* with enthusiasm; but they have no root in themselves, they do not last; the next thing is, when the word brings trouble or persecution, they are at once repelled. Another set are those who are sown "among thorns"; they listen to the word, but the worries of the world and the delight of being rich and all the other passions come in to choke the word; so it proves unfruitful. As for those who were sown "on good soil," these are the people who listen to the word and take it in, bearing fruit at the rate of thirty, sixty, and a hundredfold.'

* Omitting εὐθύς. The tendency was to add Mark's εὐθύς rather than omit it, especially when it occurred as here in the Matthew-parallel (xiii. 20).

The parable of the sower scarcely calls for comment. It is a lucid illustration of the difficulties encountered, the failures, and yet the abundantly rewarding results of one who sows the seed. The picture is of a field through which goes a footpath or road. The seed which falls **on the road** is seen by the birds and consumed. The **stony soil** refers to the familiar Palestinian condition where a rocky ledge lies a few inches underground. The soil is overheated by the rock, the seed sprouts quickly, but withers because of a lack of earth. Other seeds are **choked** by thorns after they begin to grow. But in spite of these difficulties and losses the sowing is worth the while, for that which does come to harvest produces a rich yield. The reference to this abundant harvest is not hyperbole. The soil of the plain of Gennesareth—the section around Capharnahum—was proverbially rich. Josephus speaks of its fertility and perfect climate in the most eulogistic terms (*War*, iii. 10. 8).

The point of the parable is obviously one of encouragement to those who **sow the word**. Though much of their labour be in vain, they need not be discouraged. It is more likely that such a parable was spoken late in Jesus' ministry, after the sending out of the disciples. It embodies Jesus' confident faith in God.

The interpretation of the parable which is given in verses 13-20 was scarcely one given by Jesus. In the first place, as pointed out above, it is the only interpretation which appears in this list of parables, requires that Jesus be in private with His disciples in contradiction to the rest of the chapter, and clearly was an accretion to the parable document as it was first drawn up. The internal evidence of the interpretation corroborates the external indications. The interpretation makes the parable an allegory. Each difficulty of the sower which is mentioned is said to represent a particular difficulty encountered by the missionary. If all the details had such specific meaning, it may be said confidently that the group who listened certainly would not have understood the allusions. The other parables—that of the prodigal son, for example—have rather one main point which the story makes clear. The interpretation here presented gives the impression of having been elaborated after the parable had been an object of interest for its own sake, and of speculation as to the meaning of its various details.

iv. 21-25 : Two Parables on the Revealing of Hidden Truth

He also said to them, 21
  ' Is a lamp brought to be placed under a bowl or a bed ?
  Is it not to be placed upon the stand ?
  Nothing is hidden except to be disclosed, 22
    nothing concealed except to be revealed.
  If anyone has an ear to hear, let him listen to this.' Also 23 He said to them, 'Take care what you hear ; the measure you 24
  deal out to others will be dealt out to yourselves, and you
  will receive extra.
For he who has, to him shall more be given ; 25
  while as for him who has not, from him shall be taken even
  what he has.'

The parables here cited are really a catena of short sayings. They are not to be regarded as belonging originally to this context, nor to be connected with each other in this sequence. Matthew and Luke have every sentence of this group, but in widely differing contexts and connections. Evidently in the

'Q' source or sources they appeared as isolated sententious sayings which had to be worked into the Gospels as best the editors could. The meanings of the figures of speech or parables are quite obvious, but their original application is no longer recoverable. In its present setting the parable of the lamp seems to mean that the hidden mystery of Jesus' teaching is hidden only temporarily. It is destined to be revealed. Whether Mark understands this as meaning that the truth hidden from Jesus' Jewish contemporaries is now to be proclaimed to the Gentiles, or whether he thinks of the truth hidden to outsiders as now revealed to the initiated, is uncertain. In Matt. v. 15 the parable has a totally different connotation. The lamp represents the Christians, who are the light of the world and should not hide their light.

In both Matthew (vii. 2) and Luke (vi. 38) the saying **The measure you deal out to others will be dealt out to yourselves** is used to impress the truth that as men deal with their fellows God will deal with them. This was a basic thought in Jesus' synthesis of ethics and religion. In its present context it has to do with the relation between one's knowledge of divine truth and one's communication of that truth. Verse 25 was quite possibly a cynical proverb, but was applied to spiritual possessions with a new import. He who makes his own the truth he has heard, will gain more and more of the true riches.

iv. 26–29: THE PARABLE OF THE SEED WHICH GROWS OF ITSELF

26 He said, 'It is with the Realm of God as when a man has
27 sown seed on earth; he sleeps at night and rises by day, and the seed sprouts and shoots up—he knows not how.
28 (For the earth bears crops by itself, the blade first, the ear
29 of corn next, and then the grain full in the ear.) But whenever the crop is ready, he has the sickle put in at once, as harvest has come.'

Whatever be the case with reference to the series of short figurative sayings, this parable undoubtedly was part of the original collection which Mark has made use of. (It is unique in that it is the only parable which is found in Mark only.) Like the parable of the sower, it is taken from the growing of seed. A man puts the seed in the earth and then leaves it alone, **he sleeps at night and rises by day,** and **the seed sprouts and shoots up—he knows not how**—that is, he has nothing to do with it. The forces of nature bring the seed to maturity, and the only thing the man does is to harvest the crop when it is ready. So **it is with the Realm of God.**

What does the parable mean ? Many efforts have been made to interpret it as meaning that the Kingdom of God comes like the plant, **the blade first, the ear of corn next, and then the grain full in the ear**—that is, that Jesus conceived of the Kingdom as a gradual process which would take many years, or even centuries, for its maturity. But, apart from this parable and the one which follows, practically nothing of this sort is to be found in the teachings of Jesus. True, as other Jews of His day, He thought of God's realm as consisting of man's obedience to the divine will, and as existing in part, therefore, wherever fealty to God was to be found. But the evidence of His sayings is conclusive that He did not think of that universal Realm as coming by an age-long gradual development. On the contrary, He urged His hearers to repent, for that day was at hand. But, quite apart from the evidence of the other sayings, it must be carefully observed that the emphasis of the present parable falls, not on the gradual growth of the seed, but on the fact that it comes of itself, that the sower merely sows, and then waits for the earth itself to bring the seed to its full maturity. That must mean that the individual who works for the Realm of God is not the one who brings the final events to pass. His task is to do the work of preparation, to **sow the seed,** and then to wait for God to bring about the harvest.

The parable thus urged its hearers—obviously the disciples —to have faith in God to bring about His universal rule. It was an answer to a mood either of impatience or discouragement. Some have emphasized the first of these rather than the second, and have reconstructed as the occasion for the parable an effort on the part of some of Jesus' disciples to get their leader to join the Zealot movement. The suggestion is entirely possible. The spirit of rebellion was all round Jesus, and had already flared up on repeated occasions. As a prophet and teacher of the coming Realm of God, Jesus would have had to face a popular demand that He put Himself at the head of such a nationalist movement. This was what Herod Antipas and Pilate feared from Him. Their fears were groundless. His conviction was that the divine Realm would come, not by man's effort, but by God's act. ' Repent, for the Realm of God is at hand,' was His exhortation. But while this background for the parable is a reasonable and possible one, it may have been addressed merely to a mood of discouragement on the part of the disciples. Their duty was to sow the seed and then to wait, confident that the harvest would come. It is this meaning which the parable will have had for the early Church.

The question must be faced, whether this belief on Jesus' part that it is God, not man, who is to bring about the divine Realm or Kingdom does not make His teaching of little value for our day. Certainly one would grant that the good society in our day is achieved only in so far as men actively devote themselves to its establishment. An attitude which merely waits for God to accomplish that which can, and ought to, be done by human effort is weak and useless. Because of this feeling, some writers have attempted to interpret Jesus as teaching a quite modern view of social progress in the parable here and the similar one of the leaven which leavens the lump of dough. The endeavour is misguided and inaccurate. Jesus thought in eschatological terms of the universal and perfect rule of God which would be established suddenly on earth as in heaven. He did not say of this apocalyptic event that men should piously fold their hands and wait. He called for a repentance which would transform the life of the individual in all its relations into conformity to the will of God. For the consummation of that divine Realm depended upon God, not man. That is Jesus' thought. It represents a true religious instinct. Even when one translates the ethic of the New Testament from an apocalyptic framework to a world outlook which looks back on nineteen centuries of Christian history, Jesus' trust in God as the ultimate ground of hope and confidence still remains. Men must repent and bring forth fruits of repentance, but confidence in the ultimate achievement of the good depends on biological and cosmic forces deeper and more significant than human efforts. In a word, Christian faith rests ultimately on God, whether one thinks in terms of an apocalyptic transformation of the world order, or of a slow and gradual creation of human and spiritual values.

iv. 30-34 : THE PARABLE OF THE MUSTARD-SEED

He said also, 30
' To what can we compare the Realm of God ?
how are we to put it in a parable ?
It is like a grain of mustard-seed—less than any seed on 31
earth, when it is sown on earth ; but once sown it springs 32
up to be larger than any plant, throwing out such big
branches that *the wild birds can roost under its shadow.*'
In many a parable like this he spoke the word to them, so 33
far as they could listen to it ; he never spoke to them 34
except by way of parable, but in private he explained
everything to his own disciples.

This parable, like the one above, has been repeatedly misunderstood and misinterpreted. Under the influence of the practical difficulty just described, it has been maintained that the parable means that **the Realm of God** will arrive by a process of growth and development analogous to the growth of the seed to become a tree. But the point of the parable is certainly not that the mustard-seed grows, but rather the contrast between the tiny seed, **less than any seed on earth when it is sown,** and the shrub which becomes **larger than any plant.** Had the object been to emphasize the gradual slow growth of the Kingdom, some such seed as an acorn would have been far better adapted than the quick-growing mustard-plant. The object of the parable must have been, like both the preceding parables about seed, to reassure the disciples.

THE GOSPEL OF MARK

The greatness of the ultimate consummation was not to be estimated in terms of the insignificance of its beginnings. It also would have had this message for the early Church. The missionary must not be daunted by the insignificant visible results of his work.

The mustard-seed was proverbial in Palestine as an indicator of the smallest amount of anything. An illustration of this usage appears in Jesus' saying about having faith ' as a grain of mustard-seed ' (Matt. xvii. 20 and Luke xvii. 6). That it sometimes grew in Palestine to become a large shrub is indicated by a passage in the Palestinian Talmud which speaks of climbing up on it, ' as one would on a fig-tree.' The phrase in the parable in Matthew and Luke, ' and becomes a tree,' is, however, hyperbole.

Verse 33 seems to have been the ending of the original document utilized by Mark. The parables given were only a selection. So far as they could listen to it, means so far as they (the multitudes) could, by making an effort, understand. The phrase agrees with verses 2 and 9, but not with verses 11 and 34. In verse 34 we have a return to the explanation of Jesus' use of parables given in verses 11–12. The public utterances could not be understood, and Jesus explained the parables to His disciples in secret. That this note is repeated here indicates that Mark either added the difficult verses 11–12, or agreed with their contents.

iv. 35–41 : Jesus Quiets a Storm on the Sea of Galilee

35 That same day, when evening came, he said to them, ' Let us
36 cross to the other side ' ; so, leaving the crowd, they took him (just as he was) in the boat, accompanied by some
37 other boats. But a heavy squall of wind came on, and the waves splashed into the boat, so that the boat filled. He
38 was sleeping on the cushion in the stern, so they woke him up, saying, ' Teacher, are we to drown, for all you
39 care ? ' And he woke up, checked the wind, and told the sea, ' Peace, be quiet.' The wind fell and there was a
40 great calm. Then he said to them, ' Why are you afraid

CHAPTER IV, VERSES 35-41

like this ? Have you no faith yet ? ' But they were over- 41
awed and said to each other, ' Whatever can he be, when
the very wind and sea obey him ? '

There now begins a series of episodes which are related to each other and which probably have a common origin. Jesus makes a journey across the Sea of Galilee, during which He stills a storm which threatened to engulf the boat in which He and His disciples were travelling. Immediately on arriving at the east coast, in a region that was primarily pagan, He expels a host of demons from a possessed man and sends them into a herd of swine, which runs down a steep slope and drowns in the sea. He returns to familiar soil on the west coast, is surrounded by a crowd, and performs two miraculous cures. These stories are connected not only by being parts of an itinerary, but also by the amount of concrete detail which they contain. If, for example, one compares any one of these stories with the conflict narratives in chapter ii., the difference between them becomes immediately apparent. It is not possible to see clearly the source from which these accounts have come, and, in the absence of any definite facts, the early Galilean travel document which seems indicated must remain only an intriguing possibility.

Storms such as the one described are not rare on the Sea of Galilee. On the east shore the land rises precipitously to the plateau some two thousand feet above the level of the sea. Further north and east it is higher still. The wind-storms which break on the sea from the heights and through the ravines are both sudden and severe. The boat conveying Jesus and His disciples was caught in one of these squalls, and the latter feared for their lives. The remainder of the story is told in vivid and popular language. Jesus, asleep in the stern, is awakened. He ' rebukes ' the wind, and commands the sea to be quiet, just as He did the demon in i. 25 ff. It appears that the storm is thought of as the work of a demon. This was quite natural, for demons not only entered human bodies, but could locate themselves in the wind, or in stars, or other natural objects (cf. Eph. ii. 2). A great calm followed

Jesus' words. The statement of the disciples to each other points the moral of the story, a moral couched in terms of the developed faith of the Church rather than of the days of the Galilean ministry : **Whatever can He be, when the very wind and sea obey Him ?**

In attempting to understand this story one must remember that it was written down a number of years after the event which is described, and in the light of the beliefs which Christians had come to hold about Jesus. That a severe storm fell upon the small boat which once conveyed the disciples and their master from the western to the eastern shore of the Sea of Galilee, and that they were convinced either then, or later, that they had been saved by Jesus' powers, remain the salient facts. One might guess that the words of Jesus, when aroused from His sleep, were words of encouragement and faith, rather than addresses to the wind and sea. In any case, modern readers are likely to seek elsewhere for the causes for the quieting of the storm than did the disciples. But the story contributes a brief but vivid picture of the journeyings in and around Galilee, and of the impression which Jesus made upon His followers.

v. 1–20 : The Possessed Man of Gergesa

v.
1 Then they reached the opposite side of the sea, the country of the
2 Gerasenes. And as soon as he stepped out of the boat a man from the tombs came to meet him, a man with an
3 unclean spirit who dwelt among the tombs ; by this time
4 no one could bind him, not even with a chain, for he had often been bound with fetters and chains and had snapped the chains and broken the fetters—nobody could tame him.
5 All night and day among the tombs and the hills he
6 shrieked and gashed himself with stones. On catching sight of Jesus from afar he ran and knelt before him,
7 shrieking aloud, ' Jesus, son of God most High, what business have you with me ? By God, I adjure you, do not
8 torture me.' (For he had said, ' Come out of the man, you

CHAPTER V, VERSES 1-20

unclean spirit.') Jesus asked him, 'What is your name?' 9
'Legion,' he said, 'there is a host of us.' And they begged 10
him earnestly not to send them out of the country. Now
a large drove of swine was grazing there on the hillside; so 11
the spirits begged him saying, ' Send us into the swine, that 12
we may enter them.' And Jesus gave them leave. Then 13
out came the unclean spirits and entered the swine, and the
drove rushed down the steep slope into the sea (there were
about two thousand of them) and in the sea they were
drowned. The herdsmen fled and reported it to the town 14
and the hamlets. So the people came to see what had
happened, and when they reached Jesus they saw the 15
lunatic sitting down, clothed and in his sober senses—the
man who had been possessed by 'Legion.' That frightened
them. And those who had seen it related to them what had 16
happened to the lunatic and the swine. Then they began 17
begging Jesus to leave their district. As he was stepping 18
into the boat the lunatic begged that he might accompany
him; but he said, 'Go home to your own people, and 19
report to them all the Lord has done for you and how he
took pity on you.' So he went off and began to proclaim 20
throughout Decapolis all that Jesus had done for him; it
made everyone astonished.

The episode of the healing of the man who called himself
Legion is said to have taken place immediately after Jesus
and His disciples disembarked on the east coast. The location
of the incident in this area is confirmed by indications in the
body of the account. In verse 20 it is said that the man
proclaimed his cure **throughout Decapolis**. This was a term
which had been applied to ten cities which had been given a
certain amount of independence by Pompey, all but one of
them being in Transjordania east of Samaria, Galilee, and the
Lebanons. The presence of the swineherd also points to a
section which contained a Gentile population, for the raising
of swine was forbidden to Jews.

The name of the region, however, raises a number of questions. The manuscripts of Mark in verse 1 read variously 'the country of the Gerasenes,' 'of the Gadarenes,' and 'of the Gergesenes.' Gerasa, the name supported by the manuscripts which until recently were considered the best, was a well-known city, completely inland, some forty miles south of the Sea of Galilee. If this reading be correct, one would be justified in arguing, as does Bacon, that Mark was unacquainted with the most elementary features of Palestinian geography. Gadara, which also was an important place, is geographically possible, being about six miles from the sea, but the manuscript testimony for this name in Mark is weak. The third group of manuscripts, which give 'Gergesa,' was formerly regarded as of distinctly secondary value, but lately scholars have shown that this 'Cæsarean family' goes back to the earliest days, and has equal claim to acceptance with any of the other groups. Supplementing this increasing recognition of the textual value of the Gergesa reading is some archæological evidence. A small town has been located on the east shore of the Sea of Galilee, about half way down the length of the lake. The ruins are now called Kersa, and near by is a ruined town called Gerze. According to the Aramaic scholar Dalman, the development of these forms from Gergesa presents no difficulty. There is also a curious Talmudic passage in which the territory in this region is assigned to the Girgasites mentioned in Deut. vii. 1, which would be understandable if a town called something similar were in the neighbourhood. Origen and Eusebius speak of a town on the east coast called Gergesa, although their testimony is late and not entirely in agreement. Thus there seems to have been a town of this name on the eastern shore, and the reading of the Cæsarean family may be accepted as correct. The other textual forms can be explained as a misreading of the name by some scribe as the well-known city Gerasa, and then a correction of that by some copyist who was aware that Gerasa was two days' journey inland, but that Gadara was near the coast. The point is of importance since, as remarked, it involves the question whether the evangelist assumed that Gerasa, the modern Jerash, was on or near the Sea of Galilee.

The individual who **came to meet Jesus as soon as He stepped**

CHAPTER V, VERSES 1–20

out of the boat was in a most pathetic condition. He was confident that he was possessed by many demons, and accordingly called himself **Legion**. This was the Roman military unit containing six thousand men. The man dwelt **among the tombs**. Since there were no cemeteries in the modern sense, the word is to be taken to refer to a group of tombs hewn in a rock cliff near the town. Tombs were supposed to be a favourite haunt of demons, and there is a saying in the Talmud that one who had spent a night in the tombs was a suspicious character. From the description of the man's behaviour it is clear that he was mad, but the popular character of the story prevents any more exact diagnosis of his derangement. That he had been **bound with fetters and chains** many times may have been due to a desire to protect the community, or simply to the sort of cruelty which has always been seen in the treatment of the insane.

The account states that the unfortunate individual ran up to Jesus immediately on catching sight of Him, made obeisance, and addressed Him as **Jesus, son of God most High**. To the evangelist this instantaneous recognition of Jesus by the demoniac presented no difficulty, for he believed that the demons possessed supernatural knowledge (cf. 1. 24 and iii. 11 f.). Modern writers are not quite so sure on this point, and are rather inclined to draw from this detail the conclusion that the episode did not follow the crossing of the sea as immediately as the narrative now states. The demon, with an oath, urges Jesus not to torment him—a reference to the general belief that Satan and the demons will be punished in the Age to Come (cf. Rev. xx. 10). Jesus asks the name of the man (or of the demons) and learns that it is Legion. The demons, recognizing that they are to be exorcised, **begged him earnestly not to send them out of the country**. A similar detail appears in the story of Tobit's struggle with a demon: when driven out, the demon goes away 'into the uppermost parts of Egypt,' far from its familiar haunts. They request that they be sent into a herd of swine feeding near by. Jesus permits this, whereupon the latter rush down the cliff and are drowned in the sea.

This strange story, reflecting the demonology of the day, is told with considerable gusto. It is difficult to bring the part about the swine into relationship with the purposes or procedures of Jesus. If it be regarded as historical, one would naturally explain it as a misinterpretation on the part of the disciples. A herd of swine feeding on a slope might easily be stampeded by a maniac who runs shrieking and waving his arms in their direction, and the disciples would certainly have regarded their rush over the cliff as due to the demons which had just been expelled. But the original story may have grown in its retelling. Montefiore thinks that a popular tale has been attached to the narratives about Jesus. The change from the singular in verses 2, 7, and 8 to the plural in verse 10 may indicate such a growth. The request for the name of the man or demon, nothing further being said about it, is also curious. Demons or spirits are not supposed to give their names so freely. To know the name of one is to have it in your power. This is an old and widely prevalent idea. These details would be explained if the tale had been told differently at one time—perhaps a story of the expulsion of a demon on the eastern shore, then enlarged by the addition of a popular tale with the necessary modification of certain features, among the latter, possibly, the dropping out of the use of the demon's name in the exorcism. As it stands, however, the narrative is a good story which should not be spoiled. But one has the feeling that the verdict of the thirty-nine Articles on the Apocrypha applies here as well: while it may be read for an example of life and instruction of manners, it is a precarious basis on which to establish any doctrine.

On learning of the loss of the swine the people of the region are said to urge Jesus to leave their borders. **As He was stepping into the boat,** the man who had been healed asked to be permitted to go with Him, but was told instead to go and announce to his **own people** what God had done for him. This has been understood as giving Jesus' sanction to a Gentile mission. But nothing has been said to suggest that the man was a Gentile, and in any case the Greek phrase here would mean only ' your own household ' (cf. viii. 26).

CHAPTER V, VERSES 21-43

v. 21-43: THE HEALING OF JAIRUS' DAUGHTER AND AN UNNAMED WOMAN

Now when Jesus had crossed back in the boat to the other side, a 21 large crowd gathered round him ; so he remained beside the sea. A president of the synagogue, called Jairus, came 22 up, and on catching sight of him fell at his feet with earnest entreaties. ' My little girl is dying,' he said, ' do 23 come and lay your hands on her that she may recover and live.' So Jesus went away with him. Now a large crowd 24 followed him ; they pressed round him. And there was a woman who had had a hemorrhage for twelve years—she 25 had suffered a great deal under a number of doctors and 26 had spent all her means but was none the better ; in fact she was rather worse. Hearing about Jesus, she got behind 27 him in the crowd, and touched his robe ; ' If I can touch 28 even his clothes,' she said to herself, ' I will recover.' And at once the hemorrhage stopped ; she felt in her 29 body that she was cured of her complaint. Jesus was at 30 once conscious that some healing virtue has passed from him, so he turned round in the crowd and asked, ' Who 31 touched my clothes ? ' His disciples said to him, 'You see the crowd are pressing round you, and yet you ask, "Who touched me ? " ' But he kept looking round to see 32 who had done it, and the woman, knowing what had 33 happened to her, came forward in fear and trembling and fell down before him, telling him all the truth. ' Daughter,' 34 he said to her, 'your faith has made you well ; go in peace and be free from your complaint.' He was still 35 speaking when a message came from the house of the synagogue-president, ' Your daughter is dead. Why trouble the teacher to come any further ? ' Instantly Jesus 36 ignored the remark and told the president, ' Have no fear, 37 only believe.' He would not allow anyone to accompany him, except Peter and James and John the brother of James. So they reached the president's house, where he 38 saw a tumult of people wailing and making shrill lament; and on entering he asked them, ' Why make a noise and 39

40 wail? The child is not dead but asleep.' They laughed at him. However, he put them all outside and taking the father and mother of the child as well as his companions
41 he went in to where the child was lying; then he took the child's hand and said to her, ' Talitha koum '—which may
42 be translated, ' Little girl, rise, I tell you.' The girl got up at once and began to walk (she was twelve years old);
43 and at once they were lost in utter amazement. But he strictly forbade them to let anyone know about it, and told them to give her something to eat.

The above section continues the narration of a series of wonderful works performed in connection with a journey across the Sea of Galilee and back to the western side. The impression is conveyed that it took place immediately on Jesus' return. Verse 21, with its now familiar picture of Jesus teaching crowds by the sea (cf. ii. 13, iii. 7, and iv. 1), seems, however, to be one of Mark's techniques for connecting unrelated episodes or filling in gaps between them.

The **president of the synagogue** was the official who had general oversight of the building and the services. It was his task, for example, to name those who would say the prayers for the congregation, read the Scriptures, and translate. Each synagogue had only one such official, and he was naturally one of the leading citizens of the community. The present text of Mark gives his name as **Jairus,** but the name is lacking in a number of manuscripts of the Western family, and it does not appear in Matthew. Furthermore, the proper name is lacking in verses 35 and 38, where it would have been much simpler to have said ' Jairus' house ' than **the house of the synagogue-president.** The identification of unnamed individuals in the Gospel stories was a favourite practice of early Christian writers, and it would seem as if the name of Jairus is such an addition. In this case it may have been brought back into Mark from the Gospel of Luke. For the wording of the short phrase in the Marcan manuscripts which have it varies, and **one** group—the Cæsarean family—follows the wording as it is in Luke.

CHAPTER V, VERSES 21-43

Jesus goes with the synagogue-president toward his home. During the journey we are told that a woman was healed by touching His garment. We have already had occasion to note Mark's fondness for inserting one story within another. Whether the setting here is due to this tendency or to historical recollection cannot be said with assurance. There is nothing unreasonable about the latter, though the lack of chronology which nearly all the Gospel stories exhibit prevents one feeling any special confidence in the arrangement. The woman did not openly avow her complaint, but pressed through the crowd, believing that if she only touched His garment she would be healed. That Jesus is said to have been **conscious that some healing virtue had passed from Him** represents a popular explanation of how His wonderful works were accomplished.

Before reaching the house of Jairus, if that was his name, messengers came announcing the child's death. The father is told to have faith. On reaching the house, Jesus says to the mourners, **The child is not dead but asleep.** The evangelist certainly does not take this to be a literal statement. Had he done so, there would have been no miracle to narrate. Up to this point Jesus had not seen the body. Mark either understands the word to refer to the sleep which lasts until the resurrection day, or, perhaps, a sleep from which Jesus knew that He would awaken the child. Going into the room with three of His disciples, He takes her by the hand and says, **Little girl, rise, I tell you.** The word ' to rise ' means in Greek, as in English, both to get up and to rise from the dead.

This is the only instance of a resurrection of the dead by Jesus which Mark preserves. Dogmatic statements obviously are not in order. We do not know the illness from which the child suffered, and we have only the opinion of the relatives and friends that she had died a few minutes before Jesus reached her. In the parallel account in Matthew the father reports that the child is dead when he first requests that Jesus come and put His hands upon her.

The words employed by Jesus to awaken the child are in Aramaic. The original reason for this was, no doubt, the feeling that the wonder-working words should be preserved literally. Origen states that spells and incantations lose their power if translated into another language, and something of the same feeling was felt perhaps with reference to the words used by Jesus to cure and revive. The Aramaic word *ephphatha*, ' be opened,' is preserved also in vii. 34 in connection with another cure. But it was evidently not the author of the Gospel who was primarily responsible for leaving these Aramaic words in a Greek text, for he is quite satisfied to reproduce in Greek the utterances which drove out the demons, cleansed the leper, forgave the sins of and healed the paralytic, restored a withered arm, and even stilled a storm. The most natural explanation of these Aramaic words is that Mark was working here with a Greek document, in which the wonder-working words of Jesus were preserved in Aramaic. He preserves the actual words, as had his documentary source.

In verse 43 it is stated that Jesus **forbade them to let anyone know about it.** This is the characteristic point of view of the evangelist. If the story is told accurately, the command would have been impossible of fulfilment, since those who had announced that the child was dead and who had been excluded from the room were bound to see her living again. Such injunctions must be considered along with the commands to the disciples and the demons not to reveal the Messiahship. They represent in part the author's awareness that Jesus was not regarded as the Messiah during His lifetime by the Jewish people, in part his desire to magnify the healing work of Jesus by insisting that He endeavoured to keep these stories from spreading, and possibly in part, as has been suggested, some actual tradition that He had tried to avoid the role of healer of the sick.

vi. 1–6 : THE REJECTION AT NAZARETH

vi.

1 Leaving there, he went to his native place, followed by his
2 disciples. When the sabbath came, he began to teach in the synagogue, and the large audience was astounded. ' Where did he get all this ? ' they said. ' What is the meaning of this wisdom he is endowed with ? And these

CHAPTER VI, VERSES 1-6

miracles, too, that his hands perform ! Is this not the 3 joiner, the son of Mary and the brother of James and Joses and Judas and Simon ? Are not his sisters settled here among us ? ' So they were repelled by him. Then Jesus 4 said to them, 'A prophet never goes without honour except in his native place and among his kinsfolk and in his home.' There he could not do any miracle, beyond 5 laying his hands on a few sick people and curing them. 6 He was astonished at their lack of faith.

It is often suggested that at this point a new section of the Gospel begins which lasts to viii. 26. In this section Jesus is pictured as moving restlessly from one place to another, now to Nazareth, then across the Sea of Galilee, and back again ; then He abandons Galilee and journeys through pagan territory to the north. The section is also marked by stress on the opposition to Jesus by the people of Nazareth, by Herod, and by the religious leaders. There may be a convenience in so dividing the Gospel story, but in reality there is no break or division between this section and what has preceded. The section contains the same sort of material as that which has been examined—episodes and incidents of Jesus' ministry. Nor are the themes which receive special emphasis in the section new ones. So far as the evangelist knows, the Galilean ministry was from its beginning an itinerant one (see i. 39). And the opposition to Jesus by the scribes and Pharisees—even the plot to put Him to death—has already been made plain. What we have in this middle part is simply the continuation and development of themes which have already appeared and which are, indeed, characteristic of the entire work.

The opening narrative of this section—the rejection at Nazareth—is one of unique biographical value. True, some recent scholars have explained it as an imaginative development from the saying, ' A prophet is not without honour except in his native place and his own home,' supporting the suggestion with the further argument that one of the favourite themes of the early Church was that Jesus was rejected by His own people and accepted by the Gentiles. The suggestion, however, has little to commend it. The rejection of Jesus by His own community was bound to have appeared as something of a reflection upon Him until one had become accustomed to the idea. It is difficult to believe that Christian theology would have invented such an episode outright. In the second place, the story carries rather plainly the implication that Jesus' family did not oppose the attitude of their fellow-townsfolk. Yet members of His family were known to have been leaders in the Church. 1 Cor. ix. 5 shows that 'the brothers of the Lord' were prominent workers, and one of them, James, was the head of the Jerusalem Church. A story which so definitely involved Jesus' family would have required some support in fact or tradition to have been accepted. Nor can one discount the factual details which the story contains —the enumeration of Jesus' brothers, the reference to His sisters, and the statement of His inability to accomplish there any mighty works. Finally it is clear that, if the proverb which has been quoted was current as one of Jesus' own sayings, it in itself is proof of the historicity of some such rejection. To deny the episode involves also denying the authenticity of the saying. One would have to assume that the proverb was first attributed to Jesus, and then the episode was invented to illustrate it. Such complete scepticism is unnecessary to explain the facts, and is a less reasonable explanation than that we have before us the literary deposit of an authentic tradition.

There can be little doubt that by **his native place** Mark means Nazareth. He has twice referred to Jesus as being from there, and this Gospel never mentions Bethlehem or suggests that Jesus was born there. When the Sabbath came, He went into the synagogue, as was His custom (i. 39), and took advantage of the invitation to speak which the president of the synagogue would have extended Him in advance. Mark's story knows nothing of the details of his address. It states that the audience **was astounded** at His **wisdom** and accepted the accounts of His miracles, though they could understand neither. These notes do not accord well with the rejection of Him, which is the main theme of the story. One

CHAPTER VI, VERSES 1–6

suspects that they are due to the evangelist, since they echo phrases from the scene in the synagogue of Capharnahum, where the people were said to have been 'astounded at His teaching' (i. 22 ff.). The rest of the story expresses disrespect rather than surprise and admiration. The home audience refused to be impressed. They knew the speaker, and could see in Him only the local carpenter or joiner, whose mother and brothers and sisters were well known.

As remarked, the words of disapproval which the people of Nazareth express are of outstanding biographical value. Unfortunately, just at this point the manuscripts vary, creating a problem as to what is the correct text.

The reading, **Is not this the joiner, the son of Mary?** which is printed above, is supported by the majority of the manuscripts. But a number of others, the most important being fam. 13, 33, 565, 700, and P45 (the recently discovered third-century Chester Beatty Papyrus), along with a number of old Latin versions and the testimony of Origen, read, 'Is not this the son of the joiner, and of Mary?' This is the form of the question in Matthew. This reading was thus that of the Cæsarean family. The reading probably spread from this group to other manuscripts.

It is difficult to decide between these two readings, but the weight of the argument seems to fall definitely in favour of the reading, **Is not this the joiner?** The major considerations are the following : (1) If the evangelist had wished to mention whose son Jesus was, it is reasonable to suppose he would have given His name, not His occupation. The rest of the family are all mentioned by name. (2) The Cæsarean reading gives a very awkward order of the Greek words. (3) Had the original reading been, 'Is not this the son of the joiner?' there seems no good reason why it should have been changed. The explanation that it denied the Virgin Birth is not applicable, for in Matthew, which tells of the Virgin Birth, this reading is allowed to stand unchanged. (4) On the other hand, it is easy to explain the rise of the Cæsarean reading. Assimilation of the text of Mark to that of Matthew is one of the commonest sources of textual corruption.

Assuming that this was the wording of Mark's text, there seems no reason to question the accuracy of the tradition which the writer used. The story would not have been invented. Celsus, the first literary critic of the Church, writing about the middle of the second century or earlier, sneers at the idea that the Saviour was a manual labourer, and Origen takes pains to deny the fact. This general feeling may have been the reason for Matthew's modification of Mark's sentence to ' Is not this the son of the joiner ? ' At any rate, in a choice between Matthew and Mark in parallel passages, all things else being equal, the latter is to be preferred. Since these two passages are the only references in the New Testament which bear upon the subject, it appears that there is no reliable evidence for the traditional picture of Joseph as a carpenter or joiner. The best ground for maintaining it is the likelihood that Jesus would have followed His father's craft.

The word translated **joiner** by Moffatt can mean an artificer in wood, stone, or even metal. Justin Martyr and the apocryphal *Gospel of Thomas* both say that Joseph—here they follow Matthew—made ploughs and yokes. This testimony probably rests on no new information, but only on a knowledge of the conditions of Palestine. For most of the construction there was, and is to-day, primarily of stone, a fact which justifies Moffatt's adoption of the word **joiner** rather than the traditional ' carpenter ' to represent the Palestinian worker with wood. If this is not the meaning, one would think of a stonemason, a view which finds some support from a number of the parables of Jesus. How long Jesus had practised this craft we do not know, but the remarks of the villagers are proof that He had not been trained as a scholar or scribe. One can well understand the contempt which the scribes of Jerusalem would have for an unschooled Galilean artisan, who undertook to correct their interpretation of the Mosaic legislation. The independence and courage of Jesus are correspondingly thrown into clearer light by these facts.

In the enumeration of the family of Jesus the omission of Joseph is best explained as due to his death earlier. See the remarks on iii. 31. Joseph is not mentioned in the New

CHAPTER VI, VERSES 1-6

Testament outside of the birth-stories and the genealogies. The Christian tradition knew nothing about him. That James, Joses, and the others were full brothers and sisters of Jesus has been vigorously denied, two alternate views having been proposed. The older of these is to regard them as children of Joseph by a former marriage. This is the view of the Greek Church. Its earliest witness is the *Protevangelium*, or *Gospel of James*, according to which Joseph was an old man when he married Mary. The second view is that of the Latin Church, which regards the children as cousins of Jesus, this interpretation going back to Jerome. Both views are obviously motivated by the desire to defend the doctrine of the perpetual virginity of Mary, and have no warrant in the earliest evidence.

That Jesus could perform no remarkable works in Nazareth is emphasized by the word for **sick people**. It means those who were ailing or sickly rather than those seriously ill.

vi. 7-13 : THE MISSION OF THE TWELVE

Then he made a tour round the villages, teaching. And summoning the twelve he proceeded to send them out two by two ; he gave them power over the unclean spirits, and ordered them to take nothing but a stick for the journey, no bread, no wallet, no coppers in their girdle ; they were to wear sandals, but not to put on two shirts, he said. Also, he told them, ' Wherever you enter a house, stay there till you leave the place. And if any place will not receive you and the people will not listen to you, shake off the very dust under your feet when you leave, as a warning to them.' So they went out and preached repentance ; also they cast out a number of dæmons and cured a number of sick people by anointing them with oil. 7 8 9 10 11 12 13

The event described in these few verses is one of the most significant of all those which the Christian tradition has preserved of the active life of Jesus. We are told little about it—little more, indeed, than the bare fact that Jesus sent the disciples out. What the objective was, what was the field of their labour, when did the event take place, who were sent out, whether there was only one mission or a number of them, did the event intensify the opposition to Jesus—none of these questions is answered.

Like nearly everything else in the Gospels, the historicity of the event has been questioned. Some have thought that the whole story is only an idealization of the apostolic office and a reading of the later Christian missions back into the lifetime of the Founder. But there are too many indications in the earliest Christian sources of some sort of mission preaching on the part of the disciples to doubt the main fact. In Matthew and Luke there is preserved an independent account of the instructions given by Jesus on this occasion, and Luke knows of a mission of seventy disciples. One of the most original and striking sayings of Jesus is bound up with the return of the disciples from such a tour (Luke x. 18). In Mark ix. 38 we read of unauthorized representatives of Jesus. In 1 Cor. ix. 14 Paul records a saying of 'the Lord' which implies a missionary activity on the part of His disciples.

The event, then, may be accepted as a fact. Its significance must not be overlooked. Jesus undertook to arouse the nation. To His own efforts He added those of such followers as He could trust. His was no quiet, peaceful programme of teaching, but an undertaking that challenged and quite evidently aroused the whole nation. In the light of this programme, it is not surprising that Herod was alarmed. And the recognition of this programme makes it possible to understand why the national leaders and religious authorities should have been so concerned about the Galilean teacher as to endeavour to secure His execution. The leaders evidently believed that they had no alternative but to accept Jesus or get rid of Him by force.

The account before us is clearly composite. In verse 8 the instructions, which have been given in indirect discourse, change to direct quotation. In verse 10 a new beginning is made with the phrase, **Also he told them.** Nothing is said of preaching in verses 7 and 8, but it is implied in verse 11. In view of the interest which the early Church had in these

CHAPTER VI, VERSES 7-13

instructions to Christian missionaries, as is evidenced by the 'Q' document and Paul's citation in 1 Corinthians, it is not surprising that there were in circulation various copies of some of these sayings. The roughness of Mark's account is due clearly to the use of more than one of these copies, either by the evangelist or his source.

Verse 7 says that Jesus sent **the twelve**. But at the conclusion of the mission (verse 30) we read of **the apostles** who returned. Luke tells of seventy being sent out, and Paul's words are more general still. Probably there was more than one mission. It is usually assumed that the Twelve were sent out first and others later.

As regards time and place, the story hangs in the air. According to the location of the account in Mark's scheme, it took place when the Galilean ministry was at its height, and this seems reasonable enough. Mark implies that the disciples were sent throughout Galilee, but the parallel account in Matthew and the probabilities in the case suggest a wider field of work. Matt. x. 6 commands the workers not to go to the Gentiles nor into a city of the Samaritans, and Matt. x. 23 speaks of a limitation 'to the cities of Israel.' This latter verse is greatly disputed, but the genuineness of the former is most probable, and implies a mission to all the people of Israel. Why should Judea have been left out of such a programme ? Was it left out ? The story of the last visit to Jerusalem suggests at points that Jesus was known in the capital before that visit. The concern of the Jerusalem authorities over Jesus' work also suggests that He or His disciples had invaded Judea. The fact, furthermore, that twelve disciples were selected for some special itinerary or mission argues strongly that Jesus' programme was nation-wide in its scope. It seems most likely that Jesus sent His representatives to all corners of the nation, though the headquarters of the movement remained in Galilee.

The specific instructions to the emissaries are given in brief terms. They should go in pairs. Travelling alone, especially at night, was quite objectionable in Jewish eyes. Nor were the Christian missionaries to collect alms. Thus they were forbidden to carry the **wallet** in which religious mendicants put things given them. Their equipment was to be the simplest possible—no luggage, only one tunic (and not two, as has the traveller whom Josephus tells of in *Ant.* xvii. 5. 7), no money in their girdle. Only a staff is permitted. They were to stay in one house so long as they remained in one place. These regulations are strikingly like the ones which Josephus says the Essenes observed when they travelled : ' They carry nothing whatever with them on a journey, except arms as a protection against brigands. In every city there is one of the order expressly appointed to attend to strangers, who provides them with raiment and other necessaries ' (*War*, ii. 8. 4).

The practice of the Essenes thus seems to have been the pattern for the Christian missionaries, for the instructions here in Mark were certainly followed in the Palestinian Church. Whether they all go back to Jesus is questionable. At one point it seems unlikely. The command to remain in one house, rather than to move about, would seem more applicable to conditions after there were Christians in the various towns who would serve as hosts, rather than to the days when the mission was just beginning. Outside of the direct instructions there are two details which probably reflect later belief and practice. In verse 8 it is said that Jesus **gave them power over unclean spirits.** That Jesus could thus transfer His power to His disciples is not borne out by other evidence, and smacks of the magical. A story later in the Gospel tells how the disciples could not cast out a demon, and had to wait until their master arrived. The statement in verse 8 thus looks like a later popular assumption. Verse 13 states that the disciples **cured a number of people by anointing them with oil.** This is probably an anachronism based on later Church practice. Jas. v. 14 indicates that it was a Christian practice in Palestine. There is evidence also that it was a common Jewish means of healing, as can be illustrated by the treatment which the Good Samaritan gave the man whom he found injured. But there is no other evidence, apart from the passage here, that Jesus or His disciples during His lifetime adopted such well-known therapeutic measures. It is interesting to note that these adjustments—if they are that—to later missionary practice point to Palestinian missionary methods rather than those of the Hellenistic world. These instructions to the disciples will first have been put in writing in Palestine itself.

In summing up the work of the disciples, Mark records that they did three things on their journey : they **preached repentance, also they cast out a number of dæmons and cured a number of sick people.** In other words, the evangelist conceived of them as carrying on the work which Jesus was doing. Compare, for example, the editorial summary of Jesus' activity in i. 15 and iii. 9–12.

vi. 14–16 : POPULAR RUMOURS ABOUT JESUS

Now this came to the hearing of king Herod, for the name of 14 Jesus had become well known ; people said,* ' John the Baptizer has risen from the dead, that is why miraculous powers are working through him ' ; others said, ' It is 15 Elijah,' others again, ' It is a prophet, like one of the old prophets.' But when Herod heard of it he said, ' John has 16 risen, the John I beheaded.'

* Reading ἔλεγον with B D and the Old Latin.

These three verses, giving the popular rumours about Jesus which came to the ears of Herod and the opinion which the latter expressed concerning Jesus, are used by the evangelist to fill in the interval between the sending out of the disciples in verse 13 to their return in verse 30. Other instances of this same technique have been observed, and additional examples follow in the Gospel. The connecting words, however, are misleading. They indicate that what Herod heard was of the sending out of the disciples. But the rumours which are reported relate not to this but to Jesus' **miraculous powers** (verse 14). To make the story fit, one must generalize the opening sentence—stories about Jesus' work came to Herod's ears.

The relationship between Jesus and Herod hardly stopped with a remark by Herod about Him. Had that been the case, the Christian tradition would scarcely have preserved the recollection of it. In this case a saying preserved independently by Luke supplies the answer which otherwise would have been a guess. From Luke xiii. 31 ff. we learn that Herod at one time determined to kill Jesus, but that the latter was warned by some friendly Pharisees. It has often been noted that Jesus is found frequently outside of Herod's territory: in the Decapolis, in the tetrarchy of Philip, and in the regions of Tyre and Sidon. In the answer which in Luke xiii. Jesus sends back to Herod there is defiance, but at the same time a definite statement that Jesus did not propose to die at Herod's hands. One is justified consequently in assuming that Herod's attempt compelled Jesus to change the area of His work at least once. The original tradition from which these words in Mark have come quite likely contained something of all this, and it is possible that the suggestion of a flight on Jesus' part led to the elimination of the rest of the story.

King Herod, strictly speaking, is an error, for Herod Antipas, son of Herod the Great by his Samaritan wife Malthace, was only tetrarch. Matthew and Luke both make the correction in parallel passages. But it is quite likely that Herod was popularly called a king. In Matt. ii. 22 similar language is used about Archelaus, who occupied a similar status.

The views which are expressed concerning Jesus bring out sharply the deep impression which He made. The opinions fall into two groups. Some said that He was **a prophet like one of the old prophets.** Montefiore aptly remarks that this ' hit the mark most nearly. His freshness and originality, his power and confidence, his assurance of direct divine inspiration, are all points of resemblance between him and them. Like them, "he spoke with authority and not as the scribes."' He might have added that the reports of the wonderful deeds which He performed also reminded the pious of the wonders wrought by the prophets of the olden days. Others went even further. He was not only a prophet, He was one of the great prophets who had come back to life. Elijah and John the Baptist are the ones mentioned, both mighty figures in the popular imagination, the one the forerunner of the hoped-for

CHAPTER VI, VERSES 14-16

Reign of God, the other the prophet who so recently had announced the imminence of the New Age, had defied the pagan tetrarch and died at his hands. Herod Antipas himself is said to have adopted the latter identification. To an outside observer there was a striking similarity between the work and message of Jesus and that of John. The main difference seems to have been that wonders were reported of Jesus which had not formed part of the reputation of John. This was accounted for by the whisper that Jesus was John *redivivus*, and hence possessed supernatural power. This statement is attributed to popular rumour. Herod is said to have accepted this rumour, but it is possible that the Christian tradition has taken his opinion too literally. His original statement which came to be quoted may only have meant that Jesus was, so far as he could see, the *alter ego* of the man whom he had beheaded. Some such a view seems more in line with Herod's endeavour to put Jesus to death.

vi. 17-29 : The Death of the Prophet John

For this Herod had sent and arrested John and bound him in prison on account of his marriage to Herodias the wife of his brother Philip ; John had told Herod, 'You have no right to your brother's wife.' Herodias had a grudge against him ; she wanted him killed, but she could not manage it, for Herod stood in awe of John, knowing he was a just and holy man ; so he protected John—he was greatly exercised when he listened to him, still he was glad to listen to him. Then came a holiday, when Herod held a feast on his birthday for his chief officials and generals and the notables of Galilee. The daughter of Herodias came in and danced to them, and Herod and his guests were so delighted that the king said to the girl, ' Ask anything you like and I will give you it.' He swore to her, 'I will give you whatever you want, were it the half of my realm! ' So she went out and said to her mother, 'What am I to ask ? ' 'John the Baptizer's head,' she answered. Then she

hurried in at once and asked the king, saying, ' I want you to give me this very moment John the Baptist's head on a
26   dish.' The king was very vexed, but for the sake of his
27   oaths and his guests he did not care to disappoint her ; so the king at once sent one of the guard with orders to bring his head. The man went and beheaded him in the prison,
28   brought his head on a dish, and gave it to the girl ; and the
29   girl gave it to her mother. When his disciples heard of it, they went and fetched his body and laid it in a tomb.

This story of John the Baptist's death serves further to fill in the gap between verses 13 and 30. Mark shows a fondness for such colourful stories, as can be illustrated by reference to the story of the Gergesene demoniac and the swine, and that of the young man who fled without his garment from the garden of Gethsemane.

Josephus tells of the death of John, but, while his account touches Mark's at several points, it runs along different lines. Herod Antipas had visited his half-brother Herod Philip in Rome, and while there fell in love with Herodias, his wife. The two agreed that she would desert her husband and join Antipas, provided that he would divorce his own wife, who was the daughter of King Aretas of Petra. But the latter, learning of the affair, left Galilee and returned to her father's Court. As a result, Aretas, at the first good opportunity, made war on Herod and defeated his army. This was interpreted by the people, says Josephus, as a divine punishment on Herod Antipas for his execution of John the Baptist. He then describes John's preaching and tells of his death. Herod, ' who feared lest the great influence John had over the people lead to a rebellion (for they were ready to do anything he should advise), thought it best by putting him to death to prevent any mischief he might cause.' Accordingly he was sent a prisoner to the fortress at Machærus, and there put to death (*Ant.* xviii. 5. 2).

The two accounts are different in character and in interest. Josephus' is the narrative of a historian writing sixty years after the event, interested in explaining the cause of the war with Aretas. The story in Mark is a popular legend interested in the death of the hero prophet who had rebuked the ' king ' for his personal morals. This popular legend has developed along the lines of the Old Testament story of Jezebel, who stirs up Ahab against Elijah and against Naboth. Sober history states that the populace connected the defeat of Herod by Aretas specifically with John's execution, and the latter's rebuke of Antipas has all the appearance of truth. Even Josephus, writing years later, comments on the scandal of the Court as having ' confounded all the laws of our country ' (*Ant.* xviii. 5. 4). If John publicly denounced this marriage, one can be quite sure that Herodias would have resented it even more than Antipas. Mark's story thus appears to be a popular account of how the great prophet had been brought to his death by the woman whose desertion of her husband— Jewish law did not permit her to divorce him—and adulterous marriage to the tetrarch the prophet had publicly denounced. The dance of Salome at the king's banquet, indeed, seems entirely beneath the dignity of a princess, but the Herodian family was not very scrupulous on many points of morals, and there may have been some foundation for the story.

Mark's account is in error on one point. The first husband of Herodias was not Philip, but Herod of Rome. The confusion is due, no doubt, to the fact that Salome married Philip the Tetrarch of Ituræa. It has been alleged that Mark is also wrong in describing Salome, the daughter of Herodias, as a girl at this time, it being asserted that she was a middle-aged woman. The only evidence for this is that Philip, whom she married, assumed his tetrarchy at 4 B.C. and must have been, therefore, at the time of John's execution (*cir.* A.D. 28) fifty years old or more. But this is no proof that Salome was his equal in years. There is evidence to the contrary. There are two ways in which her approximate age may be calculated. The first is by means of the age of Herodias, her mother. Shortly after 7 B.C. Herod the Great made a speech in which he referred to the children of his sons Alexander and Aristobulus (among them being Herodias) as ' little children ' (*War*, i. 28. 2). Herodias' grandfather would scarcely have called her a ' little child ' if she had been over ten years of age at the time, and her marriage would hardly have been before the beginning of our era. Salome, then, could hardly have been born before A.D. 1 or 2. In the year in which John the Baptist was executed she would have been not older than in her late twenties—how much younger than that we cannot tell. A second calculation gives a similar result. Philip, Salome's husband, died in A.D. 34. Salome then married Aristobulus, and we know she bore him three children. In the light of this fact we may assume that she came to Aristobulus not much older than her middle thirties at the most. This again would indicate that Salome was not more than in her twenties at the time of John's execution. These calculations do not prove, of course, that Salome danced before the tetrarch and charmed him into promising to give her even half his realm, but at least it proves that she was young enough to have done so. That is some comfort at least for those who do not like to see a good story spoiled by the allegation that if Salome danced at all, it was at the age of forty-five or fifty.

The fortunes of the Herodian family are beside our purpose, however, and must not be pursued further. Only a few familiar facts may be mentioned. Herodias ultimately proved Antipas' downfall. When her brother Agrippa received from Caius the title of king over the neighbouring territory which had belonged to Philip, she persuaded Antipas to journey to Rome to endeavour to secure the same honour. Agrippa, however, sent letters to the emperor accusing Antipas of intriguing against the Government, and, instead of being made a king, Antipas was banished to Gaul. It must be said, however, that at the end of the story Herodias played her part with nobility and courage, which partly atones for the sordid tale of infidelity and ambition which preceded. The Emperor, when he learned that she was the sister of Agrippa, his favourite, exempted her from the banishment to which her husband was sentenced. Whereupon she replied that she who had been 'the partner of Antipas in his prosperity, preferred to share his misfortunes also.' Caius then banished her along with Antipas and gave her private estates to Agrippa.

CHAPTER VI, VERSES 17–29

Before leaving this story one point must be mentioned to avoid misunderstanding. In verse 22 some manuscripts read that the *danseuse* before the king was 'his daughter Herodias,' and this reading appears in the Authorized translation. As a result there is considerable confusion in popular thought as to the figures in this story. There can be no doubt that Herodias was the mother—the 'Jezebel' who was responsible for the prophet's death.

vi. 30–44 : THE FEEDING OF THE FIVE THOUSAND

Now the apostles gathered to meet Jesus and reported to him all 30 they had done and taught. He said to them, 'Come away 31 by yourselves to some lonely spot and get a little rest' (for there were many people coming and going, and they could get no time even to eat). So they went away privately 32 in the boat to a lonely spot. However, a number of people 33 who saw them start and recognized them, got to the place before them by hurrying there on foot from all the towns. So when Jesus disembarked, he saw a large crowd, and out 34 of pity for them, as they were like sheep without a shepherd, he proceeded to teach them at length. Then, as the 35 day was far gone, his disciples came to him, saying, 'It is a desert place and the day is now far gone ; send 36 them off to the farms and villages around to buy some food for themselves.' He replied, 'Give them some food, 37 yourselves.' They said, 'Are we to go and buy ten pounds' worth of food and give them that to eat ? ' He said, 'How 38 many loaves have you got ? Go and see.' When they found out they told him, 'Five, and two fish.' Then he 39 gave orders that they were to make all the people lie down in parties on the green grass ; so they arranged them- 40 selves in groups of a hundred and of fifty; and he took 41 the five loaves and the two fish, and looking up to heaven he blessed them, broke the loaves in pieces which he handed to the disciples to set before them, and divided the two fish among them all. They all ate and had 42 enough ; besides, the fragments of bread and of fish which 43

44   were picked up filled twelve baskets. (The number of men who ate the loaves was five thousand.)

With verse 30 Mark picks up the thread of the narrative which had been dropped with verse 13. The disciples return and narrate what they have done. Jesus bids them to retire to some place of quiet where they can rest. This they do by boat, yet the crowd sees them going and precedes them on foot, so that when they disembark a crowd is waiting. All of this was natural enough, but a scrutiny of the verses suggests strongly that they are editorial in character, and simply make the connection with the story which comes next. The disciples are present in the episode to be narrated, and so they must be brought back. Note that while it is stated that they **reported to Him all they had done and taught,** there is no word as to the content of that report, nor even whether or not the mission had been successful. The next episode takes place in **a lonely spot,** but the crowd is still present. Hence Jesus must go off, but He is followed. Note that Mark does not know anything about where the place was. The rest of these introductory sentences might be described as stage scenery, familiar already from the section iii. 7–9—the crowd pressing on Him, the boat in which He seeks rest, and yet His inability to escape. If this be so, we need not bother about the questions which have perplexed many exegetes, whether or not people on foot could get around the northern shore of the lake and arrive on the other side before the boat. For those to whom this seems an arbitrary treatment, however, it might be pointed out that there is nothing in the text which says that the boat in which Jesus and His disciples set out went to the eastern shore. If the boat headed a few miles north or south, it would have been possible for the crowd to keep it in view and even to be waiting on the shore when the boat came to land.

With verse 34 the new episode begins. The story is distinctive in that it is the only episode of the Galilean ministry which all four of the Gospels narrate. Furthermore, it is the one episode which is reported twice in Mark's Gospel, the story of **the feeding of the four thousand** in viii. 1–10 being universally regarded as a doublet of the narrative here. It is evident that the story was a favourite one in Christian circles.

At first glance the account of the feeding of the five thousand would seem to contain the reminiscences of an eyewitness. The meal took place in the evening. The disciples suggested sending the multitudes away. Jesus asked them to go and see how much food they had already. They report the exact number of loaves and fishes. The crowd is then made to sit down in **parties on the green grass.** They arranged themselves in orderly groups. The disciples divided the food which Jesus had blessed. We are even told how many baskets full of fragments were taken up. But if one looks at the second story of this episode in viii. 1 ff., one is made to hesitate, for here is a second account of this feeding, and these details are either absent or are different. It is, of course, possible that we have in the account given here a story which goes back originally to some eyewitness, while the second account is a derived one, an off-shoot of the main tradition from which the realistic details have been lost. But this is only one of two possibilities. Those who told these stories, probably for several decades before they were put into writing, were not devoid of an artistic sense. The picture of the crowds drawn up in orderly groups on the green grass which is lacking in the second account may be picturesque accretions to the story. We must therefore hesitate to lay much weight on these details. This is particularly unfortunate as regards **the green grass,** for this is one of the few chronological indications in all the material which Mark records. Grass in Galilee is green only in the springtime, before and a few weeks after Passover. But, even if the detail be authentic, it could not be argued that a year had elapsed since the episode of the plucking of the ripe grain recounted in ii. 23 ff., for the Marcan arrangement is not chronological. Both episodes may have occurred at practically the same time, or at a considerable interval.

The main question, however, is whether the narrative has any foundation in fact. Many scholars have doubted this, quite apart from the question of miracle, because of the Old Testament parallels and because of the anticipations in the story of the common meals of the Christian Church and the celebration of the Eucharist. It is the general belief of the writer of this commentary, however, that the Gospel narratives are not free untrammelled constructions of Christian thought, but had their rise, for the most part at least, in actual events, which, of course, may have been modified or misunderstood in the subsequent retelling. Even in the present story this may have been the case, though I would not deny the influence of the Old Testament stories, particularly of 2 Kings iv. 42-44.

The belief that the story anticipates the Christian Eucharist centres on the striking wording of verse 41. **He took the five loaves . . . broke the loaves in pieces which he handed to the disciples to set before them** (cf. Mark xiv. 22). Perhaps the form of wording has been influenced by the more familiar story of the Eucharist, but the deed itself is not an echo of that ceremony, but quite in place. As Billerbeck has shown in his commentary from the rabbinic writings, the approved ritual for beginning a meal when guests were present was for the host, or the most distinguished person present, to take bread, to pronounce the blessing over it, break it, give portions to the guests present, and to begin the meal by eating a portion of it. It certainly seems more reasonable to assume that there was a memorable meal in a lonely place initiated by Jesus, and that this was developed into a miracle of the multiplication of loaves and fish, than to assume that it was invented quite without any beginning point in the tradition.

On this assumption the story can be reconstructed in its main outlines. All day Jesus had been teaching the people, speaking of the coming Realm of God and its basic principles of fellowship and mutual assistance. Someone calls to His attention that it is late and there is no way to procure food in that place. Jesus sends His disciples to find out how much food they have brought, for there is no suggestion in the Synoptic Gospels that the loaves and fishes were provided by a boy. That is only in John. He makes the people sit down in companies which form eating groups such as the Jews were familiar with when they ate their sacred meals in Jerusalem at the time of the festivals. At His suggestion all the company

CHAPTER VI, VERSES 30-44

share with others what they have with them. All are fed, and the lesson of love and service to one's neighbour and of the joy of so doing has been driven home. Even the detail about picking up the fragments was true to form. In the present story the object of mentioning this was merely to show how much food was left over, but, if what took place was a social meal, this was not the original reason for the act. To gather up at the end of the main course the larger pieces which had fallen on the floor was one of the fixed rules of procedure at polite Jewish dinners. There is a Talmudic story, somewhat later than the Gospels, which indicates that the practice rested on the superstitious belief that by so doing one kept away the demon of poverty. The story forms an interesting parallel to the one under consideration. A demon has been pursuing a man for a long time, and, at last seeing him eating his meal on grass, is confident that he will gain possession of him. The man thwarts the demon, however, by cutting down the grass and throwing it and the fragments which had fallen on it into a near-by stream. The custom, then, applied even to eating on grass. Apparently the disciples in gathering up the fragments were endeavouring to carry out the dictates of good manners.

But if for a brief hour beside the sea, with the words of the Teacher still ringing in their ears, the crowd entered into the spirit of that fellowship under God which He had described, and if this was the origin of the story, it did not remain so simple. The loaves and fishes fetched by the disciples became the only food, and this by the Lord's blessing was miraculously multiplied. Furthermore, the story became symbolic to the early Christians. The meal became an anticipation of the Eucharist. Bread and fish appear frequently in frescoes in the catacombs as symbols of the Eucharist. The celebrant of the mass in the Western Church still looks **up to heaven** when he consecrates the elements. In this way a tradition gathers meaning and becomes rich with significance as it is transmitted from hearer to hearer and from generation to generation. No one should object to such growth in richness and suggestiveness as the stream of Christian tradition flows on. But these acquired meanings have to be stripped off if one's object is to get back to the earliest scenes and ideas.

vi. 45–52 : JESUS WALKS UPON THE WATER

45 Then he made the disciples at once embark in the boat and cross before him towards Bethsaida, while he dismissed the
46 crowd ; and after saying goodbye to them he went up the
47 hill to pray. Now when evening came the boat was far out in the middle of the sea, and he was on the land alone ;
48 but when he saw them buffeted as they rowed (for the wind was against them), he went to them about the fourth watch
49 of the night, walking on the sea. He could have passed them by, but when they saw him walking on the sea they
50 thought it was a ghost and shrieked aloud—for they all saw him and were terrified. Then he spoke to them at
51 once ; ' Courage,' he said, ' it is I, have no fear.' And he got into the boat beside them, and the wind dropped. They
52 were utterly astounded, for they had not understood the lesson of the loaves ; their minds were dull.

This story seems to have been connected with the previous one in one of Mark's written sources. For the words in verse 45, in which Jesus makes the disciples embark in the boat and proceed toward Bethsaida while He dismisses the crowd, presuppose the previous situation. Nor can these words be regarded simply as editorial connecting links, for, in that case, whence came the mention of the town Bethsaida ? Mark has no interest in these Galilean place names, makes no use of the town in his story, and one can conceive of no reason for the place having been mentioned had it not been present in some very definite form in some source which he was using. It would appear, therefore, that verse 45 was not composed by the evangelist, or, putting it conversely, that the connection between the story of the feeding of the five thousand and the walking on the water had already been made in one of his source documents.

CHAPTER VI, VERSES 45-52

The mention of Bethsaida in this verse is the beginning of a series of place names that strikes one as surprising. After the disciples are sent toward Bethsaida, in verse 45, we read in verse 53 that they landed at Gennesaret. In vii. 24 Jesus departs for the regions of Tyre, then comes back to the territory of the Decapolis (vii. 31); in viii. 10, crosses the sea to 'the district of Dalmanutha,' recrosses the sea again (viii. 13), reaches Bethsaida a second time (viii. 22); and in viii. 27 is mentioned as being near Cæsarea Philippi. These movements are vague and at times confused, as the detailed notes will show. The place names do not play any important part in the episodes which are recounted. But the sudden appearance of this series of place names is definitely of interest.

From the opening of the public ministry of Jesus to vi. 45 Mark has not given the names of any locations with the exception of Capharnahum, 'His native place,' and 'the country of the Gergesenes.' It is evident that the evangelist has not inserted these names to give definiteness to his account, else he would have put them in also in the earlier chapters. As remarked in the Introduction, there seems to be a source or sources which has supplied them. The delineation of such a document or documents, however, in the present state of our knowledge is largely guess-work.

The Bethsaida of verse 45 was in all probability the Bethsaida Julias, mentioned by Josephus, which lay on the eastern side of the Jordan river at the point where it emptied into the Sea of Galilee. It had been rebuilt by Philip, tetrarch of Ituræa, in 4 B.C., and named after Augustus' daughter. He built a palace there in which he died in A.D. 34. Some have conjectured that there was a second Bethsaida somewhere on the western shore because of the difficulties of harmonizing verse 45 with verse 53, but there is no evidence of any such. That the name Bethsaida does not have its recently bestowed additional name Julias is perhaps because the populace continued to use the older name for the town.

The story which follows, of Jesus overtaking the boat when it was in the middle of the sea and walking on the water up to it, can only be described as a pious legend. Some have thought

THE GOSPEL OF MARK

that it took its rise from some saying of Jesus, but none such is cited—as would be expected in such circumstances. There are no Old Testament parallels to the story. It seems easiest to suppose that there was some incident which furnished the starting-point for the legend, but it is idle to conjecture exactly what happened. The story of the storm at sea (iv. 35 ff.) seems to have coloured the account to some extent. Note the wording of verses 48 and 51. **The fourth watch of the night** was about 3 a.m. This division of the night into four watches was the Roman mode of reckoning in contrast to the older Jewish system of three night watches of four hours each. The Roman reckoning seems to have passed over into local Jewish usage, due no doubt to the presence of the Roman troops in Palestine (see Acts xii. 4, the four divisions in Mark xiii. 35). The detail, therefore, is no sure clue as to the provenance of the Gospel. The Jewish reckoning of three watches remained, however, in the temple.

In verse 52 we have the statement that the disciples **had not understood the lesson of the loaves ; their minds were dull.** The translation of the last phrase is not quite strong enough. Literally it reads, " Their hearts were hardened "—reminiscent of the biblical story of Pharaoh. The thought of the evangelist is that the disciples were not permitted to understand these events until after the resurrection. The explanation seems to reveal a consciousness on the part of Christian groups that much of its theology, and even to an extent its tradition of the events of Jesus' life, was a subsequent development.

vi. 53–56 : THE SICK CROWD AROUND JESUS WHEREVER HE GOES

53 **On crossing over they came to land at Gennesaret and moored**
54 **to the shore. And when they had disembarked, the people**
55 **at once recognized Jesus ; they hurried round all the district and proceeded to carry the sick on their pallets,**
56 **wherever they heard that he was ; whatever village or town or hamlet he went to, they would lay their invalids in**

CHAPTER VI, VERSES 53-56

the marketplace, begging him to let them touch even the tassel of his robe—and all who touched him recovered.

This general statement is similar to the ones which have appeared at iii. 7-12, vi. 7, and probably at vi. 30-33. The writing of **Gennesaret**, however, is so pointless that it must be due to a written source. Mark may have had before him some note that Jesus landed at Gennesaret and the people brought their sick to Him, which he expanded into the present general statements.

Gennesaret was the name of a remarkably fertile and thickly populated plain on the north-west side of the Sea of Galilee. That the disciples set out for Bethsaida (verse 45) and landed at Gennesaret is explained either on the assumption that head winds led them to alter their course, or, more likely, that these place names are remains from an earlier tradition from which the connecting links have dropped out.

The **tassel of His robe** was the blue fringe or tassel required on the corners of the robe of every male Jew by the law of Numbers xv. 38. By this tassel a Jew could always be distinguished from a Gentile. That Jesus wore these tassels is only one of the many points which shows His loyalty to the religion of the Torah.

vii. 1-16: THE CONTROVERSY OVER THE RITUAL WASHING OF HANDS

vii.

Now the Pharisees gathered to meet him, with some scribes 1 who had come from Jerusalem. They noticed that some of 2 his disciples ate their food with ' common ' (that is, unwashed) hands. (The Pharisees and all the Jews decline to 3 eat till they wash their hands up to the elbow, in obedience to the tradition of the elders ; they decline to eat what 4 comes from the market till they have washed it ; and they have a number of other traditions to keep about washing cups and jugs and basins and beds.) Then the Pharisees 5 and scribes put this question to him, 'Why do your disciples not follow the tradition of the elders ? Why do

6   they take their food with 'common' hands?' He
    said to them, 'Yes, it was about you hypocrites indeed
    that Isaiah prophesied!—as it is written,
        This people honours me with their lips,
        but their heart is far away from me:
7   *vain is their worship of me,*
        for the doctrines they teach are but human precepts.
8   You drop what God commands and hold to human tradition.*
9   Yes, forsooth,' he added, ' you set aside what God com-
10 mands, so as to maintain your own tradition! Thus, Moses
    said, *Honour your father and mother*, and, *He who curses*
11 *his father or mother is to suffer death*. But you say that if a
    man tells his father or mother, " This money might have
    been at your service, but it is Korban " (that is, dedicated
12 to God), he is exempt, so you hold, from doing anything for
13 his father or mother. That is repealing the word of God in
    the interests of the tradition which you keep up. And you
14 do many things like that.' Then he called the crowd to
    him again and said to them, ' Listen to me, all of you, and
    understand this :—
15   nothing outside a man can defile him by entering him ;
        it is what comes from him that defiles him.
16 If anyone has ears to hear, let him listen to this.'

* Omitting βαπτισμοὺς ξεστῶν καὶ ποτηρίων καὶ ἄλλα παρόμοια τοιαῦτα πολλὰ ποιεῖτε.

The first question in connection with this important section must be that of the hand-washing ritual here referred to.

In the comment on the story of Jesus eating with publicans and sinners (ii. 13-17) it was pointed out that the Pharisees were a body of pietists, zealous for religion, who had undertaken to recover the ideal of a law-observant and ceremonially clean nation. This was in its ultimate motive, and many of its results, an admirable programme. But it had its special dangers. One of these was the inevitable tendency of the programme to become further and further elaborated and refined, particularly as regards its demand for separation from things unclean. Pharisaism did not go as far as asceticism, but it did elaborate its requirements to a point where they went

CHAPTER VII, VERSES 1–16

beyond the actual requirements of the biblical and traditional laws. They wanted Israel to be not merely an obedient people, but a 'holy people,' who would go beyond the strict letter of the law to obey what they felt to be its intention or ideal. Illustrations of the working out of this tendency are to be seen in the exaggerated ritualism of the Essenes, and in such acts as the voluntary sacrifices by some pietists of many more animals than the law required.

The hand-washing with which the above story is concerned was another and very clear illustration of this tendency. The older law had required it only of the priests and their families when they ate 'holy food '—namely, food which came to the priests in connection with the sacrifices in the temple or other regulations of the cultus. Originally not even the priests were required to perform the rite when they ate ordinary food. Laymen had no obligation in the matter whatever. But by the second century the Pharisaic emphasis on ceremonial purity had extended the practice to the entire laity and made it obligatory for all food. It was made one of the primary requirements for membership in the Pharisaic associations: new members were first instructed in the rite of hand-washing and afterwards in the further rules of purity. If they would agree to keep the hand-washing rite, they were admitted to the organizations (see Strack and Billerbeck, *Kommentar*, ii, pp. 502 ff.). But practically all references to the custom are second-century ones, the earliest explicit ones being in connection with stories of the rebellion of the Jews under Hadrian. This was a century after Jesus' death. Hence some Jewish scholars have insisted that the above account is anachronistic, or else that Jesus' disciples were all priests and so were obligated to the rite at an earlier period. But there is a record of a discussion of the practice by the rabbinic schools in the second half of the first century, and it seems likely that some Pharisaic leaders in Jesus' day were already demanding that those who would be especially religious should not eat without purifying their hands in this manner. The evidence, however, makes it clear that this rite was not a practice of **all the Jews** in Jesus' day—not even of all the Pharisees.

The parenthesis which begins with verse 3 is in error, therefore, in its sweeping statements concerning the extent of the practice. But there are other difficulties with this parenthesis, some of which are obscured in Moffatt's translation. Proposals have been made to eliminate one of these dealing with the form of the rite by assuming a confusion between certain similar Aramaic words. But to carry these statements back to the Aramaic stage of the Gospel tradition makes them even more difficult to understand. As stated in the Introduction, either the parenthesis was a later explanatory addition to Mark's text, or else it would seem evident that the author did not have any first-hand knowledge of the conditions of Jewish life. For reasons already stated, the former seems the more reasonable of these alternatives.

As in iii. 22, we are told of **scribes who had come** down from **Jerusalem.** It is unnecessary to add further to what is said in the comment on that verse except to note that the reappearance of these *dramatis personæ* suggests that Mark drew both episodes from the same source. One notices that again the objection of these scribes is levelled against the negligence of Jesus' disciples. It is plain that these were drawn from a class of non-scrupulous Jews, those who would have been called ' the people of the land ' by the scribes.

Jesus' reply begins with verse 6, but the words which follow are not a unit. It would be more accurate to speak of three replies of Jesus, i.e. verses 6–8, 9–13 and 14–23. Each of these sections is complete within itself, has its own introductory statement, and presents different lines of defence to the criticism. Note that verses 14–23 are said to have been uttered to a different audience. These three groups of sayings are clearly diverse in origin, and there can be but little doubt that they represent the collocation by the evangelist of various sayings of Jesus about the Pharisees and their rules of ritual cleanness, which the tradition had preserved. This fact in itself is o fimportance : there were certainly more conflicts between Jesus and the leaders of Jewish religion than are recorded in the Gospels.

According to verses 6–8, Jesus answered His critics by

CHAPTER VII, VERSES 1-16

labelling them hypocrites, applying to them the words of Isaiah xxix. 13, and declaring that they neglected the law of God to keep a human tradition. The quotation from Isaiah, however, was scarcely made by Jesus. For it follows the wording of the Septuagint (Greek) version rather than the Hebrew, and it is just the deviation of the Greek text from the Hebrew which is the point of the quotation—the *doctrines they teach are but human precepts*. Paul also describes the Jewish ritual laws as 'human precepts' (Col. ii. 22), and a similar phrasing appears in Titus i. 14. From the second century on, this polemic appears constantly in the Christian Fathers. Irenæus, for example, says that the Jewish elders not only violated the true law of God, but 'they set over against it their own law, which to this day is called the Pharisaic.' In the thought of this section we are moving within the circle of ideas of early Christian apologetic, and it is not surprising that the tradition of Jesus' words has had added to it the apposite words in the Greek of Isaiah. There is, however, no good reason for not regarding verse 8 as a genuine word of Jesus—indeed, as His reply to the criticism expressed in verse 5. For the words exactly apply to the case in hand. The hand-washing rite was not required of laymen by the law, either written or oral. That Jesus and His disciples should keep it was merely a contention of certain Pharisaic teachers. The statement that the scribes and Pharisees neglected the true law of God to pay a great deal of attention to a matter not required by the Torah sounds true to Jesus' outlook and temper. One is reminded of another passage— 'Woe unto you, Pharisees, for you tithe mint and rue and every herb, and neglect justice and the love of God.' That Jesus condemned a false emphasis within the requirements of the law leaves no doubt that He would have condemned even more readily an emphasis on matters of ritual which were Pharisaic additions to the Jewish ceremonial code.

That verses 9-13 were uttered on a different occasion from the words of 7-8 is clear from the new introduction—' And he said to them . . .' (Moffatt, **he added**)—and from the fact that it deals with annulling one of the ethical precepts of the law, whereas the previous discussion dealt with the neglect of God's law. This section goes further than the previous one in its attack on Jewish legalism. Instead of mere neglect we have now the charge of a violation of the divine law to keep the Pharisaic tradition.

The case of **Korban** had nothing to do with money given to the temple, as is sometimes said. The word was simply a formula for an oath or vow. Jewish law regarded vows as inviolable. The moral difficulties which arose from time to time as a result of unwise or harmful vows was a subject of grave concern to the scribes, and by A.D. 150 it was ruled that a vow could be annulled by going before a scribe. There is Talmudic evidence that vows not to help or assist certain individuals or groups were a familiar practice of the period. That vows of this sort between parents and sons sometimes occurred can also be given documentary proof. In such cases the conflict of moral obligation between the duty of keeping one's vow and the duty of caring for parents was obvious. By about A.D. 90 the scribes were agreed that where the matter was between parents and sons ' the door was open,' the vow could be annulled (*Ned.* ix. 1). In other words, some half a century later the scribes accepted the same position that Jesus had maintained, but the passage under review is evidence that in A.D. 28 the scribal ruling upheld the validity of such oaths. This ruling Jesus wrathfully attacked.

The issue involved was plainly one of the conflict of two laws, both of them biblical. Jesus seems to have felt that in such a case of conflict it was obvious that the abstract law of the validity of oaths should give way before the law commanding respect and care for parents. The ruling that the former should be observed He deemed as simply human tradition. It was not from God. The scribes, of course, in reply could have cited Deut. xxiii. 21. But there are other instances which we shall encounter wherein Jesus appears to have been indifferent even to the text of scripture where it ran counter to His conception of God's will. And this imperative prophetic consciousness of God's will was formulated in terms which gave the right of way, in cases of conflict, to

CHAPTER VII, VERSES 1-16

human needs and interests. Within half a century Judaism adopted the same position. ' The scholars agreed with R. Eliezer that when the affair was between son and parents the door was open on account of the honour that is due to parents.'

This brings us to verses 14-16, and to the explanation of this section in verses 17-23 which seems quite plainly secondary and homiletical. Verse 15, the heart of the passage, may be said almost to sum up Christian ethics and to contrast it with Jewish ethics. The authenticity of the saying is seriously questioned by many scholars. Others allege that Jesus meant by it something quite different from the way the Gentile Church understood it. The argument against it is the point that, had Jesus said, in so categorical a fashion as He is here quoted as saying, that nothing from without could make the man unclean, the controversy which nearly split the early Church in two would have been impossible. The saying is thus regarded as a reflection of the point of view of the Hellenistic wing of the Church. Their beliefs were read back into the teachings of Jesus. It is also maintained that the saying abrogates too much of the Pentateuch and too much of everyday Jewish practice to have been uttered by Jesus.

These are telling points. They force us, I think, to agree that the saying was scarcely uttered by Jesus in quite so clearcut a form and with so explicit and radical an application. Nevertheless, there are reasons for hesitating before discarding the saying or attributing it to Paul and his collaborators. There can be no doubt that Jesus showed a pronounced indifference to questions of ceremonial cleanness. He ate repeatedly in the houses of ' the people of the land,' and by so doing faced presumptive defilement, not only from furniture and vessels, but from the food itself. Certainly He ate untithed food freely. In a saying given independently by Matthew and Luke, He condemned the Pharisees 'who cleansed dishes and cups from ceremonial defilement, but who themselves were full of extortion and wickedness ' (Luke xi. 39, and Matt. xxiii. 25). If Mark ii. 25 be genuine, He approved David's example in eating illegally the loaves of the shewbread. His own conception of the essence of God's will was a positive and ethical one. Engaged in an urgent endeavour to bring to the outcasts and irreligious the good news and meaning of the Realm of God, He found Himself criticized and opposed by individuals who seemed to Him to substitute a scrupulous attention to foods and similar matters for that loving service which God requires. Righteousness, as determined by what and how one ate, was an issue which arose repeatedly between Jesus and the scribes. We see it involved in the controversies over eating with ' the people of the land,' in the saying about clean dishes, in the criticism over uncleansed hands. It would be surprising in the light of His bold restatement of the biblical laws on divorce, and His rejection of the law of the validity of oaths where care of parents was concerned, if He had never affirmed that men were not made unclean in God's sight by what and how they ate.

But, so far as we can see from the Gospels, Jesus' criticisms of Judaism were occasional and specific rather than general. If He spoke about man's acceptableness with God as resting upon the state of his heart rather than upon what he ate, it is likely that the saying was in connection with some specific issue and was probably *ad hoc*, and not so detached and sweeping as we have it here. His handling of the law of the Sabbath furnishes probably the safest analogy. He never abrogated the Sabbath nor its laws. But He did ignore and reject the laws against Sabbath work on occasions when human needs were at stake. In line with this, it would probably be too much to maintain that, in the saying in vii. 15, Jesus abrogated the food codes of Leviticus and declared that one could eat swine or camel with freedom. But He may very well have declared, in connection with some specific case that arose, that a good man who was engaged in doing a good deed did not become evil in God's sight through the food which he ate, that men were defiled rather by what came from their hearts. Since we know that Jesus was criticized severely for eating with publicans and sinners, one naturally thinks of some such situation as the occasion of the saying, but there were any number of opportunities for an issue of this sort to have arisen. The scribal insistence on the food laws was simply

CHAPTER VII, VERSES 1-16

because they were commanded in the Scriptures. Jesus had a much freer attitude toward the Scriptural commands. His attitude was more intuitive and untrammelled. He had not been trained in the scribal schools.

I suggest, therefore, that the saying of verse 15 is basically authentic, but that the original utterance was less sweeping and categorical than it here appears. The moral judgment that foods do not make men unclean in God's sight relates itself to much of Jesus' teaching, and the assumption that Jesus gave expression to it does not seem unwarranted. How He related such a judgment to the requirements of the law is not preserved in the tradition. The probability is that the organizing and systematizing of His ethical judgments were the work of those who followed Him.

Verse 16 is absent from a number of the most valuable manuscripts. It is more likely that it should be regarded as an importation into the text from chapter iv. after the important saying of verse 15.

vii. 17-23 : THE MEANING OF THE SAYING IN vii. 15

Now when he went indoors away from the crowd, his disciples 17 asked him the meaning of this parabolic saying. He said 18 to them, ' So you do not understand, either ? Do you not see how nothing outside a man can defile him by entering him ? It does not enter his heart but his belly and passes 19 from that into the drain' (thus he pronounced all food clean). ' No,' he said, ' it is what comes from a man, that 20 is what defiles him. From within, from the heart of man, 21 the designs of evil come : sexual vice, stealing, murder, 22 adultery, lust, malice, deceit, sensuality, envying, slander, arrogance, recklessness, all these evils issue from within, 23 and they defile a man.'

The conflict over the Jewish legal observances which broke out in the early Church was inevitable, since the founder had been loyal to the Jewish faith and was believed to have fulfilled Jewish hopes, yet on many an occasion had expressed an impatience with, and rejection of, a number of the Jewish precepts. As the Church spread among Hellenistic Jews and Gentiles, the non-ritual element won the leadership. Sayings of Jesus which had been responsible for this non-legalistic spirit in the movement from its beginning were now collected and developed. The interpretation of the parabolic saying in this section represents in all probability such a process of late reflection on the meaning and significance of the saying. Verse 15, if original, was no doubt struck off in the heat of criticism and conflict, and represented a broadside of defence on the part of Jesus with reference to some act of Himself or His disciples which violated Pharisaic scruples. In the 'explanation' here, with its long list of sins which come from the heart, one feels the cooler atmosphere of later exegesis. The saying is now seen to imply an entirely new ethic from the Jewish one, and its implications are developed in detail. One notes that this exegesis of the saying is presented by means of the device of Jesus teaching the disciples privately what He meant. This is Mark's belief as to what took place (cf. iv. 34). He is no doubt sincere in reading back into the first events an understanding of them which was the product of time and struggle.

The significant phrase in this interpretation is the parenthesis in verse 19, **thus He pronounced all food clean.** Some have thought that this is due to a later copyist whose marginal comment crept into the text. While this is always possible, there is no good reason for not attributing it to the evangelist. Short parenthetical insertions are found often in the Gospel —compare, for example, xiii. 14—and from the standpoint of content no objection can be taken to this comment. It is obvious from the entire discussion that the evangelist regards the Jewish food laws as abrogated.

vii. 24–30 : A Syrophœnician Girl is Healed

24 Leaving there, he went away to the territory of Tyre and Sidon. He entered a house and wanted no one to know of it, but

CHAPTER VII, VERSES 24-30

he could not escape notice ; a woman heard of him, whose 25
daughter had an unclean spirit, and she came in and fell at
his feet (the woman was a pagan, of Syrophœnician birth) 26
begging him to cast the dæmon out of her daughter. He 27
said to her, ' Let the children be satisfied first of all ; it is
not fair to take the children's bread and throw it to the
dogs.' She answered him, ' No, sir, but under the table the 28
dogs do pick up the children's crumbs.' He said to her, 29
' Well, go your way ; the dæmon has left your daughter,
since you have said that.' So she went home and found the 30
child lying in bed, with the dæmon gone from her.

The topographical details absent from the previous section
now return. **Leaving there** seems to refer back to the Plain
of Gennesaret of vi. 53, since this was the last place mentioned.
The geographical references in the account of a tour to the
north, however, are vague and very general. The words, **and
Sidon**, should probably be dropped from verse 24. They are
lacking in many manuscripts, and verse 31 reads as if Sidon
had not already been mentioned. **The territory of Tyre**
bounded Galilee on the north. Nothing is said about visiting
the city itself, and the impression the story makes is of a
journey of some weeks in the quiet of a near-by pagan region
where Jesus was unknown. Burkitt thinks that the journey
lasted nearly nine months, because of the reference to the green
grass in the feeding of the five thousand a little before the
journey, which would be in the spring, and the journey to
Jerusalem for the Passover on Jesus' return to Galilee. But
this is surely to attach an importance and accuracy to the
order of Mark's narrative which the loose connection of the
stories does not suggest.

Mark knows practically nothing about this journey except
that it was not a missionary tour. It is scarcely possible to
suppose that he invented the tour simply to give a setting for a
story about the healing of the Syrophœnician girl, however,
for Gentiles were to be found all over Galilee. Had the journey
been imagined, we would also expect to find by all odds some
sanction for the later Gentile mission of the Church. It seems

likely, therefore, that Mark had some indication in his materials of such a journey. As to why Jesus should have withdrawn from Galilee to heathen soil, one can only surmise. We have already had occasion to note that Herod Antipas attempted to kill Jesus at one point in His life and that Jesus sent word back that He did not intend to die outside Jerusalem (see Luke xiii. 31 ff.). A departure from Herod's territory seems to be related to this threat, especially since it is stated that Jesus did not wish His presence in this new region to become public knowledge. If the location of the incident at this point in Mark's story could be accepted without question, there would be strong confirmatory evidence of this interpretation of the journey. For on His return to Galilee, Jesus remains in concealment (ix. 30), and shortly afterwards transfers His work to Judæa. On this view the journey to the north would have been both an escape from Herod and an opportunity to think out His future plans. It must be said, however, that none of this is mentioned in Mark, and is arrived at only by piecing together information in the different Gospels. While reasonable and attractive, this interpretation must remain conjectural.

Mark knows of only one incident of that journey. In the light of the strongly Hellenistic character of the Gospels it is a wonder that the story was preserved in this form at all. Apparently it had served a double purpose. It served the interests of those Jewish Christians who had been opposed to Gentile missions. Such episodes as this one, and such sayings as that of Matt. x. 6—'Do not go among the Gentiles, rather make your way to the lost sheep of the house of Israel'— had evidently been used by them in the discussion of the desirability of preaching to other peoples. On the other hand, the story of how a Gentile woman, by the exercise of great faith, won for herself the spiritual privileges and blessings which were first proclaimed for Jews, would have served equally well those who believed in the Gentile mission. The story of the healing of the centurion's servant in Matt. viii. 5, has the same point. There was not much in the tradition which could be utilized in support of this programme, and

CHAPTER VII, VERSES 24-30

those who were ready to forget racial barriers had to make the most of what there was. It is interesting to note that Matthew, which preserves at a number of points the tradition of this distinctly Jewish Christianity, has the story of the Syrophœnician woman in a much more definitely anti-Gentile form than has Mark.

The wording of verse 24 implies that Jesus made a stop of some duration at a home, probably that of a Jewish resident of the section. Here He was recognized, and a Gentile woman of the native Phœnician stock, hearing of Him, came to beg Him to heal her daughter. The term **Syrophœnician** is used to designate the Phœnicians of the Syrian coast in contradistinction to those who had settled around Carthage. The use of the word suggests the viewpoint of one writing away from Palestine. Josephus speaks often of the Phœnicians, but he never feels it necessary to say which Phœnicians he means. On the other hand, the same term that Mark uses is found in Justin Martyr of Ephesus, Juvenal of Rome, and other Hellenistic writers. The girl is said to have had **an unclean spirit**, a popular explanation of illnesses that were not otherwise understood.

In Matt. xv. 24, in answer to the woman's request, Jesus is represented as first replying, ' It was only to the lost sheep of the house of Israel that I was sent.' This is the essential meaning of the words in verse 27 in Mark, which Matthew gives in answer to the woman's further importunities : **it is not fair to take the children's bread and throw it to the dogs.** There is every reason to regard the main idea of this saying as a true reflection of the thought of Jesus. His mission was to His own people. He felt Himself called of God to preach to Israel as had the prophets of the past. He lived in a world in which the presuppositions of thought of Palestinian Jews and the neighbouring Gentiles were so basically different that it was virtually out of the question for one to serve both peoples. Jesus did not begin the evangelization of the Gentiles. As a matter of fact, neither did the early Christian missionaries begin it. Pharisaism and the Jews of the Diaspora in general had undertaken that task long before the Christian movement ever appeared, and with considerable success. Jesus' contribution was to emancipate and broaden the religion to which the Gentiles were being converted.

The difficulty with the saying of Jesus in this incident is not so much with its main thought as with the form in which the thought is expressed. The difficulty has been variously met: (1) That ' we must content ourselves with the surmise that the harsh words . . . were spoken by one or other of the disciples '—so Warschauer. (2) That ' the allusion to dogs has been thrown back into Jesus' words from the woman's reply, and that she was the first to mention them '—so T. R. Glover. (3) That the statement was a sort of pedagogical device in which Jesus gave expression in the presence of the disciples to the attitude of bigoted and chauvinistic Jews in order that they might be shocked by hearing such words in His mouth and realize acutely the incompatibility of such an attitude with His teachings—so several popular writers. All of these explanations seem arbitrary and unsatisfactory. A picture of the life of Jesus which is built on a virtual denial of the Gospel story is neither a sound basis for faith nor even good apologetics.

Perhaps the best explanation of this strange story is to view it against the background of the particular crisis which Jesus faced at the time. It has been remarked that the most probable explanation of this journey on pagan soil was that Jesus was faced with the prospect of John the Baptist's fate if He remained in Galilee, and the implacable opposition of Jewish leaders no matter where He worked. Travelling on foreign soil, He did not wish to be known. To grant the woman's request would be the beginning of a wonder-working activity among the Gentiles. That which was denied to the people of Israel He was now asked to bestow on Gentiles. His words to the woman are not so much an answer to her request as an expression of His deep feeling over the crucial issue which He faced. This interpretation does not eliminate the harshness of the comparison between the Jews and Gentiles, but it makes Jesus' statement one directed to His own problem rather than a gratuitous insult to the woman. In confirmation of this interpretation it can at least be pointed out that the thought of

CHAPTER VII, VERSES 24-30

confining His work and that of His disciples to the Jews does reappear in the Gospel tradition, but the note of contempt for the Gentiles does not. On the contrary, Jesus seems to have entertained generous feelings toward the Samaritans, and to have kept free from that bitter hatred of the Romans which was felt by so many of His compatriots.

The statement, **Let the children be satisfied first of all**, is not found in the Matthean version of the incident. It has been thought to be an additional touch to soften the harshness of the story. It could be read even as enjoining a Gentile mission after the Jews had first ' been fed.' The account of the cure is remarkable in that it is the only one in Mark which takes place at a distance. But the centre of interest of the story was in the saying of Jesus, and the ' form critics ' are perhaps right in regarding the conclusion of the story as conventional.

vii. 31–37 : ' HE MAKES THE DEAF HEAR AND THE DUMB SPEAK '

He left the territory of Tyre again and passed through Sidon 31 to the sea of Galilee, crossing the territory of Decapolis. And a deaf man who stammered was brought to him, with 32 the request that he would lay his hand on him. So 33 taking him aside from the crowd by himself, he put his fingers into the man's ears, touched his tongue with 34 saliva, and looking up to heaven with a deep sigh he said to him, ' Ephphatha ' (which means, Open !). Then his ears 35 were at once opened and his tongue freed from its fetter —he began to speak correctly. Jesus forbade them to tell 36 anyone about it, but the more he forbade them the more eagerly they made it public ; they were astounded in the 37 extreme, saying, ' How splendidly he has done it all ! He actually makes the deaf hear and the dumb speak ! '

The route given for Jesus' return journey is curiously expressed. Since Sidon is further north than Tyre, the statement that He **passed through Sidon to the sea of Galilee** is puzzling. The story was in Aramaic at one time, as verse 34 shows, and it is possible that a corruption of the text has taken place in the transition of languages. As stated in the discussion of the author in the Introduction, it is more likely that Mark had a confused statement in one of his sources, and that this accounts for the obscurity of his sentence than that he was ignorant of the general relationship of Tyre, Sidon, the Decapolis, and the Sea of Galilee. As the wording now stands, Jesus' route would have been over the Lebanons, southward and eastward through the territory of Philip, and then westward back to the Sea of Galilee. Some such route would have been constantly outside of Herod Antipas' jurisdiction, which fits in with the interpretation which has been advanced as one of the reasons for this journey. The next two episodes take place in the Decapolis region, however, and part of the description of the route may be due to the editorial necessity which Mark constantly faced of fitting his sources together.

In the cure which is recounted there is no suggestion that the condition was due to a demon, as in so many of the cases already narrated. There is also the further difference that in this case Jesus uses physical means. In this the evangelist is consistent. Demons are driven out by a command (see i. 25, v. 8, and ix. 25), but in the case of those who are regarded as sick there is always physical contact between Jesus and the sufferer (cf. i. 31, v. 28 and 41, vi. 56, and here). There are two exceptions to this rule—the story of the paralytic man, which is complicated by the controversy with the scribes, and the restoration of the sight of Bartimæus, where physical contact is not mentioned, though not denied. Back of this consistency is the idea that demons are bound to obey the word of their conqueror, but that sickness is cured by the flow of healing power from the person of Jesus.

Here, and in viii. 22 ff., Jesus is said to have made use of spittle. This was regarded as having curative powers by both Jews and Gentiles in the ancient world, though the associations of its use were often magical. Well known is the story of the cure by this means of a blind man, in Alexandria, by the Emperor Vespasian. If Jesus actually made use of it, the fact should probably be explained as due to His belief in its value and His faith that God would make it effective for a cure.

CHAPTER VII, VERSES 31-37

But the absence of any reference to the use of spittle by Jesus in any of the accounts in Matthew or Luke, or in other stories in Mark, makes it dubious whether it was part of His method. It is possible that the detail is merely filled in by Mark in accordance with the accepted ideas of the age as to how wonderful cures were performed.

The words of the crowd, **He actually makes the deaf hear and the dumb speak!** are a reference to the words of the Messianic prophecy of Isa. xxxv. 5 : ' Then shall the eyes of the blind be opened and the ears of the deaf unstopped. Then shall the lame man leap as the hart and the tongue of the dumb shall sing.' In such a citation one sees the theological interpretation of Jesus' career by the early Christians entering into, and influencing the telling of, the story. How much it has influenced it in individual cases it is often impossible to say.

viii. 1-10: THE FEEDING OF FOUR THOUSAND

viii.

In those days, when a large crowd had again gathered and when they had nothing to eat, he called his disciples and said to them, ' I am sorry for the crowd ; they have been three days with me now, and they have nothing to eat. If I send them home without food they will faint on the road. Besides, some of them have come a long way.' His disciples replied, ' Where can one get loaves to satisfy them in a desert spot like this ? ' He asked them, ' How many loaves have you got ? ' They said, ' Seven.' So he ordered the crowd to recline on the ground, and taking the seven loaves he gave thanks, broke them, and gave them to His disciples to serve out. They served them out to the crowd, and as they also had a few small fish, he blessed them too, and told the disciples to serve them out as well. So the people ate and were satisfied, and they picked up seven baskets of fragments which were left over. (There were about four thousand of them.) Then he sent them away, embarked at once in the boat with his disciples, and went to the district of Dalmanutha.

The story is obviously a doublet of the great feeding recounted in vi. 30 ff. The situation is the same, and the details are for the most part the same—a suggestion by Jesus, astonishment expressed by the disciples, the crowd made to sit upon the ground, the blessing, breaking, and distribution of the bread, and the fragments which are left over gathered up. The differences are the numbers of everything, the people, the loaves of bread, and the baskets of fragments, and also the statement that the crowd had been with Jesus **for three days.** It should also be noted that the account contains no hint of a knowledge of a previous feeding. Had the tradition meant to describe two separate incidents, the disciples would certainly not have been described as so astonished on the second occasion.

The narrative is therefore of further interest chiefly for the light which it throws on the transmission of the tradition. One is struck by the presence of exact figures for the various items. If one had this story only, one might insist that this citation of the exact number of the loaves of bread and of the baskets full of fragments indicates the recollections of a participant in the event. But it is evident, from a comparison with those of the other story, that they have no actual value; they are due to the necessities of the story-teller's art, a factor which plainly must be allowed for in attempting to understand and evaluate these early stories. One notes also the dropping out of the introduction or setting which the episode has in vi. 32–34, and yet the reappearance in the body of this account of the striking statement of Jesus' compassion on the crowds (cf. viii. 2, and with vi. 34). The presence of the doublet confirms the impression which Mark's record has given of the use of written sources. Both of two such similar accounts would scarcely have been taken over by an editor from a tradition orally circulated. Only the details stated differently in writing would have made him think of them as referring to different episodes.

This story of the miraculous feeding closes, curiously enough, with a statement very similar to the conclusion of the previous account of a feeding in the desert. At the end of that

CHAPTER VIII, VERSES 1–10

story the disciples were sent ahead in a boat towards Bethsaida while Jesus stayed to dismiss the crowds. Here we are told that Jesus dismissed the crowds and then **embarked in the boat with His disciples and went to the district of Dalmanutha.** This latter district is quite unknown. Matthew, in the parallel passage, reads Magadan, or Magadala, the manuscript evidence favouring perhaps the former spelling. But evidence concerning the location of Magadan is almost as completely lacking as concerning Dalmanutha.

viii. 11–13 : The Demand for a Sign

Now the Pharisees came out and started to argue with him, 11
asking him for a Sign from heaven, by way of tempting
him. But he sighed in spirit and said, 12
  ' Why does this generation demand a Sign ?
  I tell you truly, no Sign shall be given this generation.'
Then he left them, embarked again, and went away to the 13
opposite side.

A sign, or wonderful work, gave confirmation of one's claim to authority, either authority in teaching or authority of one's person. Thus a scribe who ruled on the law contrary to the opinion of the majority gave ' signs ' to try to convince his colleagues. Another scribe, similarly, on announcing when the Messiah would come, is asked for a sign (*Sanh.* 98*a*). So it is said in the late rabbinic commentary, *Pesikta Rabbati*, that the Messiah Himself when He came would stand on the roof of the temple, announce to the people that their salvation was at hand, and point those who doubted to a light which would stream over Him from heaven (Strack and Billerbeck, *Kommentar*, i, p. 641). In Josephus there are indications that Messianic pretenders felt the demand for signs and promised them to their credulous followers. He tells, for example, of one named Theudas, who promised the multitudes that the Jordan river would divide at his command and that they would pass over dryshod.

The recent French biographer of Jesus, Goguel, thinks that the demand for a sign in the passage here should be interpreted in this Messianic fashion, namely, 'the sign for the rallying of His followers and the signal for the beginning of the Messianic revolt.' This, however, is not supported by the data in the Gospels. A sign is demanded in proof of one's claims, and there is no evidence that Jesus made any public claim to the Messianic office. The more natural explanation is in connection with His teachings. He claimed authority for His interpretations of the divine law, the same authority that John the Baptizer had exercised. Could He give a sign from heaven as proof that He was a prophet?

The answer which Mark records Jesus as giving is surprising. One would expect a reply which would point to His healings and other 'mighty works.' The answer given is contrary to the whole tendency of the Christian apologetic. One recalls how the Fourth Gospel dwells upon 'the signs' which Jesus performed. And one notes that both in Matthew and in Luke the demand for a sign is answered at least partly in the affirmative. In Matt. xii. 40, xvi. 4, and Luke xi. 29 it is said that no sign will be given 'except the sign of Jonah,' while in Luke xi. 20 it is suggested that the casting out of demons by Jesus was sign enough. The completely negative answer which Mark records must owe its existence, therefore, to an actual saying of Jesus. Even His answer was put to polemic use: a generation such as that of Jesus' opponents deserved no sign and would be given none (see Matt. xii. 39 and the other passages cited above). But there were signs to the inner circle. In Mark viii. 19, for example, Jesus is made to remind the disciples of the miracle of the loaves and fishes.

But if Jesus gave the answer which is recorded of Him in verse 12, it is clear that one must revise the impression that the Gospels give as to the extent to which the ministry was filled with miraculous deeds. It would indicate that we are right in rationalizing the stories of the feeding of thousands in the desert, of the walking on the water, and of the storm at sea. While it has been maintained in this commentary that the stories of exorcisms and healings have an authentic basis, they were no doubt less numerous than the evangelist repeatedly suggests. But it is also doubtful whether these latter

CHAPTER VIII, VERSES 11–13

could have been presented as signs ' from heaven.' The ' sons of the Pharisees ' also cast out demons on occasion (Matt. xii. 27), and healings of the sick belonged to the same category. What was demanded was a voice from heaven, or a light, or some other heavenly indication.

This refusal of Jesus to give a sign seems difficult to correlate with indications in the Gospels that the exorcisms and healings which He performed were to His mind proof that the power of Satan had been broken and the universal rule of God was shortly to be established. The reader is referred to the discussion of this difficulty in the comment on iii. 22–27. The contradiction is not so much between the refusal to give a sign and the appeal to these ' mighty works,' as it is between the appeal to these works and the injunctions which Mark attributes to Jesus that those who had been healed were to tell no one. Between these alternatives the injunctions to silence appear to be secondary and possibly even editorial. The refusal to give a sign does not contradict Jesus' conviction that the power of God was working through Him in these unusual occurrences. His refusal may very likely have rested merely on the knowledge that He could not perform these works at will—a fact which even Mark betrays—and His unwillingness to tempt God by endeavouring to give a demonstration of His power.

As remarked above, Matthew and Luke both add to this refusal of a sign the words, ' except the sign of Jonah.' This, however, is not contrary to the essential meaning of the saying here, for the Lucan form of the longer saying shows that the sign referred to was that of Jonah preaching to the men of Nineveh. In other words, both the Marcan and the Lucan version agree that Jesus refused to attempt a miraculous proof of His authority.

viii. 14–21 : ' BEWARE OF THE LEAVEN OF THE PHARISEES AND OF HEROD '

They had forgotten to bring any bread, and had only one loaf 14 with them in the boat. So he cautioned them, ' See and 15

beware of the leaven of the Pharisees and the leaven of
Herod.' 'Leaven?' they argued to themselves, 'we have
no bread at all!' He noted this and said to them, 'Why do
you argue you have no bread? Do you not see, do you not
understand, even yet? Are you still dull of heart?
You have eyes, do you not see?
you have ears, do you not hear?
Do you not remember how many baskets full of fragments
you picked up when I broke the five loaves for the five
thousand?' They said, 'Twelve.' 'And how many
basketfuls of fragments did you pick up when I broke the
seven loaves for the four thousand?' They said, 'Seven.'
'Do you not understand now?' he said.

We have no means of knowing whether Mark is responsible for placing these verses in their present context or whether this had been done by his source. The former appears more likely. The connection in any case seems verbal. These sayings were said to have been uttered in a boat, and this required that they be connected with some reference to a journey across the lake. The mention of the **one loaf** of bread must be an actual reminiscence, since, unlike the number of loaves in the stories of the feedings in the desert, it is not essential for the story and, indeed, is contradicted by it. The figure of the leaven, too, is distinctly Jewish, and suggests that the central saying belonged to the earliest tradition.

Mark does not record the attempt of Herod to kill Jesus and the latter's message to the tetrarch. It has been suggested that this passage preserves an echo of Jesus' flight from Antipas' territory. That we have a journey across the lake, without provisions, coupled with a warning to the disciples to beware of the Pharisees and Herod, makes the suggestion plausible. In iii. 6 a combination of 'the Pharisees and the Herodians' against Jesus was mentioned, but Mark seems to have had no details concerning it. Conjectures, however, even when plausible, should not be confused with facts, and the fact is that the occasion of this saying has been lost.

The kernel of the section is the saying, **See and beware of**

CHAPTER VIII, VERSES 14-21

the leaven of the Pharisees and the leaven of Herod. Exactly what was meant is not explained. Leaven is used in the rabbinic writings in three senses. It is used in the sense of ordinary bread—that is, bread with leaven in it—particularly in passages discussing the requirements of the feast of Passover. It is in this sense that the disciples understand the saying, as verses 16 and 17 show, concluding evidently that Jesus meant that they should not eat the bread of the Pharisees and Herod. This misunderstanding is rebuked, but the correct use of the figure of leaven is not given. We are left to choose between the other two Jewish uses of the figure. It appears in at least one passage to refer to the teaching of the law; in a number of others to refer to the evil disposition which leads men astray. Of these two the latter appears the more likely, since one could not warn against the teaching of Herod. The other Gospels provide no help in the interpretation. Matthew changes the saying to read, ' Beware of the leaven of the Pharisees and the Sadducees,' which might mean the interpretation of the law which these groups advocated. Luke drops the reference to Herod, and adds that Jesus meant the hypocrisy of the Pharisees. The Marcan form would appear to be the original form of the saying.

The rebuke of the disciples in verses 19 ff. has every indication of being secondary and due to the evangelist. The disciples' dullness of understanding has been mentioned before (vi. 52). The reference to the two great feedings could not have been written until after the two stories had been combined into a single narrative. The thought seems to be, Do not think of bread that one eats; I can supply your deficiencies in this respect, as the feedings of the multitudes show. You must perceive the spiritual truths.

viii. 22-26 : JESUS RESTORES THE SIGHT OF A BLIND MAN IN BETHSAIDA

Then they reached Bethsaida. A blind man was brought to 22 him, with the request that he would touch him. So he 23 took the blind man by the hand and led him outside the

	village ; then, after spitting on his eyes, he laid his hands
24	on him and asked him, ' Do you see anything ? ' He began to see and said, ' I can make out people, for I see them as
25	large as trees moving.' At this he laid his hands once more on his eyes, and the man stared in front of him ; he
26	was quite restored and saw everything distinctly. And Jesus sent him home, saying, ' Do not even go into the village.'

The healing here described duplicates to a striking degree the cure of the deaf stammerer in vii. 32 ff. Both wonders take place outside Galilee. In both cases the afflicted person is brought to Him with the request that He would touch him. In both instances Jesus takes the man away from the crowds. In both cases spittle is used in the cure, and the afflicted part is touched. It is no doubt the meaning of verse 26 that in this instance as in the other the man is instructed not to tell of the miracle. It is not surprising, therefore, that the two stories have been regarded as variants of each other, or as a pair of miracle stories.

There are a number of striking parallels between this account and Hellenistic healing stories, as well as between this one and the narrative of vii. 32 ff. The removal of the sufferer from the crowd, the insistence on the completeness of the recovery, and the injunctions to silence are all characteristic traits. The use of spittle for a similar purpose is found in the story already referred to of Vespasian's healing of a blind man in Alexandria. The mention of the first objects as appearing like trees can be partially paralleled from an inscription recording a cure in the temple of Asklepios, in which it is said that the first things seen were the trees in the temple precincts. These points of relationship to Hellenistic stories of healings indicate that this and probably the companion account in vii. 32 ff. were developed, if not originated, in the syncretistic atmosphere of the Hellenistic world.

IV. THE MESSIAH IN SECRET
(viii. 27–xiii. 37)

AT this point in the Gospel a definite change takes place both in content and in tone. To this point we have had accounts of Jesus as a public figure, teaching the multitudes, healing the sick, sending His disciples out to proclaim His message. In the section now beginning the primary interest is in the relationship of Jesus to His more intimate disciples, their recognition of Him as the Messiah, and His teaching of them as to the necessity of His sufferings and death. These themes are not completely new. Private instruction of the disciples has been mentioned, the term ' Son of Man ' has crept into the narrative twice, and the Passion itself has been mentioned. But that which has been incidental or anticipatory now becomes explicit and primary.

That there was a basis in fact for this increasing concern with the questions of Jesus' fate and His function or rôle would seem obvious. Nevertheless it is the evangelist who has made this thought of a suffering Messiah the dominant one as the Gospel approaches its close. He has done this by choice of the incidents and sayings to be recounted, by their arrangement, and by certain general statements with which he interprets the story. Mark does not minimize or apologize for the death on the cross, but regards it and the resurrection as the climax of his narrative. The Gospel is not a tragedy; the tragic note is never present. It is rather epic drama, the story of a Saviour who was put to death by evil powers, but who rose from death to assure His followers of His ultimate victory and their reward. In this we see the evangelist interpreting the career of Jesus in accordance with the faith of Hellenistic Christianity. Bultmann and others have described the Gospel as a cult story, not a biography. Perhaps one might say more accurately that it is a biography of Jesus as this was recalled and cherished in the Christian cult.

viii. 27-33 : 'Thou Art the Christ!'

27 Then Jesus and his disciples set off for the villages of Cæsarea Philippi. On the road he inquired of his disciples 'Who
28 do people say I am?' 'John the Baptist,' they told him, 'though some say Elijah, and others say you are
29 one of the prophets.' So he inquired of them, 'And who do you say I am?' Peter replied, 'You are the Christ.'
30 Then he forbade them to tell anyone about him. And he
31 proceeded to teach them that the Son of man had to endure great suffering, to be rejected by the elders and the high priests and the scribes, to be killed and after three days to
32 rise again ; he spoke of this quite freely. Peter took him
33 and began to reprove him for it, but he turned on him and noticing his disciples reproved Peter, telling him, 'Get behind me, you Satan! Your outlook is not God's but man's.'

The story of Peter's confession is given a locality, though not an exact one. The villages of Cæsarea Philippi would be the outlying hamlets of Philip's capital. Since the discussion which is recounted took place on the road it is probably meant that the city was not actually entered, just as we never read of Jesus entering Tiberias, the residence of Herod Antipas. Since the mention of the town has no particular pertinency for the account which follows, it is best explained on the assumption that the name represents an actual recollection which had been preserved by Mark's source.

The account under consideration is one of the crucial ones in the Gospel. It recounts a declaration by Peter that Jesus was the long-awaited deliverer of the Jewish people. Is this history, or pious imagination? Some of the ablest scholars are convinced that the latter is the case, and have described it as 'a legend of faith.' But the reason for so regarding it is not based on the story itself, but on the general conviction that Jesus did not regard Himself as the Messiah, and was not so regarded until after the resurrection. This faith of the early Church was then carried back, it is believed, to Jesus' own

CHAPTER VIII, VERSES 27-33

consciousness, and to Peter, the leading disciple, was given the distinction of having made the first confession. It is thus necessary at this point to discuss the general question.

DID JESUS REGARD HIMSELF AS THE MESSIAH?

The main facts as they appear in the Gospel account can be stated quite simply, though the solution of the problem is beset with the greatest difficulties.

The facts are as follows : Mark makes it clear that Jesus made no public claim to Messiahship, enjoining silence on demoniacs and on the disciples when they conferred the title upon Him. At the final trial no witnesses that He made this claim could be produced. It is, however, recorded that Peter, and presumably the other disciples, privately acknowledged Him as the Messiah. Mark does not record an explicit acceptance of the title by Jesus, but states that, having charged them ' to tell no one,' He proceeded to speak of His approaching Passion, referring to Himself as ' the Son of Man.' From this point on, this phrase appears repeatedly in Jesus' mouth, particularly in sayings concerning His death, resurrection, and future glory. There is no clear assertion of Messiahship, although the account of the request of the sons of Zebedee seems to imply it, until one reaches the account of the trials. Here, in answer to a question of the high priest, ' Art thou the Christ, the Son of the Blessed ? ' Jesus is said to have answered, ' I am. And ye shall see the Son of Man seated on the right hand of power and coming on the clouds of heaven.' To Pilate's question, ' Art thou the King of the Jews ? ' Mark records an ambiguous answer—' Thou sayest it.' A placard placed over the cross carried the wording, ' The King of the Jews.' These are the major facts in the case.

Thus there is only one instance in which Jesus is said to have declared unequivocally that He was the Christ—in His reply to the high priest. But it so happens that this scene in Mark, the story of the Jewish trial, is the one element in the final events most open to question. As an exact historical record it is of very doubtful dependableness. The grounds for this statement will be presented in the commentary, but even Professor Burkitt, who championed so persuasively the historicity of Mark, admitted that ' the grounds against treating Mark xiv. 53-65 with the same measure of historical respect that one accords to the rest of Mark xiv. are sound.' One is faced, therefore, with a baffling set of facts : in spite of the conviction of the early Church that Jesus was the expected Messiah, the Synoptic Gospels record only one dubious instance in which Jesus affirmed this, but do record numerous instances in which He spoke of Himself as the ' Son of Man.' One turns first, therefore, to a consideration of this term.

The Son of Man

This phrase, originally a Semitic idiom meaning simply ' man '—as in the familiar passage, ' What is man, that thou art mindful of him ? and the son of man, that thou visitest him ? '—came to be, through its use in Daniel and Enoch in connection with the heavenly being of the visions, a title for a heavenly individual who would come on the clouds at the last day to preside over the Great Judgment and the New Age. In the Gospels a few instances of the meaning ' man ' seem to have been mistaken for the title, the clearest being perhaps ii. 28. These can be set aside. A number of others have no unifying thought, the title merely taking the place of the first personal pronoun in certain sayings of Jesus. This group is clearly secondary. Jesus did not use the title as an habitual designation of Himself. The greater number of the uses of the phrase are in contexts which refer to Jesus' approaching sufferings and death and His return in glory. It is with this group that we need to concern ourselves. The reader is referred to the lucid discussion of this phrase in Jackson and Lake's *Beginnings of Christianity*, Vol. I, pp. 374 f., for the details of these several uses.

As soon as one raises the question whether Jesus applied to Himself this exalted title of apocalyptic literature, one incontrovertible fact emerges : the bridge by which the person of Jesus, the prophet and teacher, could be connected with

CHAPTER VIII, VERSES 27-33

that of a heavenly 'Son of Man' at the right hand of God, must have been a conviction of Jesus' death and resurrection. Only by death and resurrection could Jesus enter into that heavenly region whence He would come on the clouds at the end of the age. This knowledge, it is often assumed, Jesus possessed by anticipation and by faith. He believed God would raise Him up after death, and so expected to become the Son of Man. The alternate view would be to assume that it was the early Church after the resurrection which identified Jesus with the heavenly Son of Man. According to Acts ii. 33 the Church thought of Jesus as 'raised to God's right hand,' and 'to be kept in heaven until the restoration of all things' (Acts iii. 21).

In attempting to decide between these alternatives the balance of probability is strongly in favour of the view that it was the early Church which applied this title to Jesus:

(1) The only use of the title which is found in both of the earliest sources, Mark and the 'Q' sayings of Matthew and Luke, is in sayings referring to the return of Christ in glory. Mark uses it repeatedly in connection with the Passion, but this use is never found in the 'Q' sayings. Where these two documents agree, there will be found, surely, the earliest and most dependable tradition. This earliest use of the title thus referred not to the Passion, but to the glorified Christ. This would seem to indicate clearly that its use originated with the early Church. To the early Church the resurrection was the starting-point of a new theology. It overshadowed and wiped out the crucifixion. The Church's interest was Christ's return for judgment, which was now possible. To Jesus, on the other hand, the later events would have had meaning and significance only in connection with the approaching ordeal. That the title seems to have been unrelated in the earliest tradition to the Passion argues against Jesus having applied the title to Himself.

(2) In the second place, for Jesus to have thought of Himself as the apocalyptic Son of Man it would have been necessary not only to have foreseen His death and to have believed that God would raise Him up to have a part in the Age to Come,

but also to have believed in a special resurrection for Himself immediately after death, or at least before the time of that great event. The normal expectation of a devout Jew who accepted the Pharisaic belief in the resurrection was that after death the body was placed in the tomb and the spirit went to the place appointed for the spirits until the last day. Then body and soul would be reunited and raised up together. The Son of Man, however, was supposed to wait in heaven until He came to inaugurate the new day. The thought of such a special individual resurrection was not impossible in the first century, as can be easily shown. But it does burden the hypothesis that Jesus thought of Himself as the heavenly Son of Man more than its proponents often recognize. Indeed this view comes very near requiring the older conception of Jesus' complete foreknowledge of the events that were to follow.

(3) For Jesus to have regarded Himself as the apocalyptic Son of Man requires that He must have accepted the certainty of His approaching death long enough in advance to have completely reorganized in His mind contemporary apocalyptic thought. The Son of Man was a heavenly personage already existing who had been ' chosen and hidden before God before the creation of the world.' To have brought the work of a Galilean prophet and servant of God into relationship with this figure involved a radical rethinking of the entire apocalyptic scheme. This would have been the work of months of meditation on the mystery of His fate. But the evidence of the Gospels, in spite of much reading back of later events into the earlier period, does not suggest such an early recognition of what the final result would be. The prayer in the Garden of Gethsemane, if historical even in its general tenor, indicates a sudden realization that He must actually ' drink the cup.' We know very little about Jesus' final efforts in Jerusalem, but the impression left by the record is that He endeavoured up to the last to win the nation to genuine repentance, hoping for success. Nor do the words at the Last Supper give any indication of so vital a reconstruction of current apocalyptic hopes. Aside from the sacramental features, the thought

CHAPTER VIII, VERSES 27-33

expressed is that He and His disciples will be gathered together again at the great banquet in the Kingdom of God.

The point is often made in reply that the title is used so rarely in the New Testament as to indicate that the Church would not have originated it. The reply overlooks the fact that the New Testament is a collection of Greek documents. The title belongs to the earliest stage of the Church when it spoke Aramaic. We have only traces of this Aramaic Christian literature—namely, the early chapters of Acts and some of the traditions incorporated in the Gospels. In both of these the title is present. It meant nothing to Greek Christianity, which quickly dropped the term.

I conclude, therefore, that the series of ideas which viewed Jesus as the Son of Man to come in glory on the clouds of heaven, with the holy angels, was the theological achievement of the Palestinian Church. The sanction for these beliefs was naturally found in Jesus' teachings, and the title inevitably became part of the oral tradition, and later the written tradition of His words. But it never appears in the Gospels in the mouths of the disciples, probably for the following reason : It was known that this view of Jesus was not entertained by the disciples during Jesus' lifetime. In the tradition this fact took the form of the oft-repeated thought that the disciples did not understand until later what Jesus was endeavouring to teach them.[1]

The Messiah

The above conclusion has seemed to many scholars to mean that Jesus made no claim to special or unique dignity, and that the title, ' the Messiah,' or the ' Anointed One,' is also to be attributed to the early Church. Jesus, it is maintained, only thought of Himself as a prophet. After the belief in the resurrection was established, His followers acclaimed Him as the Messiah or Christ, and this was read back into the earlier

---

[1] The view that Jesus used the title 'Son of Man' but meant by it not Himself, but the heavenly figure of whom John the Baptist spoke, has not been considered in these remarks. It will be discussed in the commentary on viii.. 38. (See pp. 156–159)

history. In this way the 'Messianic secret' of Mark is explained: there was nothing of this Messiahship in the familiar story of tradition; hence it was assumed that Jesus had imposed on the disciples a decree of silence.

This reconstruction of the facts is attractive from a number of standpoints, but it has certain difficulties to face which are almost insuperable:

(1) In the first place it seems certain that Jesus' intimate disciples during His lifetime regarded Him as the Messiah. The story of Cæsarea Philippi seems to go back to a definite historical recollection in which the place and chief spokesman are recalled. It is confirmed by the request of the sons of Zebedee for the places on Jesus' right and left hand in His glory—a story which would hardly have been invented. The strongest evidence of this belief, however, is the virtual impossibility of assuming that the belief in Jesus' resurrection, His Messiahship and His apocalyptic office would have arisen after His execution had there been no such belief earlier. But this evidence of the disciples' belief during Jesus' lifetime indicates that Jesus Himself held some such conviction. Had Jesus held no such thoughts concerning Himself, He certainly would have eliminated these false ideas and expectations.

(2) Jesus was executed by the Romans. At the public trial Pilate asked Him, 'Art thou the King of the Jews?' and received an answer that was not a denial. Over the cross was placed a placard which read, 'The King of the Jews.' Had Jesus never regarded Himself as the Lord's 'Messiah' or 'Anointed One,' it seems unbelievable that He would have allowed Himself to be executed without protest on such false grounds.

(3) Supplementing the above, though without significance alone, are those sayings which show that Jesus attached to His hour, His teaching, and His person a special and unique significance. Here the data are all so coloured by later Christian beliefs that it is practically impossible to make a distinction between the sayings which are probably later and those which seem to be genuine. But all of these cannot be eliminated. He believed that the end of the age was at hand. In His own

CHAPTER VIII, VERSES 27-33

exorcisms and cures He saw the evidences of Satan's power being broken. The cities of Galilee He upbraided because they had not repented at works greater than any which had been done in Sodom and Gomorrah. Many prophets and kings had desired to see the things which were transpiring in His day. He called for men to follow Him, and to obey His teachings of the divine will. According to one saying, He declared that one's status in the Day of Judgment would be determined by the attitude they adopted toward His words. Other sayings promise rewards to those who suffered on His account. How much of all this picture is genuine it is very difficult to say, but there is certainly enough to make one hesitate at describing Jesus' conception of His mission in ordinary terms.

Thus we have a mystery of history. There is no dependable record that Jesus claimed to be the Messiah, but His intimate disciples believed it to be true, and His enemies put Him to death after a public trial in which He was charged with this belief. It is possible that Jesus kept silent at every suggestion of Messianic dignity, but not that He consistently denied it. And if He kept silent, His refusal to answer has significance.

There is an old answer to the problem which has more recently been put in a new light. In an essay in Jackson and Lake's *Beginnings of Christianity*, G. F. Moore has shown with great care that the term ' Messiah,' or ' Anointed One,' was applied to various individuals and groups in the sense of ' appointed ' or ' consecrated ' by God to a unique task or mission. It had been applied to the patriarchs, to the people of Israel as a whole, to the prophets, to the kings of Israel, even to Cyrus the conqueror of Babylon. It had also been applied to the apocalyptic heavenly man in the visions of Enoch. In Jesus' day it was applied especially to the hoped-for warrior-king who would deliver the nation. Basically the term meant ' one appointed by God,' though in Jesus' day the reference to the one who would bring about the great deliverance of the nation was closely associated with the phrase.

In view of these facts it seems reasonable in itself, and in accordance with the evidence, to assume that Jesus, believing Himself divinely commissioned to proclaim the nearness of the Realm of God and also its true character, opposed in this work by virtually all the accepted leaders of the day, threatened with death, yet striving to create a repentant and righteous nation ready for the imminent judgment, should have felt that He was ' the anointed one ' whom God had sent for this task. The people expected a warrior-king. Jesus rejected such concepts. ' The kings of the Gentiles lord it over you and their great ones exercise authority. Let it not be so with you. He who would be greatest, let him be the servant of all.' The evidence asserts that Jesus accepted from His disciples the title, ' the Lord's Anointed,' while at the same time endeavouring to teach them that His work was not one of conquest but one of service and perhaps even of death in supreme obedience to the will of God. This seems entirely reasonable. And may not His refusal of an answer to the pagan Pilate have been for the reason that, though unwilling to deny His great vocation, He knew that the procurator would misunderstand His claim, and regard His admission as a legitimate reason for His immediate execution ?

This seems on the whole the most satisfactory solution. The records have been so overlaid with the later beliefs that proof and absolute certainty are out of the question. But without the assumption that Jesus accepted His disciples' expression of faith in Himself as ' the Anointed One,' the story of His last days and of the rise of the Christian movement becomes a series of unrelated and almost incomprehensible facts.

. . . .

With this conclusion we return to the account of Peter's confession in Cæsarea Philippi. According to the text, Peter, in answer to a direct question, declared, **You are the Christ.** In Matthew, a Gospel somewhat later in date and with more developed theological concepts in many respects, this is followed by an ejaculation of praise on Jesus' part. But there is none of that here. Instead we read (1) that He **forbade them to tell anyone,** (2) that He proceeded to teach them that **the Son of Man had to endure great suffering,** (3) that Peter began to

CHAPTER VIII, VERSES 27-33

rebuke Him for saying this, and (4) that Jesus turned on him and . . . reproved Peter, telling him, 'Get behind Me, you Satan !' This is surely not an imagined scene. The rebuke you Satan to the chief of the apostles must be based on some actual incident. Nor is the story an outright acknowledgment of Messiahship by Jesus such as might readily be attributed to the early Church. It would appear that we are dealing with an authentic tradition, though one which may have undergone some modification.

Peter declared that Jesus was the Christ. Jesus certainly did not deny this, else there would have been no special significance attached to the scene in early Christian memory. The text states that He began to speak of His sufferings, and, to Peter's remonstrance at this, He spoke out in the sharpest terms. This all seems fairly well in accordance with the view which has been advanced—that Jesus did regard Himself as God's 'Anointed,' sent to prepare the nation for the establishment of the universal reign of God, but that He knew this to be a mission of service and sacrifice, not of ease and glory. Peter's belief was in line with the popular hope. But this had to be corrected. Jesus was a different sort of divine messenger.

But into this primitive account the intrusion of later thoughts can be traced. The title **the Son of Man** is introduced in verse 31 without any explanation of the change from **the Christ** of verse 29. The reason for the change is that the tradition—probably before Mark—regards Jesus' remonstrance as meaning that His Messiahship was to be of the apocalyptic sort, one gained by the path of death, rather than that of the warrior-king. The view maintained in this volume is that it was neither, but a belief in a Messiahship of service in the divinely appointed task. Verse 31 also describes the events of the Passion with an exactness of detail which indicates a formulation of the words after the events they describe. Lastly one notes the familiar process of the growth of the account by the accretion of sayings which were originally independent units in the tradition. But this brings us to verse 34.

viii. 34–ix. 1 : SAYINGS ON THE CONSEQUENCES OF DISCIPLESHIP OR ITS REFUSAL

34 Then He called the whole company to him with his disciples, saying to them, 'If anyone wishes to follow me, let him deny himself, take up his cross, and so follow me ;
35 for whoever wants to save his life will lose it, and whoever loses his life for my sake and the gospel's will save it.
36 What profit is it for a man to gain the whole world and to
37 forfeit his soul ? What could a man offer as an equivalent for his soul ?
38 Whoever is ashamed of me and my words in this disloyal and sinful generation, the Son of man will be ashamed of
ix. him when he comes in the glory of his Father with the
1 holy angels. I tell you truly,' he said to them, ' there are some of those standing here who will not taste death till they see the coming of God's Reign with power.'

The connection of these verses with the preceding story of Peter's confession is obviously editorial. The introduction of **the whole company** is apparently because of the feeling that the first of the sayings is addressed to those who were considering discipleship, rather than to the Twelve.

With the exception of the last verse, these sayings deal with the necessity of sacrifice and suffering by the disciples of Christ, and of the reward which those who take up their own cross can anticipate. Their presentation in this setting is interesting. It shows that to Mark the major point of the previous section was not Peter's acclaim of Jesus, but Jesus' reply that the Messiah must suffer and die. This provided, in the evangelist's view, one of the best occasions for presenting sayings concerning similar experiences on the part of His followers. From this point on in the Gospel these two thoughts appear constantly—Jesus, the Messiah, keeps teaching the disciples that His career will be one of humiliation, suffering, and death, and that they should expect to meet with like experiences.

CHAP. VIII, 34–CHAP. IX, 1

Verse 34 seems to have been especially popular in the early Church, for it appears not only here, but twice in Matthew and Luke—in Matt. x. 38=Luke xiv. 27, and Matt. xvi. 24=Luke ix. 23. This is understandable, since the early Christian movement had to undergo persecutions both from the Jews and the Gentiles. The verb, to **deny himself,** is the same used in xiv. of Peter's denial. It means: to refuse to recognize, disavow, deny utterly. The figure, **take up his cross,** comes from the Roman practice of requiring the condemned person to carry his cross to the place of execution. Executions by crucifixion were common in Palestine, and it has been maintained that Jesus chose this figure to express ' the idea of severest suffering and ultimate risk.' The figure would not have been particularly pertinent, however, nor very clear, since crucifixion was always a legal execution of a condemned criminal. The figure seems to point rather to a time in the early Church when crucifixion always brought to mind the sufferings of Christ. That it was a familiar item in the Christian vocabulary is illustrated repeatedly by Paul's writings (cf. Gal. ii. 20, ' I have been crucified with Christ ').

The same fact of early Christian influence on the wording of the sayings is to be seen in verse 35. The contrast between saving one's life here and losing it in the final judgment may well have been Jesus' own language, possibly even the phrase **for My sake** (cf. Matt. v. 11). But the word **gospel,** meaning the Christian message of salvation, betrays the language of a later decade. Mark likes the expression and repeats it in x. 29, but the word is early Christian, and Jesus' own expression seems rather to have been ' for righteousness' sake ' (Matt. v. 10), or, ' for the sake of the Kingdom of God ' (see Matt. xix. 12, Luke xviii. 29). The same contrast of the gaining of life here and the loss of it in the world to come is the thought in verses 36–37. The word translated **soul** is the same one translated **life** in the preceding verses. To avoid an imagined contrast or difference, it had best be rendered ' life ' in both places. The thought is of the futility of wealth and power in the light of the Great Judgment which is impending. The language here is reminiscent of rabbinic sayings and parables.

But in verse 38 the thought takes a different turn. The previous sayings have pointed toward the persecutions and martyrdoms of the early Church. But what if one be ashamed of such a cause and desert it in the hour of trial ? The answer is that **the Son of man will be ashamed of him when He comes in the glory of His Father with the holy angels.** The general meaning of the verse to the readers of the Gospel is clear enough. To them the phrase **the Son of man** was simply another name for Jesus, and the saying reminded them of the Great Judgment, which would be based upon the attitude which they took toward Jesus and His words. But the historian, patiently examining the record of the words of Jesus, is brought up sharply by this passage. Here the term **Son of man** appears again, but this time it would seem to indicate a figure which is contrasted with that of Jesus : **Whoever is ashamed of Me ... the Son of Man will be ashamed of him.** This verse is not the only one which gives this impression. The view has been maintained, therefore, that such passages indicate that Jesus did use the title, Son of Man, but not to refer to Himself. He spoke rather of a heavenly figure whom He expected to come to inaugurate the New Age. John the Baptizer had spoken of such a figure, and Jesus, it is maintained, echoed his teachings in this respect. The more important passages on which this view is based are, besides the one here : Matt. x. 23, Luke xii. 40, Mark xiii. 26, and the several sayings in the apocalyptic discourse in Luke xvii. 22–37. In support of the thesis it is also urged that the application of the title and functions of the Son of Man to Jesus by the early Church would be easier to understand if Jesus had already spoken of such a figure, and the idea needed only to be transferred to Him after the resurrection.

This makes a strong case, and one which cannot be easily denied. It is weakened, however, by two considerations. The first of these is the fact that the early Church, in its appropriation and development of the ' Son of Man theology,' inserted it into the tradition of Jesus' sayings in so many places where one can be sure that it did not stand originally that one

CHAP. VIII, 34–CHAP. IX, 1

questions how much of the evidence can be carried back to Jesus. We have already had occasion to note the way in which, both in Mark and in the ' Q ' sayings, the title has been extended to several types of contexts in which it was admittedly not original. In apocalyptic sayings, one can see the extension of the title and idea by comparing Mark ix. 1, with Matt. xvi. 28 (the coming of God's Reign is changed to, ' the Son of Man coming in His Kingdom ') ; or by comparing the two forms of the ' Q ' saying, Matt. xix. 28, and Luke xxii. 30. In Mark the three solemn prophecies of Jesus' death and resurrection in which the title appears (viii. 30, ix. 31, and x. 33) are the work of the editor, and Luke xxi. 36, which contains the striking phrase about ' standing before the Son of Man ' at the Judgment, looks as if it may be a similar editorial statement designed to provide a conclusion to the apocalyptic discourse. The passage Matt. x. 23, which enjoins the disciples when persecuted in one city to flee to the next, since they will not have gone through the cities of Israel ' until the Son of Man be come,' seems to fit the early days of the Church a great deal better than the Galilean ministry of Jesus. The description of the Great Judgment contained in Matt. xxv. 31 ff., in which the Son of Man is the Judge, is generally regarded as a later Christian product. Perhaps the strongest evidence, besides the saying here in Mark and its parallels, that Jesus spoke of the coming of a heavenly Man, not Himself, is provided by the two apocalyptic discourses in the Gospels, namely, Mark xiii. 26, and Luke. xvii. 22–37. But it is in this area of apocalyptic that we know that the thought of the Church in the earliest period was most active and creative. Paul's letters to the Thessalonians indicate how freely Christian belief developed along these lines, and an analysis of Mark xiii. suggests the same conclusion. In the light of all this evidence of early Christian extension of this idea, the belief that the use of this title goes back to Jesus Himself becomes difficult to hold with any assurance.

The second consideration is the absence of any reference to this figure of the Son of Man in the specific ethical teachings of Jesus. In these sayings, which have been less coloured by the developing theology of the Church, when Jesus speaks of the reward of the righteous, it is God who will bestow it. 'Your Father which seeth in secret will reward you openly' (see Matt. vi. 1, 4, 6, 18). Jesus' concept of the judgment seems revealed in the following sayings : 'If you forgive men their trespasses, your heavenly Father also will forgive you. If you forgive not men their trespasses, neither will your Father forgive your trespasses' (Matt. vi. 14 f. ; compare the even stronger statement in xviii. 35). In the entire three chapters of the Sermon on the Mount there is no reference to the Son of Man. In the parallel collection in Luke vi. there is only one mention of the term, an obviously unoriginal instance. And yet had Jesus thought of the final reward and punishment as being administered by a heavenly agent of God, one would expect some suggestion of it in the promises of the Beatitudes or the references to the final judgment which Matt. v.–vii. contain. This approach to the question suggests that Jesus Himself thought of God as the judge and rewarder of men, and that it was the early Church which introduced the concept of the Son of Man.

Thus, though the possibility that Jesus accepted John's teaching of the heavenly Man cannot be denied, it seems on the whole quite likely that this aspect of Christian apocalyptic belief was the work of the Christian community after the resurrection. If Jesus did repeat the idea it was clearly conventional and subordinate to His vivid sense of God's direct care of the individual. As regards the Christian adoption of the idea, it can be adequately explained, quite apart from Jesus' teachings. Two forces would have helped to establish it in Christian circles. On the one hand, the disciples had believed that their master and teacher was going to reveal Himself as the Messiah of Old Testament prophecy. In this they had been disappointed, but the resurrection suggested a different interpretation of their hopes. In addition, it must be remembered that John the Baptist had described a heavenly figure who was coming soon to execute the final judgment, and John's influence was strong in the early years of the Church. Just as the latter's use of the rite of baptism was adopted after

CHAP. VIII, 34–CHAP. IX, 1

Jesus' death, so would his teaching of the heavenly One have helped the Church find its way to its new faith.

These references to the sufferings of the followers of Christ and to the coming of the Son of Man suggested the saying, in ix. 1, as to the nearness of the time : ' I tell you truly . . . there are some of those standing here who will not taste death till they see the coming of God's Reign with power.' This saying, like the preceding one, has occasioned endless debate. The study of the last twenty-five or thirty years, however, has made it clear that the reign of God means the eschatological establishment of God's universal rule, and not the gradual growth of the influence of the Church, as it used to be argued. But the more exact dating, **some of those standing here,** looks suspiciously like an endeavour on the part of a later teacher to encourage a generation whose faith in the coming of the End was beginning to waver. There is every reason to think that Jesus proclaimed that the divine Event was near. But it is very doubtful if He formulated any such exact chronology of its arrival as the passage here presents. As stated in the Introduction, the saying provides a valuable clue as to the date of the Gospel.

ix. 2–8 : JESUS IS TRANSFIGURED BEFORE HIS DISCIPLES

Six days afterwards Jesus took Peter, James and John, and 2 led them up a high hill by themselves alone ; in their presence he was transfigured, and his clothes glistened 3 white, vivid white, such as no fuller on earth could bleach them. And Elijah along with Moses appeared to them, 4 and conversed with Jesus. So Peter addressed Jesus, 5 saying, ' Rabbi, it is a good thing we are here ; let us put up three tents, one for you, one for Moses, and one for 6 Elijah ' (for he did not know what to say, they were so terrified). Then a cloud came overshadowing them, and 7 from the cloud a voice said, ' This is my Son, the Beloved, listen to him.' Suddenly looking round they saw no 8 one there except Jesus, all alone beside them.

THE GOSPEL OF MARK

This strange story is a puzzle to modern readers. For those Christians for whom the Gospel was composed its meaning is not difficult to determine. It meant the confirmation to the disciples of Peter's confession, and Jesus' restatement of it in terms of the heavenly Son of Man. Now Jesus appears in the glory which was to be His after His sufferings. The word **transfigured** means to become changed in form or nature. A good illustration of the meaning is provided by 2 Cor. iii. 18. The **clothes which glistened white, such as no fuller on earth could** bleach them, are heavenly garments. The angel whom the women met in the tomb of Jesus was clad in white (Mark xvi. 5), and Enoch lxii. 16 refers to the ' garments of glory . . . which shall not grow old ' with which the righteous shall be arrayed after they shall have risen from the earth. The Gospel of Matthew adds to the passage here that Jesus' face shone as the sun, a detail which belongs to similar contexts and descriptions. Readers of the Pentateuch would also recognize in the **cloud overshadowing them** the Shekinah, or presence of God. The first part of the words of the heavenly voice come from Isa. xlii. 1—the passage which speaks of God's chosen servant on whom He shall pour His spirit. They are the same words spoken by the heavenly voice at the Baptism. The remaining clause, **listen to Him,** remind one of Moses' statement in Deut. xviii. 15 : ' God will raise up unto thee a prophet from the midst of thee of thy brethren, like unto Me. Unto Him shall ye hearken.'

Various views have been suggested as to the origin of this story. It has been said to have been a vision by which Peter became convinced of Jesus' Messiahship. Or it has been described as a post-resurrection experience, the **six days afterwards** referring to that event. A third explanation is that it is a piece of Christian symbolism, Moses and Elijah, representing the law and the prophets, being made to testify to Jesus' Messiahship.

The details of the story throw considerable light upon its origin. As has been remarked, Jesus appears transfigured in revelation of His future glory as the heavenly Son of Man. But this is a conception of Jesus which the disciples certainly

CHAPTER IX, VERSES 2-8

did not hold during His lifetime. We are not dealing, therefore, with a vision of Peter—unless it was one he had much later—for Peter's vision would have pictured Jesus rather as an earthly and regal Messiah. The story thus expresses the early Christian belief. And it presents not one of these, but several. The quotation from Isaiah would be regarded as a declaration that Jesus was the Son of God in the Hellenistic sense of the term. The setting from which these words come speaks of the Servant of Jehovah, which was one of the titles which the New Testament writers confer on Jesus (Acts iii. 13, iv. 27, etc.). The words from Deuteronomy imply that Jesus was that prophet like unto Moses whose coming had been foretold (see Acts iii. 22). Thus one can see in the story the intertwining of several threads of primitive Christian Christology. The story in its present form represents, no doubt, a growth or development over a period of time. What its original nucleus was, there is no way now of telling.

Thus far, the fact that the words of the heavenly voice are practically identical with those of the voice at the time of the Baptism has been ignored. This is a curious fact. It must be considered in the light of the further fact that both accounts deal with a heavenly designation of Jesus' Messianic office. The two stories appear, therefore, to be different forms of the same basic tradition, one that declared that a heavenly voice at a significant moment in Jesus' life spoke out appointing and declaring that Jesus was the Messiah. The two accounts have plainly developed along different lines. One is connected with the Baptism and the pouring out of the Spirit on Jesus; the other, as the mention of the disciples shows, is thought of as occurring at a point during the course of Jesus' public ministry.

But this raises a real problem. Why should there ever have been in circulation a story which placed the heavenly declaration of Jesus' Messiahship during the course of His ministry? The logical place for such a story was after the resurrection (cf. Acts ii. 36), or at the Baptism, or at the birth of Jesus. The answer which suggests itself is that there was a recollection in the Christian tradition that it was late during the ministry of Jesus that the Messianic element entered the story—that is to say, that some such story as Peter's confession at Cæsarea Philippi was a well-known element of Christian knowledge, and that this story was connected with it. The alternative would be to assume that the story was a completely detached unit of the tradition which Mark has brought into its present context. It does not seem likely that an account of the heavenly declaration of Jesus' Messianic office would have been quite so stripped of all reference to the rest of the story.

Several details of the narrative remain to be noted. The two figures of Elijah and Moses are difficult to explain. Why these two? The usual view that they symbolized the law and the prophets seems to break down from the fact that Elijah is mentioned first in Mark and is the more prominent of the two. It is possible that these two are mentioned because neither had tasted of death. The translation of Elijah was, of course, a familiar fact. There is some evidence of a belief that Moses was translated, though the usual view, certainly in rabbinic circles, was that he died. But had the thought been primarily of bodily translation without death, one would have expected the names of Elijah and Enoch. Perhaps the answer is that among the beliefs which the exuberant eschatology of that period produced, there was one that both Moses and Elijah would return before the Final Day. Of the existence of such a belief there are two hints. The Revelation of John speaks of two prophetic witnesses before the last days (xi. 3), and the description of them seems to indicate Elijah and Moses. In the rabbinic commentary on Deuteronomy, *Debarim Rabbah*, a saying of Johanan ben Zakkai is quoted that Elias and Moses would come before the End. If some such popular belief is not the explanation, then it must be sought simply in the importance of both figures. The dating **six days afterwards** calls for some explanation. No completely satisfactory one seems to have been found. In the absence of any, I suggest the following: This story reminds one of the account of Moses going up into the holy mount to receive the tables of stone, which is told in Exod. xxiv. 12-18. That story reads: 'And Moses went up into the mount, and a cloud

CHAPTER IX, VERSES 2-8

covered the mount. And the glory of Jehovah abode upon Mount Sinai, and the cloud covered it six days: and the seventh day He called unto Moses out of the midst of the cloud.' Perhaps in the original form of the story the voice to Jesus and His disciples was six days after they went up on the mount.

ix. 9–13: JESUS FORBIDS THE DISCIPLES TO TELL WHAT THEY HAD SEEN, AND EXPLAINS THE PROPHECY OF ELIJAH'S RETURN

As they went down the hill, he forbade them to tell anyone 9 what they had seen, till such time as the Son of man rose from the dead. This order they obeyed, debating with 10 themselves what ' rising from the dead ' meant. So they 11 put this question to him, ' Why do the Pharisees and scribes say that Elijah has to come first ? ' He said to 12 them, ' Elijah does come first, to restore all things ; but what is written about the Son of man as well ? This, that he is to endure great suffering and be rejected. As for 13 Elijah, I tell you he has come already, and they have done to him whatever they liked—as it is written of him.'

Two themes appear in this conversation which is said to have taken place on the descent from the Mount of Transfiguration. The first furnishes confirmation of the interpretation of that story given above. Jesus is said to have placed on the disciples an injunction of silence **till such time as the Son of man rose from the dead.** This order they obeyed, although it is insisted that they did not understand what this latter meant. The command carries an important implication. This story of the Transfiguration was not known even by the body of the disciples until after the resurrection—a fact which weighs heavily against the view that this was an actual vision by Peter. The injunction to silence which is one of Mark's major themes is here given a time limit, and this is stated in terms of an individual, special resurrection from the dead, which it is admitted the three disciples could not understand at this time. The object of this injunction seems to be to

THE GOSPEL OF MARK

explain why it was that this convincing proof of Jesus' supernatural office was not known earlier.

With verse 11 a new theme is developed, the current expectation of the coming of Elijah. The connection with what has preceded is purely verbal, however, since there is no connection in thought between the two references to Elijah.

The question which the disciples ask here was of considerable importance to the early Church. For one of the Jewish objections to accepting the Messiahship of Jesus was, as Justin's debate with Trypho shows, that Elijah had not come. Mark gives the Christian answer, the main point of which is clear. Elijah had come, as prophesied in Mal. iv. 5, but had been rejected, as the Scriptures foretold.

This saying is not explained, but there can be little doubt that it is John the Baptist who is referred to. This is the answer which Justin Martyr gives to Trypho's argument. It is also explicitly affirmed in Matt. xi. 14—' And if you care to believe it, this is the Elijah who is to come.' In Luke i. 17, the angel announces to Zechariah that the son who is to be born to him will go before the Lord ' in the spirit and power of Elijah.' The Fourth Gospel, on the other hand, denies explicitly that John was Elijah (i. 21). In answer to questions, John describes himself merely as ' the voice of one crying in the wilderness, Prepare the way of the Lord,' as prophesied in Isa. xl. 3. This passage of Scripture, we have seen, probably stood alone in the words about John in Mark's introduction (i. 2). It would appear, then, that the early Christian views about John took two forms, or rather developed in two stages. Some were content to say that he was the prophet who fulfilled the words of Isa. xl. 3—' the voice in the wilderness.' Others went on to identify him with Elijah, quoting also Mal. iii. 1, and iv. 3. The Gospel of Mark seems to occupy a sort of transition stage in this development. In i. 2 ff., there is no hint that John was Elijah, nor is this suggested in the long story about the death of John. In the saying placed here, however, the belief is implied. Unless, therefore, the present passage be regarded as an addition to his text, Mark incorporated both views.

CHAPTER IX, VERSES 9-13

The chief factor which led to the recognition of John as Elijah was, of course, the scriptural and scribal teaching as to his reappearance before the Day of the Lord. But there were other strong suggestions and influences. John loomed large in Christian tradition and consciousness. He represented a prophetic survival which was the more striking because of its previous absence. He wore the dress of Elijah (2 Kings i. 8). Elijah defied and opposed King Ahab, and John publicly rebuked Herod, the tetrarch. Elijah's chief opponent was Jezebel, the queen, and John was beheaded at the instigation of Herodias. It is not surprising, thus, that early Christianity saw in John the fulfilment of the current expectation.

The last words of verse 14, **as it is written of him,** create a definite difficulty. No such prophecy of an Elijah who would return to be rejected can be found. Rawlinson thinks that the meaning of the saying is that, if one interpreted the Scriptures properly, he would realize that Elijah would have to suffer on his return just as in his first lifetime, and points to 1 Kings xix. 2-10. The one other explanation which seems to have been advanced is that some apocryphal document, now lost, contained the passage in question.

This view that the identification of John as the expected Elijah was the work of the early Church rather than Jesus Himself rests on several considerations. In the first place, the identification seems to be an answer to an objection to Jesus' Messiahship by Jewish critics. In the second place, the endeavour to find Scriptural anticipations and prophecies of the events of Jesus' life seems to belong to the reflective period of the early Church rather than to the stirring days of the actual ministry. In the third place, the Gospels themselves, as we have seen, do not agree that John was Elijah. Had Jesus asserted this fact, the denial of the Fourth Gospel would be incomprehensible.

ix. 14-29: THE HEALING OF AN EPILEPTIC BOY

On reaching the disciples, they saw a large crowd round 14 them, and some scribes arguing with them. On seeing him 15

the whole crowd was thunderstruck and ran to greet him.
16 Jesus asked them, 'What are you discussing with them?'
17 A man from the crowd answered him, 'Teacher, I brought
18 my son to you; he has a dumb spirit, and whenever it seizes him it throws him down, he foams at the mouth, grinds his teeth, and turns rigid; I told your disciples
19 to cast it out, but they could not.' He answered them, 'O faithless generation, how long must I still be with you? how long have I to bear with you? Bring him
20 to me.' So they brought the boy to him, and when the spirit saw Jesus it at once convulsed the boy; he fell on the ground and rolled about, foaming at the mouth.
21 Jesus asked his father, 'How long has he been like this?'
22 'From childhood,' he said; 'it has thrown him into fire and water many a time, to destroy him. If you can do
23 anything, do help us, do have pity on us.' Jesus said to him, ' " If you can "! Anything can be done for one who
24 believes.' At once the father of the boy cried out, 'I do
25 believe; help my unbelief.' Now as Jesus saw that a crowd was rapidly gathering, he checked the unclean spirit. 'Deaf and dumb spirit,' he said, 'leave him, I
26 command you, and never enter him again!' And it did come out, after shrieking aloud and convulsing him violently. The child turned like a corpse, so that most
27 people said, 'he is dead'; but, taking his hand, Jesus
28 raised him and he got up. When he went indoors, his disciples asked him in private, 'Why could we not cast it
29 out?' He said to them, 'Nothing can make this kind come out but prayer and fasting.'

This narrative involves little that we have not already met, except the realistic details of the condition of the sufferer. The afflicted boy seems to have suffered from epilepsy or something similar. The astonishment of the crowd is not over any special appearance of Jesus, due to His recent transfiguration, but over the impressive arrival of the wonder-worker in the nick of time. The rebuke of verse 19 is addressed to the whole crowd and seems literary and artificial, a prophet's condemnation of a generation without the faith to deal with such situations. The reaction of the evil spirit in the presence of Jesus is typical. It throws the boy into a convulsion. Jesus' command to the demon to **leave him ... and never enter again** is so phrased because the complaint was a recurrent rather than a constant one, and the thought evidently was that the demon only possessed the boy at the time of his attacks.

The question of the disciples in verse 28 as to why they could not effect the exorcism involves a change of scene and is probably an addition to the original story of the cure. There is an uncertainty concerning the text, the words **and fasting** being omitted by some important manuscripts. If genuine, they probably reflect the difficulties of the early Church. Jesus Himself was criticized for not requiring His disciples to fast (ii. 18), and there is no indication that He practised fasting in order to have power over demons. But fasting was a religious exercise of importance in the early Church (cf. Acts xiii. 2, xiv. 23, etc.), this being taken over from contemporary Judaism. The word thus looks like an exhortation to those who had failed in their attempts to cast out demons, to practise a greater piety.

The answer is thoroughly Jewish. Fasting was always a support to prayer, and prayer, in the views of the rabbis, was effective against the demons.

ix. 30–32 : THE SECOND PREDICTION OF THE PASSION AND THE RESURRECTION

Leaving there they passed through Galilee. He did not want 30 anyone to know of their journey, for he was teaching his 31 disciples, telling them that the Son of man would be betrayed into the hands of men, that they would kill him, and that when he was killed he would rise again after three days. But they did not understand what he said, 32 and they were afraid to ask him what he meant.

The last topographical reference was to Cæsarea Philippi in viii. 27. This lay in the territory of Philip and outside Galilee.

Mark thus means to say that Jesus and His band now crossed Galilee, but in secret. The evangelist's explanation is that Jesus is now engaged in teaching His disciples of His approaching death and subsequent elevation to glory. The contents of this instruction are identical with those in viii. 31 ff. In x. 33 the same predictions are made a third time. This threefold announcement of a rejection, death, and resurrection which awaits the Son of man—the title appears in each announcement—gives the narrative a solemn and dramatic tone which marks it off from the narrative of the Galilean ministry. This is clearly intended by the evangelist. The secret hidden at the beginning, and only perceived by evil spirits, has at last been recognized by the disciples. From viii. 27 on, Jesus instructs them in the doctrine of the suffering, dying, and rising Son of man.

But the evangelist knew well the story of what took place at Jerusalem. When the events occurred, the disciples, taken apparently by surprise, fled. A threefold, detailed explanation of what was to come could only be reconciled with this result on the theory that the disciples did not understand what they were told. Modern readers are more likely to conclude that Jesus' predictions were not as detailed as Mark describes them.

ix. 33-37: ON TRUE GREATNESS AND ON SERVICE IN THE NAME OF CHRIST

33 Then they reached Capharnahum. And when he was indoors he asked them, 'What were you arguing about on the
34 road?' They said nothing, for on the road they had been
35 disputing about which of them was the greatest. So he sat down and called the twelve. 'If anyone wants to be first,'
36 he said to them, 'he must be last of all and the servant of all.' Then he took a little child, set it among them, and putting his arms round it said to them,
37   'Whoever receives one of these little ones in my name receives me,
     and whoever receives me receives not me but him who sent me.'

CHAPTER IX, VERSES 33-37

A good deal has to be said in any study of early Christianity about the theology of the early Church. But it is necessary always to remember that this theology was only one side of early Christianity—its thought side. The practical side was a fellowship with others who professed this ' Way ' and tried to maintain its ethical standards.

These two sayings need little comment. The saying in verse 35 must have been one of Jesus' most frequent utterances, for it appears in the Gospels repeatedly with slight variations in form (see here, Mark x. 43 f., Matt. xx. 26 f., and Luke xxii. 26 ; Matt. xxiii. 11, and Luke ix. 48*b*). The ethical ideal which it formulates is identical with the sayings about the chief commandments, the so-called Golden Rule, and the saying of Jesus preserved in Acts—' It is more blessed to give than to receive.' Indeed, while many doubts may exist as to the exact apocalyptic and theological beliefs of Jesus, it may be fairly stated that the content of His ethical teaching is known to us beyond cavil. The importance of this to Christian thought and teaching is often overlooked.

The occasion of the utterance of the saying in verse 35 is said to have been a contention **on the road** of travel as to **which of them was the greatest.** The dispute is often interpreted as a debate concerning priority in the coming New Age. This is quite possible. We know from x. 37 that such questions were discussed. It is suggestive that both Matthew and Luke interpret the story in this way.

The scene portrayed in verses 36 and 37 of Jesus taking the child in His arms, and declaring that **whoever receives one of these little ones in My name receives Me, and . . . Him who sent Me,** namely God, is one of the most beautiful in the Gospels. Along with the similar story of the blessing of the children in x. 13 ff., it presents a tender, affectionate aspect of Jesus' character which the Church especially cherished. The scene was no doubt independent of the preceding verses, since the duty and privilege of *receiving* a child has no connection with the question of who is greatest. The phrase **in My name,** on the basis of Talmudic passages, would mean ' on My account,' or ' for My sake,' but this does not seem to fit the context so well as to interpret it as meaning, ' because I have commanded it '—i.e. ' as a part of Christian duty.' The word *receive* in the present instance can only mean ' to accord kindly treatment to.' This is declared to be equivalent to *receiving* or showing kindness to Christ, and thereby to God. Montefiore rightly stresses the value of this saying in Christian practice : ' The dynamic effect . . . has been enormous. All social service wrought in Christ's name and spirit is wrought to him. Who can measure or count the deeds of sacrifice and love to which this saying has prompted ? '

So much for the meaning and value of the saying. Critically examined, the saying would appear to have some connection with two others which appear in Matthew. At the close of the mission charge to the disciples, Jesus declares, ' He who receives you receives Me, and he who receives Me receives Him who sent Me ' (Matt. x. 40 ; cf. Luke x. 16). The mission charge closes with the saying, ' And whoever gives one of these little ones even a cup of cold water . . . shall not lose his reward ' (x. 42). The saying here seems to be a variant or conflation of these two. If the Marcan form be regarded as a conflation of the two similar sayings current in the tradition, then the introductory scene will have to be taken as due to the evangelist or his authority as an explanation of the **little ones** of the saying. It is thus possible that the form of the saying is due to the repetition and reworking of Jesus' sayings in the Christian tradition. All one can say with assurance is that the saying goes back to, and is genetically related to, genuine sayings of Jesus, and that the scene is in His character and spirit. But this really is all that it is necessary to say.

ix. 38–41 : THE EXORCIST WHO WAS NOT A FOLLOWER

38 John said to him, ' Teacher, we saw a man casting out dæmons in your name ; but he does not follow us, and so we
39 stopped him.' Jesus said, ' Do not stop him ; no one who performs any miracle in my name will be ready to speak
40 evil of me. He who is not against us is for us.
41 Whoever gives you a cup of water because you belong to Christ, I tell you truly, he shall not miss his reward.'

CHAPTER IX, VERSES 38-41

This is a curious story, its connection with the preceding verses being, apparently, the verbal connection of the phrase **in My name**. But it is obvious that the meaning of the phrase is different in the two passages. In the preceding section it meant, ' on My account,' or, ' at My command.' Here it refers to the utterance of the name as a wonder-working formula. The situation here presented may have arisen during Jesus' lifetime, but is more likely to have occurred subsequently. Effective Christian employment of the name of Jesus in exorcisms and healings (see Acts iii. 6, and Acts xvi. 18) would quickly give rise to its use by others. The magical papyri and ostraka now being recovered in great numbers point to the frequency of such usage of the names of great individuals and divinities. Acts xix. 13 ff. shows that the early Church had considerable difficulty with individuals who used the name of Jesus in this way but had no connection with Christian brotherhoods. The passage before us gives a tolerant answer to the problem. It states that the Church had no quarrel with people who used the name of Jesus to do a good work, and uses one of the very general sayings of Jesus—**He who is not against us is for us**—to support the view. This seems the most plausible view of the passage. On this interpretation the original meaning of the saying is lost, since that depends entirely on its occasional purpose.

One of the weak points of early Christian ethics was its inability to recognize any good whatever in the motives and beliefs of rival cults and religious teachers. It is pleasant, therefore, to note this indication that the Church could at times be more tolerant than, for example, was Paul in his address to his rival, Elymas, on the isle of Cyprus—' O full of all guile and all villainy, thou son of the devil, thou enemy of all righteousness ' (Acts xiii. 10).

Verse 41 elaborates the general injunction in verse 39 not to stop the exorcist. In the Greek text both verse 40 and verse 41 are introduced with a causal conjunction, and the translation should have ' for ' or ' because ' inserted at the beginning of each verse. The saying in 41 gives the positive side of the truth stated negatively in the preceding verses.

THE GOSPEL OF MARK

No one who does a good deed in the name of Christ shall lose his reward. The wording **because you belong to Christ** is certainly early Christian, rather than a phrase of Jesus, but the emphasis on even a gift of cold water receiving its reward is in line with Jesus' saying about men being judged by their idle words, and His commendation of the widow's gift in the temple.

It is well to keep in mind that the sharpness of the distinction between Christians and outsiders represented by the motive **because you belong to Christ** is characteristic of the early Church. It was a by-product of the effort to emphasize the fellowship of Christians and to create an organization. One thinks of Paul's words, ' Do good to all men, but especially to the household of faith,' and similar injunctions. Organization involved the Church immediately in distinctions on the basis of membership. Such a development did not contradict the ethic of Jesus, but it certainly complicated it. One cannot help but feel that the motive for a good deed **because you belong to Christ**, or, with Matthew, ' because he is a disciple,' is a less worthy one than that implied in the injunctions of Matt. v. 44-46 : ' But I say unto you, love your enemies . . . that you may be sons of your Father in heaven. . . . For if you love only those that love you, what reward have you ? '

ix. 42-50 : Sayings Concerning Hindrances

42 ' **And whoever is a hindrance to one of these little ones who believe, it were better for him to have a great millstone hung round his neck and be thrown into the sea.**

43   **If your hand is a hindrance to you, cut it off :**
      better be maimed and get into Life,
        than keep your two hands and go to Gehenna, to the fire that is never quenched.

45   **If your foot is a hindrance to you, cut it off :**
      better get into Life a cripple,
        than keep your two feet and be thrown into Gehenna.

CHAPTER IX, VERSES 42-50

If your eye is a hindrance to you, tear it out : 47
 better get into God's Realm with one eye,
  than keep your two eyes and be thrown into Gehenna.
 where *their worm never dies and the fire is never put out.* 48
Everyone has to be consecrated* by the fire of the discipline. 49
Salt is excellent : 50
 but if salt is tasteless, how are you to restore its flavour ?
 Let there be " salt between you " ;
 be at peace with one another.'

* The Greek word ἀλισθήσεται literally means 'salted,' the metaphor being taken from the custom of using salt in sacrifices (cp. e.g. Levit. ii. 13 ; Josephus, *Antiquities*, iii. 9. 1). 'There is fire to be encountered afterwards, if not now; how much better to face it now and by self-sacrifice insure against the future' (Professor Menzies).

The thought of service to others suggests the opposite one of hindering or obstructing others, and this is stated in the vigorous pictorial language which was characteristic of Jesus. The saying is found not only here, but also in Luke xvii. 1 f., a passage derived from some other source. It would seem thus to have been generally current as one of Jesus' sayings. The phrase **little ones who believe** can scarcely apply to children. It is the same expression which one meets in Matt. x. 42, and must refer to those ' babes ' to whom knowledge and understanding had come, rather than to the ' wise.' We know from Luke vii. 29, and Matt. xxi. 32, that Jesus felt strongly the rejection of the message of John the Baptist and of Himself by the upper classes, and its acceptance by outcasts and humble folk. The saying, though general, may have referred particularly to the opposition of the scribes to Jesus' work, whom He charged not only with refusing to enter the Kingdom of God themselves, but also with preventing those who wished to enter (Matt. xxiii. 13).

To this warning against hindering others is added a group of sayings about hindrances to oneself. Here the sharpness of the alternatives set out, as well as the form of expression, seem characteristic of Jesus' thought. One is reminded of the parables of the pearl of great price and of the hidden treasure. The Kingdom of God is worth any sacrifice. In the verses here the thought is in terms of sacrificing a part of the body rather than the whole of life.

The contrast is stated in terms of entering **Life** or being **thrown into Gehenna**. The language is thoroughly Jewish. **Life** was often used to describe the future reward of the righteous. Gehenna, literally a valley west and south of Jerusalem, had been the site of sacrifices in worship of Moloch (Jer. vii. 31). It was desecrated by Josiah, and became a dumping-place for the garbage of the city. The name came to be used to designate the place of future punishment after the judgment. In its full development Gehenna became also a place of temporary punishment before the Great Judgment, but of that there is no suggestion in the present passage. The striking description in verse 48 is taken bodily from the last verse of Isaiah (lxvi. 24), where the prophet declares that those who shall worship Jehovah in the re-made Jerusalem of the last days shall ' go forth and look upon the dead bodies of the men that have transgressed against Me : for their worm shall not die neither shall the fire be quenched ; and they shall be an abhorring unto all flesh.' The figure is of vermin and fire perpetually destroying the refuse of the city. There is no thought of an eternal torture of living beings. Nor is any such doctrine implied in the citation of the passage by Mark.

The next verse is difficult. Literally it reads—an alternate, and probably substitute, reading being rejected—' Everyone must be salted with fire.' The most probable meaning of the figure of ' salting ' is that of purifying or preserving. **Fire** is a frequent figure for trials and persecutions, though some have thought that it should be understood to refer to the fire of the last judgment. The meaning of the verse is either, Everyone will be saved through the discipline of trials, or, Everyone who will be saved will have to pass through the fire of the last judgment. This last would be analogous to the thought of 1 Cor. iii. 12 ff. The terseness of the expression rather favours a reference to the common theme of Christian sufferings and discipline. This is the view Moffatt has adopted in his

CHAPTER IX, VERSES 42-50

translation, though the Greek text is not so unambiguous as he makes it.

Verse 50 is best understood in the light of the similar saying in Matt. v. 13 : ' Ye are the salt of the world. But if the salt lose its flavour, it is useless.' The salt is the Christian message, and its programme of peace and love. If, however, this be denied in practice, it is useless. The closing injunction— ' Have salt within yourselves and be at peace with one another '—bears out his interpretation. It reminds one of Paul's efforts to eliminate the internal dissensions of the Christian brotherhoods.

X. 1 : JESUS ENTERS JUDÆA AND PERÆA

x.
Then he left and went to the territory of Judæa over the 1 Jordan. Crowds gathered to him again, and again he taught them as usual.

At this point in the story Jesus leaves Galilee on the momentous journey to Jerusalem with which His ministry ended. The itinerary of the journey is vague and uncertain, as is so often the case with the topographical details of the Gospel. A variation in the wording of the Greek manuscripts makes it uncertain whether two countries, ' Judæa and across Jordan,' or one locality, **Judæa over the Jordan,** is meant. The latter reading, adopted by Moffatt, has the stronger support and the further confirmation of being the reading of the parallel passage in Matthew. Though an awkward phrase, it can only mean the Jewish portion of Peræa, the territory east of the Jordan which was in the jurisdiction of Herod of Galilee. Mark does not seem to have in mind a ministry in Peræa, but rather the thought of a continuous journey to Jerusalem by this route (cf. x. 17 and 32). But the evangelist is obviously poorly informed on the details of this part of Jesus' work. The statement in verse 1 is very indefinite, and the incidents which follow are not anchored to any particular places and strike one as simply floating traditions which could have happened anywhere.

The Fourth Gospel corroborates and at the same time modifies this picture. According to x. 40, xi. 7, and xi. 54, Jesus worked on the eastern side of the Jordan just before the last visit to the capital. The locality, according to John, was the section near the Jordan where John the Baptizer had worked. This Gospel presents Jesus as passing from one side of the Jordan to the other, partly to escape His enemies, and, at one time, using the wilderness as a safe retreat (xi. 54). Such a presentation has the appearance of verisimilitude. That Jesus was in this section before going on to Jerusalem is guaranteed by the fact that the departure for the capital was through Jericho. But how long He stayed in the area and how publicly He worked one should probably not venture to say.

With the departure from Galilee Mark describes Jesus as abandoning His endeavour to avoid attention. The evangelist's view of the events is clear. The avoidance of the public in Galilee was due to Jesus' desire to teach the inner group of disciples about His approaching Passion (ix. 31). Now that the period of preparation is over, the crowds are at hand, **and again he taught them as usual.**

x. 2–12 : The Question about Divorce

2 **Some Pharisees came up and asked him if a man was allowed**
3 **to divorce his wife. This was to tempt him. So he replied, 'What did Moses lay down for you?'** They
4 said, ' Moses permitted a man *to divorce her by writing out a*
5 *separation-notice.*' Jesus said to them, ' He wrote you that
6 command on account of the hardness of your hearts. But from the beginning, when God created the world,
   Male and female, He created them :
7 *hence a man shall leave his father and mother*
8 *and the pair shall be one flesh.*
9 So they are no longer two but one flesh. What God has
10 joined, then, man must not separate.' Indoors, the
11 disciples again asked him about this, and he said to them, ' Whoever divorces his wife and marries another woman is

an adulterer to the former, and she is an adulteress if she 12 divorces her husband and marries another man.'

There is nothing to indicate that this episode occurred on the final journey to Jerusalem, and, since Mark likes to fill in statements of journeys or of the passage of time, it is probable that the episodes narrated in this chapter came to him as part of the undated Christian tradition.

Along with the high appreciation of family life which Judaism had preserved from the days of its tribal organization, there had continued also a patriarchal emphasis on the dominance of the husband in marriage and his unlimited right of divorce. The latter right was affirmed in Deut. xxiv. 1: ' If she find no favour in his eyes, because he has found something unseemly about her, let him give her a bill of divorce and send her out of his house.'

As in all periods of changing societies, family institutions were under considerable discussion at the time. At one extreme were the Essenes, advocating celibacy; at the other, Hellenized individuals who had abandoned Jewish standards completely. Among the scribes there was a debate as to the divorce law itself. The School of Shammai maintained that divorce was only permissible in the case of fornication, this being the meaning, they argued, of the phrase in the law, ' if he find anything unseemly about her.' The School of Hillel, on the other hand, maintained the husband's historic freedom, on the ground that the meaning of the phrase was quite general. In the version of this episode in Matthew, it is this debate which is presented to Jesus, and He is asked to take sides on the question. According to Matt. xix. 3, the question asked was, ' Is it right for a man to divorce his wife for any cause ? ' and Jesus' answer declares that divorce except for fornication was wrong. Jesus thus takes the side of the School of Shammai in the debate. But in Mark the question is whether divorce is ever right, and Jesus' answer is correspondingly sweeping.

There are several considerations which show that Mark's account is the correct one. (1) Luke xvi. 18 gives another version of Jesus' teaching on divorce. It contains no hint that it dealt with the permissible causes of divorce or listed adultery as such. (2) Paul cites Jesus' teaching on divorce in 1 Cor. vii. 10, and again there is no indication of exceptions to his general condemnation of divorce. (3) In the third place, one notes that the rest of Jesus' answer as reported by both Matthew and Mark appeals to the teaching of Genesis over against the law of divorce in Deut. xxiv. 1. One would conclude from this that the point of the discussion was whether divorce was permissible, not on what grounds it should be granted. Thus the evidence seems overwhelming that in the First Gospel Jesus' teachings have been qualified and made to conform to the position of the School of Shammai. In accepting the accuracy of Mark's account one must assume that Jesus' opponents had some inkling as to His attitude toward divorce, and wished to force Him into a position which would contradict the words of Moses.

The answer which Jesus made declares that divorce was contrary to the divine purpose revealed in the story of creation. **Male and female created he them** (Gen. i. 27). The citation of this passage was not original with Jesus. It appears in a passage in the *Zadokite Fragment* in a criticism of polygamy (vii. 1 f.), and quite probably was the classic citation in defence of monogamy. Nor was Jesus the first to say that God joins men and women in marriage. The rabbis delighted in utterances on that subject. His point is original in that He read the scriptural passage enjoining monogamy as not merely forbidding polygamy, but also the disruption of marriage by divorce—this in spite of the Deuteronomic law. Behind this insistence on obeying Genesis rather than Deuteronomy lay, of course, a perception of the cruelty and unfairness of the law of divorce. The words of the law permitting divorce He rejected as a concession to human weakness which fell below the divine ideal which Moses himself had revealed in the story of creation. Thus in general His argument was not an attack on the law as such, but an effort to interpret it, as He felt, correctly. His attitude here is in line with that which He takes in connection with the Sabbath controversies and the matter

CHAPTER X, VERSES 2-12

of inviolable oaths. The general humanitarian teachings are appealed to in correction of specific precepts or rulings. In this repudiation of the unlimited right of divorce on the part of the husband it is obvious that Jesus became one of the outstanding historic champions of the cause of women.

This saying of Jesus on divorce strikes harshly on modern ears; it is so sweeping and unqualified, and seems so ill adapted to be the regulatory rule for the great variety of situations which modern circumstances create. Two remarks may be permitted. In the first place, Jesus was speaking to a people among whom divorce was easy, and had been so from time immemorial. The emphasis needed to be placed on the basic principle of the permanence of marriage. In the second place, it must be remembered that Jesus' teachings in nearly every instance were in general and sweeping form. He was not interested, apparently, in classifying and listing the exceptional cases which arise. As rules, His sayings are unpractical; it is as declarations of the basic ethical principles in human relations that they must be regarded.

x. 13-16: THE BLESSING OF THE CHILDREN

Now people brought children for him to touch them, and the 13 disciples checked them : but Jesus was indignant when he 14 saw this, and he said to them, ' Let the children come to me, do not stop them : the Realm of God belongs to such as these. I tell you truly, whoever will not submit to the 15 Reign of God like a child will never get into it at all.' Then 16 he put his arms round them, laid his hands on them and blessed them.

The grace and beauty of the scene here depicted calls for no comment. The request that Jesus **touch** the children means, as verse 16 shows, that He place His hands on them in bestowal of a blessing. Such blessings were commonly sought in Jesus' day. The objection of the disciples was, of course, only because they felt that their master should not be burdened with such requests. It is interesting that Mark says plainly that Jesus **was angry** with them. This earliest Gospel does not hesitate to attribute such emotions to Jesus, but Matthew and Luke carefully omit the word from their accounts.

The words of Jesus concerning the childlike character necessary for admission to God's Kingdom or **Realm** have occasioned a good deal of discussion. Verse 15, as printed above, should be corrected. The words rendered **submit to** mean to receive or accept something that is offered, or to receive some person, as in ix. 37. The change from the **Realm of God** in verse 14 to the **Reign of God** in 15, which goes with the word **submit**, is confusing, since the Greek phrase is the same in both verses. We should read, 'Whoever will not accept the Realm of God like a child will never get into it.' The childlike disposition which Jesus had in mind, therefore, was its grateful acceptance of that which was offered rather than the trait of obedience. The saying presents one of Jesus' repeated criticisms of much of the religion of His contemporaries. It was too often, He felt, associated with pride and a sense of self-righteousness. 'When you shall have done all things that are commanded you, say, We are unprofitable servants,' He once declared (Luke xvii. 10). Along the same line are the sayings, 'Blessed are the meek,' and 'Whosoever shall exalt himself shall be humbled.' He condemned all thought of a claim on God, whether of race or one's righteousness. Instead, He urged a confident and grateful trust in God's care and God's reward. It is this quality of Jesus' personal religion which comes to expression in the saying here. In Paul's doctrine of justification by faith the same attitude is enjoined.

x. 17–27: A Rich Man Asks what he Must Do to Gain the Life of the Kingdom

17 As he went out on the road, a man ran up and knelt down before him. 'Good teacher,' he asked, 'what must I do
18 to inherit life eternal?' Jesus said to him, 'Why call me
19 "good"? No one is good, no one but God. You know

CHAPTER X, VERSES 17-27

the commands : *do not kill, do not commit adultery, do not steal, do not bear false witness,* do not defraud, *honour your father and mother.*' 'Teacher,' he said, ' I have observed all 20 these commands from my youth.' Jesus looked at him and loved him. ' There is one thing you want,' He said ; ' go 21 and sell all you have ; give the money to the poor and you will have treasure in heaven ; then come, take up the cross, and follow me.' But his face fell at that, and he went sadly 22 away, for he had great possessions. Jesus looked round 23 and said to his disciples, ' How difficult it is for those who have money to get into the Realm of God ! ' The disciples 24 were amazed at what he said ; so he repeated, ' My sons, how difficult it is for those who rely on money to get into the Realm of God ! It is easier for a camel to get through a 25 needle's eye than for a rich man to get into the Realm of God.' They were more astounded than ever ; they said to 26 themselves, ' Then who ever can be saved ? ' Jesus looked 27 at them and said, ' For men it is impossible, but not for God ; anything is possible for God.'

Mark apparently knows nothing about the individual who came to Jesus with this question except that **he had great possessions.** Luke (xviii. 18) calls him a ' ruler,' meaning probably a member of one of the councils or courts. Matthew refers to him as a ' young man ' (xix. 20). As a result, Christian tradition, telescoping these three statements into one title, usually refers to the individual as the ' rich, young ruler.' But the reply of the man in Mark's account, **I have observed all these commands from my youth,** rather implies that he was no longer so young. The statement that **he ran up** to Jesus looks like a detail which has survived from the account of an eye-witness. There are other suggestions of an earlier, more prolix narrative, particularly the opening words of commendation with which the man addressed Jesus, and the latter's answer rejecting the flattering epithets. On the basis of Mark's account one would think of the questioner as a wealthy individual in early middle age—at least he still can run—

proud of his position and his wealth, who, nevertheless, had become deeply dissatisfied with the conventional teaching of the law which he had known from his youth. Quite probably he had heard Jesus speak, and eagerly availed himself of an opportunity to ask the prophet who taught with such authority what he should do.

The rich man's question, **'What must I do to inherit life eternal?'** is equivalent to ' What must I do to enter the Kingdom of God to come?' The term **life** to describe the latter, and **inherit** in the sense of ' gain entrance into,' are common rabbinic idioms. Jesus' answer, **You know the commands,** is proof of His acceptance of the Mosaic law as containing the divine law adequate for salvation, if properly understood and obeyed. The precepts which are enumerated, with one exception, come from the Decalogue (Exod. xx. 12 f. and Deut. v. 16 f.). The exception is the commandment, **Do not defraud,** which is found in Lev. xix. 13 and Deut. xxiv. 14. Its presence along with the precepts from the Ten Words, as the Decalogue was called, is rather surprising. Some have thought that it is supposed to summarize the ninth and tenth commandments. This seems, however, far fetched—Paul, for example, says plainly, ' Thou shalt not covet ' in his reference to the Decalogue (Rom. xiii. 9). An important group of manuscripts omits this precept, however, and it appears likely that this prohibition has been added to the list because of its appropriateness for the man of wealth. That such addition could easily be made can be seen from the fact that in Matthew there appears the further addition, ' And you shall love your neighbour as yourself.' It may be that the precept, *Honour your father and mother*, which is out of its proper place in the citation, is also an addition.

The question often raised as to why Jesus chose those particular precepts is out of order. The Decalogue represented the essence of the law. Jesus' reply to the man's question thus meant that the answer should not be unknown to a sincere Jew, since nothing else than obedience to the Torah was required. The rich man seems to have been disappointed. He probably expected something new and original; the

CHAPTER X, VERSES 17-27

familiar phrases had lost their freshness and meaning. Jesus, we are told, **looked at him and loved him.** He then called him to become His disciple. He should sell his possessions, give the proceeds in charity, thus laying up treasure in heaven (cf. Matt. vi. 20), and come and join His group of disciples. (The phrase **take up the cross** is missing from many manuscripts, and should be dropped. It is probably imported from viii. 34.)

Why did Jesus require that the individual give all his goods to the poor ? He did not usually make this demand on those who would be His followers. The answer must be that Jesus saw in His conversation with this man both the possibilities of the man and at the same time the way in which his wealth and possessions bound him to a conventional goodness, which he had practised from his youth. He challenged him, therefore, to make a break with all which was holding him back, to exchange his possessions for treasure in heaven, and give himself completely to the cause of the Kingdom of God. That this is the correct understanding of the story is borne out by the sequel. The man **went away,** not with offence but **sadly,** and Jesus turned to His disciples with the statement. **How difficult it is for those who have money to get into the Realm of God !**

The surprise of the disciples at this saying is quite easily understandable. One with wealth, they felt, would not be tempted as others, and, besides, would be able to perform many ' good works.' Jesus, however, reiterated His statement, using this time an expression which has caused a great deal of unnecessary bother. The explanation of the **needle's eye** as a small gate, or the **camel** as a copyist's error for the word meaning a small rope, are both gratuitous and without foundation. The expression is a hyperbole, quite in the style of one whose speech sparkled with picturesque comparisons and metaphors. The figure of an elephant passing through a needle's eye occurs twice in the Babylonian Talmud, and the figure in verse 25 is evidently a local variation. The meaning is simply to repeat in even stronger terms the thought of verse 23.

THE GOSPEL OF MARK

x. 28-31: The Reward of Discipleship

28 Peter began, 'Well, we have left our all and followed you.'
29 Jesus said, 'I tell you truly, no one has left home or brothers or sisters or mother or father or children or lands
30 for my sake and for the sake of the gospel, who does not get a hundred times as much—in this present world homes, brothers, sisters, mothers, children and lands, together with persecutions, and in the world to come life eternal.
31 Many who are first will be last, and many who are last will be first.'

The refusal of the wealthy individual to leave his possessions to follow Jesus furnished an excellent setting for a logion concerning the reward of those who have made such a sacrifice. It is more likely that the saying in verses 29-30 was originally independent of the preceding story. The chief reason for saying this is that the saying here is quite general, dealing with all followers who have left home and family for the cause. The ejaculation of Peter in verse 28 looks rather like an editorial link relating this saying to the previous words on the topic of wealth. There were current in the Christian community quite different sayings concerning the special reward of the Twelve, which, however, were not entirely consistent with each other. See the discussion on Mark x. 35 ff.

This saying reflects rather plainly the experiences of the early Church. The first Christian Church was a persecuted body, even where it was not called upon to suffer actual martyrdom. Exclusion from synagogue and civic affairs and separation from members of one's family were common experiences. The saying states the reward which all such would receive. Eternal life in the world to come was assured, but even in this present age a substitute for that which was given up would be theirs. The Christian communities were a number of brotherhoods, and into this larger family all would enter. In Acts ii. 44 and iv. 32 we are told that the Jerusalem Church had all things in common, and, while this rule was abandoned, a programme of mutual helpfulness and hospitality is revealed by all early documents. Paul, in Rom. xvi. 13, speaks of Rufus' mother as his mother also. Against the fact of early Christian social solidarity and affection, this promise of reward seems to find its fullest meaning. The saying is thus significant as pointing to a fellowship and loyalty so deep and warm that its members could speak of it as a recompense even **a hundred times** for all that they had to give up for its sake. One notes again the phrase, **for the sake of the gospel**, which belongs to the vocabulary of the early Church rather than to Jesus.

Nevertheless, the main thought of the saying goes back to Jesus, and it is possible that the saying itself rests on some word of His. The basic idea is presented in the story in iii. 31 ff., which leads up to the saying, ' Whoever does the will of God, that is My brother and sister and mother.' Jesus' teaching of the necessity of sacrificing domestic ties for the cause of the rule of God, of the duty of loving others as oneself, and of the glad fellowship that men would enjoy in the Kingdom of God, were forces that furthered the development of the Christian brotherhoods. All of His teaching insisted on the ethical principle subordinating limited interests, that one might enter into a broader group of relationships. ' If you love them that love you, what reward have you ? ' The saying under consideration thus represents Jesus' point of view, though probably as this was expressed by His followers after their experiences together.

Verse 31 is a gnomic saying, the meaning of which would depend upon its context. Here it probably means that many of those who are wealthy and powerful now, in the New Age will be last, while those who have few or no possessions will be first.

x. 32-34 : THE THIRD PREDICTION OF THE PASSION

They were on the way up to Jerusalem, Jesus walking in front 32 **of them : the disciples were in dismay and the company who followed were afraid. So once again he took the**

THE GOSPEL OF MARK

33 twelve aside and proceeded to tell them what was going to happen to himself. 'We are going up to Jerusalem,' he said, 'and the Son of man will be betrayed to the high priests and scribes; they will sentence him to death and
34 hand him over to the Gentiles, who will mock him, spit on him, scourge him and kill him; then after three days he will rise again.'

Here Jerusalem is mentioned for the first time as the goal of the journey, though it has been implied in the predictions of rejection by the 'elders, high priests, and scribes.' The predictions in this third announcement are more detailed than in either of the other two.

x. 35-40 : THE REQUEST OF THE SONS OF ZEBEDÆUS

35 James and John, the sons of Zebedæus, came up to him saying, 'Teacher, we want you to do whatever we ask
36 you.' So he said, 'What do you want me to do for you?'
37 They said to him, 'Give us seats, one at your right hand
38 and one at your left hand, in your glory.' Jesus said, 'You do not know what you are asking. Can you drink the cup I have to drink, or undergo the baptism I have to
39 undergo?' They said to him, 'We can.' Jesus said, 'You shall drink the cup I have to drink and undergo the
40 baptism I have to undergo; but it is not for me to grant seats at my right or my left hand—these belong to the men for whom they have been destined.'

This story of a request by James and John, the sons of Zebedæus (i. 19), to sit on Jesus' right and left in His glory is one of the most challenging passages in the Gospels. If authentic, it admits us behind the scenes, so to speak. For here we have recorded a conversation between Jesus and two disciples, called by name, concerning the part which they would have in the expected state of glory. Fortunately, there is no important textual question involved, nor is the terminology ambiguous. The seat at the right hand was the one of highest distinction, and the one at the left hand was second

CHAPTER X, VERSES 35–40

in honour. This was customary at banquets of all sorts, and the disciples of the scribes, when walking with their teachers, were enjoined to place themselves according to the rule of right and left hand in order of honour. The figure to **drink the cup** to refer to a fate either dire, as in Ps. lxxv. 8 ff.—' In the hand of Jehovah is a cup . . . surely the wicked shall drain the deep thereof '—or blessed, as in Ps. xxiii. 5—' My cup runneth over '—is common in Jewish literature. **Baptism** as a similar figure is not so frequent, but is well attested by such passages as Ps. xlii. 7 and Isa. xliii. 2. Both figures are found elsewhere in the teachings of Jesus with the same meaning as here. In xiv. 36 Jesus prays that ' this cup may pass from Me,' and in Luke xii. 50 He speaks of a ' baptism ' which He must undergo. The seats in mind could be thrones or seats of judgment, but it is more likely that the thought is of the Messianic banquet—one of the commonest of Jewish figures—with Jesus at the head of the table. There is, it is true, a notable variation between Mark's account and the parallel one in Matthew. According to the latter (xx. 20 ff.), the request was made by Salome, the mother of the two disciples concerned. But Matthew betrays in verse 22 that he has changed the narrative, obviously for the purpose of eliminating the selfish request of James and John.

Thus we have an unambiguous request by two of the intimate group of disciples for the seats of honour by the side of Jesus in His coming **glory.** The authenticity of the story has been denied. Bultmann, for example, who regards the entire Messianic belief concerning Jesus as a post-resurrection development, sets down both the request of the disciples and Jesus' answer as a later development. But this seems arbitrary and unjustified. The story is a discreditable one as far as the petitioners are concerned. Had it arisen after their martyrdom, we certainly would have an answer which would give some more definite promise of a reward after they had drunk the cup of suffering and death. The story does not, in its main request and answer, seem to be a natural product of early Christian piety.

Unless the narrative be rejected on general grounds, it is

important evidence of the expectations and hopes of the inner group of disciples. They believed that their leader was the one who would be at the head of the New Age when it appeared, and they expressed their hopes plainly to Him. As maintained above, it does not seem that Jesus would have allowed them to continue these beliefs had He regarded them as without foundation.

To this request the wording of Jesus' reply really gives two answers. The more definite one is contained in verse 40: **it is not for me to grant seats at my right or my left hand.** In other words, He declared that He had nothing to do with the matter. There is, however, a saying recorded in Matt. xix. 28 and Luke xxii. 28 which gives a quite different answer to the question of the future honours of the Twelve. It states that they shall ' sit on twelve thrones judging the twelve tribes of Israel.' Mark knows of no such promise. In answer to the inquiry of Peter in x. 28 he could only cite the general statement that those who had sacrificed for the Kingdom of God would gain eternal life. Thus we have two traditions, one preserved by Mark and the other by the ' Q ' source. Between these two the balance of probability lies on the side of the Marcan tradition. Three points can be mentioned in favour of it : (1) the increasing respect with which the apostles were held would tend to produce the ' Q ' saying but not the Marcan one ; (2) the Marcan passage contains details which seem to point to an early authentic tradition ; and (3) the Marcan tradition on the subject is more in accord with the reserve which Jesus seems to have exercised with reference to the conditions of the Age to Come.

But verses 38 and 39 are of a different character. In these verses it is partly assumed and partly stated that (*a*) priority in the New Age is related to a martyr's death ; (*b*) that Jesus asked if the two questioners would share the same fate that He was to undergo; (*c*) that they understood this quite clearly (in contradiction to ix. 32 and other passages) ; (*d*) that they declared themselves ready for martyrdom ; and (*e*) that Jesus foretold that this would be their fate. This last, (*e*), together with (*a*), should mean that they would be given the honours for which they had asked, but in verse 40 this logical conclusion is denied. The contradiction of these verses with verse 40, their assumption that the coming death of Jesus was well understood by all the Twelve, their concern with the priority of Christian martyrs, and their prophecy of the martyrdom of the two brothers, one of which is recorded in Acts xii. 2, make it more than probable that 38 and 39 are a later addition to the story. They seem, clearly, due to reflection on the strange fact that, of the two who requested the chief places, one certainly died a martyr's death.

From the wording of this answer to the two petitioners, one would assume that both James and John had by the time of the Gospel become martyrs. But Christian tradition records that John lived to a ripe old age in Ephesus and wrote the Fourth Gospel. The problem, of course, is too complicated to be discussed here, except to say that the evidence of the reply of Jesus is so strong as to raise the question whether the early tradition may not have confused John the son of Zebedæus with some other 'apostle' of that name.

x. 41–45 : On True Greatness

When the ten heard of this, they burst into indignation at James 41
and John ; so Jesus called them and said, 42
    ' You know the so-called rulers of the Gentiles lord it
        over them,
    and their great men overbear them :
        not so with you. 43
    Whoever wants to be great among you must be your
        servant,
    and whoever of you wants to be first must be the slave of 44
        all;
    for the Son of man himself has not come to be served 45
        but to serve,
    and to give his life as a ransom for many.'

To the story of the request of James and John there is appended a saying on true greatness. That the connection with the preceding episode is due to the editor or his source is clear from the fact that these verses do not deal with pre-eminence in the future Kingdom but among men now. It is also indicated by the fact that these verses appear in a different setting in Luke xxii. 24 ff.

These words are a variant or doublet of the sayings in ix. 33–35. Both arise from some dispute concerning priority, and both drive home the lesson that greatness and pre-eminence are to be sought for only in service. As already remarked, this was one of Jesus' most constant themes, judging from the number of times and slightly varying forms in which the teaching occurs in the Gospels.

The verses contain nothing new until one comes to verse 45. This verse has been the subject of endless controversy. The word rendered **ransom** has a wide variety of uses in the Greek Bible, meaning, among other things, the monetary compensation for the release of a captive or a slave, or the money paid as release penalty for a crime, or the equivalent accepted instead of certain sacrifices ordained by the law. The basic meaning is thus an equivalent given for something, in this case Jesus' life given for the **many.** In the light of this general meaning it is probably unfair to press the more usual specific meaning and to ask to whom the ransom was thought to be paid.

The verse can scarcely be attributed to Jesus. In the first place, there is another version of this group of sayings to be found in Luke xxii. 24–27. This follows the Marcan wording fairly closely, yet with sufficient variation to show that Luke is taking it from one of his other sources. This form of the sayings has a conclusion which is quite different from the Marcan one—namely, the simple statement, 'But I am in the midst of you as a servant.' This ending is in line with the thought of the preceding verses, and it looks more original than the highly developed theological version of the same thought in x. 45. In the second place, the thought of Jesus' death as a ransom is almost completely absent from the Gospels elsewhere. No supporting passages can be cited. There is no real evidence that it formed part of Jesus' teachings, and seems foreign to

His ideas. In the third place, the idea is so frequent in Paul's writings as to account adequately for its expression here. As illustrations of Paul's use of the figure one might cite Gal. iii. 13, 'Christ ransomed us from the curse of the law'; Rom. iii. 24, 'through the ransom provided in Christ Jesus'; and 1 Cor. vii. 23, 'You were bought with a price.'

The verse, then, must be explained as one of the instances of the influence of the apostle Paul's thought on the Gospel. Recent studies of this phase of the Gospel, however, have shown that this has often been over-stated. Many of Paul's most characteristic ideas are absent from the Gospel, and some of those which are to be found do not completely represent his thought. But the Gospel belongs undoubtedly to the Pauline school—that is, one which viewed Christianity essentially as a religion of redemption through the death of the Messiah.

If, as suggested in the Introduction, the author of the Gospel was one of the coterie of Paul's fellow workers, this influence is easily understood.

x. 46-52 : THE HEALING OF THE BLIND SON OF TIMÆUS

Then they reached Jericho; and as he was leaving Jericho 46 with his disciples and a considerable crowd, the son of Timæus, Bartimæus, the blind beggar who sat beside the road, heard it was Jesus of Nazaret. So he started to 47 shout, 'Son of David! Jesus! have pity on me.' A 48 number of the people checked him and told him to be quiet, but he shouted all the more, 'Son of David, have pity on me!' Jesus stopped and said, 'Call him.' Then 49 they called the blind man and told him, 'Courage! Get up, he is calling you.' Throwing off his cloak, he jumped 50 up and went to Jesus. Jesus spoke to him and said, 51 'What do you want me to do for you?' The blind man said, 'Rabboni, I want to regain my sight.' Then Jesus 52 said, 'Go, your faith has made you well'; and he regained his sight at once and followed Jesus along the road.

Suddenly Mark's story finds firm ground again so far as the geographical data are concerned. Apparently we have in this story an account which goes back to, and owes its details to, the reminiscences of an eyewitness. The location and time are known : it was **as he was leaving Jericho with his disciples.** The man was a **blind beggar.** The attempts of the crowd to quiet him, and the details of how he threw away his cloak and the conclusion that he followed Jesus seem definite recollections. The phrase **the son of Timæus** is a translation of **Bartimæus,** and must be due to some marginal comment on an early manuscript. The evangelist knew Aramaic too well to have made the mistake of doubling the patronymic. Some writers would reject the story of the cure completely on the grounds that this ' miracle ' goes beyond the power of suggestion. One wonders. How completely blind was this beggar who apparently makes his way to Jesus without being led ? And what was the cause of this blindness ? And how complete was his cure ? In the absence of answers to such questions it is useless to debate over which miracle stories are historical and to what degree.

Of more interest is the beggar's term of address, **Son of David.** It is not meant that the blind man knows anything of Jesus' genealogy. **The Son of David** is in this instance simply ' the Messiah,' as so often in the Talmud. If the term of address was actually used by the beggar, it would mean that there were rumours among the crowd that the Galilean prophet was to reveal Himself shortly as the Deliverer. There is nothing impossible or unlikely about this. It would certainly explain more easily the attitude of Pilate subsequently, had it been the case. But one notes that in verse 51 the man addresses Jesus simply as **Rabboni,** the polite term to use to a scribe. It may be, therefore, that the Messianic address is not an authentic detail of the story. In any case the term of address serves to prepare the way for the story of the Triumphal Entry.

THE MINISTRY IN JERUSALEM
(xi.-xiii.)

AT this point there begins a new section of the Gospel which runs to the end of chapter xiii. It presents Jesus' work in Jerusalem. It is obvious at a glance that the information which Mark has on the subject is very slight, for he devotes only three chapters to this period, and one of these is merely a record of a long apocalyptic discourse. We shall also see that a number of the episodes in this section are quite without indications of date and place, and may have happened at almost any point in Jesus' ministry.

This raises the whole question of Jesus' work in Jerusalem. Mark gives no indication that Jesus had ever been in the city before, and confines His activity at this time apparently to a period of a few days. But there are some indications that this presentation is not correct:

(1) As is well known, the Fourth Gospel states that Jesus had taught in Jerusalem on a number of previous visits (see John ii. 13, v. 1, vii. 22, and xii. 12). The historical data in the Fourth Gospel involve always, of course, a difficult problem of criticism. That evangelist seems so plainly at times to be subordinating historical to theological and religious considerations that one can never be quite sure what can be depended on. Nevertheless these repeated references to Jesus' visits to Jerusalem constitute so direct and so needless a contradiction of the Synoptic account that one can scarcely throw them all out of court.

(2) To this evidence must be added certain sayings in the Synoptic Gospels which imply a longer or more frequent ministry in Jerusalem than those Gospels now record. The most important of these is the saying in Matt. xxiii. 37 and Luke xiii. 34, ' O Jerusalem, Jerusalem, how often would I have gathered thy children together . . . but ye would not.' Unless the literal meaning of this saying be rejected on the grounds that Jerusalem here represents the people of Israel,

or the saying be attributed to the work of some early Christian prophet, this would seem to point to an effort longer than the few days of Mark's account. The statement in Mark xiv. 49 —'Daily I was with you teaching in the temple'—also suggests a longer period. It will be pointed out that the episode of the Triumphal Entry probably took place at the time of the Feast of Tabernacles or of Dedication rather than of Passover.

(3) There are also suggestions that Jesus had friends and followers in the city previous to the effort of the last few days of His life. The story of the sending of the disciples to fetch the ass on which Jesus entered the city is usually explained as an arrangement with a friend. There seem to have been friends and followers in Bethany. Joseph of Arimathæa may have been a resident of Jerusalem, and he certainly would not have taken the risks he did for one whom he had seen only a day or two before. Perhaps more convincing than these uncertain intimations is the fact that the Christian movement began in Jerusalem immediately after the crucifixion. It certainly consisted of others than a few Galilean pilgrims. Its strength and vigour point definitely toward a considerable number of residents of the city who had already become followers of Jesus before His death.

(4) The probabilities in the case point in the same direction —that is to say, make the Johannine presentation seem reasonable and likely. That a prophet and teacher, brought up in the synagogue, echoing many of the teachings of the scribes, with deep respect for the temple, living in Galilee, only three days' journey by foot from Jerusalem, had never taken part in any of the pilgrimages or visited the city, is less likely than the alternate view.

None of these indications require, however, a long period of work directly preceding Jesus' death. There is some evidence in the story of the cleansing of the temple that the episode occurred some two or three weeks before the Passover. Thus it may be that Mark's account of a stay in the city of only a short period before the crucifixion is correct. This is the Johannine version (see xi. 55, xii. 1, and xii. 12 ff.). It also is

CHAPTERS XI–XIII

suggested by the fact that the crucifixion took place at the time of the Passover. It does not seem likely that the authorities would have waited until the eve of the feast to take action against Jesus, had He been in the city for any considerable period of time.

The internal evidence of the story, as far as we can piece it out, thus indicates that Jesus had preached in the capitol before this last visit, that just previous to it He had been in Peræa or perhaps in Judæa near the Jordan, and that as the Passover approached He determined to go up to Jerusalem for a further and perhaps final effort to bring the nation to repentance and preparation for the establishment of the Realm of God.

xi. 1–11 : The Entry into Jerusalem

xi.

1 Now when they came near Jerusalem, near Bethphagê and
2 Bethany, at the Hill of Olives, he despatched two of his disciples, saying to them, 'Go to the village in front of you. As soon as you enter it you will find a colt tethered, on which no one has ever sat; untether it and bring it here.
3 If anyone asks you, "Why are you doing that?" say, "The Lord needs it, and He will send it back imme-
4 diately".' Off they went and found a colt tethered outside
5 a door in the street. They untethered it; but some of the bystanders said to them, 'What do you mean by untethering that colt?'
6 So they answered as Jesus had told
7 them, and the men allowed them to go. Then they brought the colt to Jesus, and when they had put their
8 clothes on it, Jesus seated himself. Many also spread their clothes on the road, while others strewed leaves cut
9 from the fields; and both those in front and those who followed shouted,

'*Hosanna!*
Blessed be he who comes in the Lord's name!
10 Blessed be the Reign to come, our father David's reign!
Hosanna in high heaven!'

11 Then he entered Jerusalem, entered the temple, and looked round at everything ; but as it was late, he went away with the twelve to Bethany.

The geographical details in verse 1 are quite confusing. Bethany lies on the south-east side of the slopes of the Mount of Olives, some two miles or more from the city. The road from Jericho did not pass directly through the village, but slightly to its north. The Fourth Gospel states that Lazarus and his sisters lived here, and it is evident from Mark also that Jesus had friends there and made it His headquarters, in part at least, while He was in Jerusalem (see xi. 11 and xiv. 3). Bethphagê is known only from statements in the Talmud, where it is referred to several times as on the outer edge of the city. It must have been on the western slope of the Mount of Olives, or in the valley between that eminence and the city itself. Mark's enumeration of the villages is therefore out of order. From Jericho one would come first to Bethany and then to Bethphagê. Some of the manuscripts of the Gospel solve the difficulty by omitting all mention of Bethphagê, but it appears in the parallel passages in both Matthew and Luke and has quite adequate manuscript attestation. On textual grounds one would conclude that Mark wrote both names, which would indicate that he did not know the relative position of the two villages. This would probably mean that the author of the Gospel was not the John Mark who lived in Jerusalem (Acts xii. 12). But in spite of the textual data, one cannot but feel suspicious of the present form of verse 1. The wording is awkward and unlikely : **they came near Jerusalem, near Bethphagê and Bethany, at the Hill of Olives.** Furthermore, Bethany, though present in Luke, is absent from the parallel passage in Matthew. Thus, though only three manuscripts omit it from Mark's text, one tends to suspect that it was the name of this town which has been added. Bethany was well known to readers of the Gospel, and it would have been a natural addition to, or substitution for, the little known Bethphagê. While this cannot be proved, it seems sufficiently likely to make one withhold any judgment

CHAPTER XI, VERSES 1-11

as to the author based on the present reading of the verse.

The story which follows is difficult. Mark understands it, and expects his readers to understand it, as the entrance of Zion's King into Jerusalem in fulfilment of the prophecy in Zech. ix. 9. This, of course, he believes to have been Jesus' intention. It was thus a veiled announcement, to those who had ' ears to hear,' that He was the Expected One. This marks a development in the evangelist's presentation. At first the Messiahship is kept completely secret. After the disciples perceive it, Jesus teaches them plainly, but they are to say nothing to the public. Now, as He enters Jerusalem for the last few days of His ministry, He acts and speaks in such a fashion as to suggest the truth to those able to receive it. This appears in this story of the Messianic entry, and in the parable of the vineyard in xii. 1 ff. Perhaps the evangelist thought of the words about the Messiah being other than David's son (xii. 35 ff.) as an intimation of the same sort. The final stage in this dramatic presentation is in the story of the trial, when before the Jewish high priest it is said that Jesus spoke out plainly and declared that He was none other than the Christ.

But though this is the Christian understanding of this scene, Mark does not say that the crowds recognized or acclaimed Jesus as the Messiah. Their shouts are only of the **Reign to come** and of Him *who comes in the Lord's name*. It is in Matthew that these shouts are changed to read, ' Hosanna to the Son of David.' But nevertheless Mark thinks of the multitudes as rendering unconscious homage. They put their clothes on the colt and Jesus sat on them, just as when Jehu was acclaimed king by his friends (2 Kings ix. 13). And their shouts carried an acclaim of the one in their midst which they themselves did not fully realize.

Many interpreters have regarded the presentation of Mark as in the main historically correct. Thus Rawlinson, in his excellent commentary, writes : ' On the whole it seems to be the most probable conclusion that the entry in this peculiar fashion into Jerusalem was deliberate on the part of our Lord and was meant to suggest that though He was indeed the Messiah and Son of David, yet the Messiahship which He claimed was to be understood in a spiritual and non-political sense, in terms of the prophecy of Zechariah.' But this seems difficult to maintain. Had Jesus chosen this method of declaring Himself the Messiah, would He not have explained His action? The multitudes did not understand it as a Messianic deed, nor did the disciples. On the latter point, one is justified in quoting the Fourth Gospel. After describing the entry and quoting the pertinent passage of prophecy, the evangelist makes the plain statement, 'His disciples did not understand this at first, but when Jesus was glorified, then they remembered this had been written of Him and had happened to Him' (xii. 16). This seems to show that the connection of the episode with the passage in Zechariah was not seen until much later.

Thus many would rule out the account as a 'Messianic legend' constructed on the basis of Zechariah ix. 9 and xiv. 5. The story itself does not make that impression. It carries a number of details quite unnecessary for the main theme—namely, the cutting of the boughs and the particular shouts of the crowd. This suggests that we are dealing here with the familiar phenomenon so often observed—namely, the modification of an earlier story under the influence of developing Christian beliefs.

In an article in the *Journal of Theological Studies* (Vol. xvii, pp. 139 ff.) the late Professor Burkitt has thrown a good deal of light on what must have been the original event. He calls attention to the fact that certain details of the narrative do not fit the Feast of Passover so well as certain other festivals. At the Feast of Tabernacles, which took place before the autumn rains, a characteristic feature of the celebration in the temple was the carrying of green branches by the people. During the service the Hallel (Ps. cxiii–cxviii) was recited, and at certain points the branches were waved in concert. After the sacrifice for the occasion, the people (or possibly the priests only) marched in procession around the altar, carrying their branches and intoning the Hosanna from Psalm cxviii. The

CHAPTER XI, VERSES 1–11

branches themselves are known actually to have been called 'Hosannas.' A similar ritual was followed at the Feast of Dedication, which recalled the cleansing of the temple by Judas Maccabæus in 165 B.C., and which was modelled on Tabernacles (2 Macc. x. 8). Burkitt concluded that the episode described here took place at the Feast of Dedication, and that the announced purpose of Jesus was to rededicate the temple, an act which took place on the very next day.

This last feature of Burkitt's reconstruction—that the Triumphal Entry and the cleansing of the temple both took place at the time of the Feast of Dedication—does not seem to be acceptable. For there is internal evidence in the latter story which connects it with the days preceding the Passover. But the connection of the story of the Triumphal Entry with these details of the ritual of Tabernacles is too striking to be accidental. The crowds in the story cut green branches from the fields, and while Mark only says that they strewed them on the way, yet it is said in John xii. 13, and no doubt implied in Mark, that they also carried them as they proceeded. Psalm cxviii, from which verse 9 comes, was recited on a number of occasions, but the cry *Hosanna* was just the one repeated by the procession which went around the altar. Thus a story of Jewish pilgrims carrying green branches and shouting Hosanna, seems definitely to belong to another festival than the Passover.

This result is important. It is definite evidence of an earlier effort on Jesus' part to win the sacred city for His cause. It also gives a clue for the reconstruction of this story. Jesus came up to Jerusalem, in company with a number of pilgrims, to celebrate the Feast of Tabernacles. The 'Lulab,' or branches, were difficult to secure in the city—there is a Talmudic story of the high prices paid on one occasion, and also some scribal legislation on the question of their being loaned. The pilgrims gathered the branches as they came near. As they came over the Mount of Olives, or approached from the hills to the north, the city came into view, its walls impressively strong, its temple and sacred court plainly visible, the smoke from its great altar rising before their eyes. In their midst was the prophet of Galilee, whose announcements of the Reign of God to come shortly had raised their hopes in eager enthusiasm, and whose teachings of righteousness, oft-times opposed to those of the scribes, they hoped to see put into practice. Their enthusiasm broke out in shouts of praise suggested by the branches in their hands. '*Hosanna*... O Jehovah, we beseech Thee, Send now prosperity ; *Blessed be He who comes in the name of the Lord*'—so reads the Psalm. The central cry, *Hosanna*, meant literally, save, but its ritual use gave it virtually the meaning, Help Israel, O God.

According to this view the pilgrims did not think of Jesus as the expected Messiah, and this is in line with the testimony of the Gospels elsewhere. No doubt the thought lay near at hand, and questions about the strange individual in their midst must have been asked by many pilgrims of each other. The thing that puzzled these Galileans was no doubt the fact that He made no move toward actually establishing the Kingdom of David. Constantly He had said that God would set up the Kingdom in His own time. Men must wait, and in the meanwhile repent. Thus the multitudes thought of Jesus as a mighty prophet of the Kingdom to come, but not as the Anointed One whom they expected to bring it about.

That Jesus rode into the city on the colt of an ass was no doubt accidental and an unimportant detail. Later it was made much of because it was regarded as a fulfilment of Zechariah. The evangelist thinks of the instructions to the disciples as resting on foreknowledge. If historical, we would rather think of a pre-arrangement.

xi. 12–14 : THE CURSING OF THE FIG TREE

12 Next day, when they had left Bethany, he felt hungry, and
13 noticing a fig tree in leaf some distance away he went to see if he could find anything on it ; but when he reached it, he found nothing but leaves, for it was not the time for
14 figs. Then he said to it, ' May no one ever eat fruit from you after this ! ' The disciples heard him say it.

CHAPTER XI, VERSES 12–14

This is one of the most curious stories about Jesus and one which most obviously cannot be taken as sober history. Jesus scarcely went about blasting fruit trees simply because they did not have fruit ready for Him at the moment. Mark explains that, being Passover time, it was not the season of figs, which, of course, makes the act more unreasonable. A considerable amount of scholarly energy has gone into an attempt to save the situation somewhat by proving, with great erudition, that even in the month of Nisan (Passover time) there might have been something edible on the tree, either green knops (which other scholars insist were never edible), or figs left from the previous year which, on certain varieties, ripened with the coming of the leaves in the early spring. This last possibility is well attested, but the whole argument is quite useless. It doesn't matter whether figs were possible or not, it still remains nonsensical and 'out of character' for Jesus to have forbidden the tree to have any fruit in the future simply because it did not have any at the moment.

Two explanations of the story have been advanced. One would regard it as having developed from the parable of a barren fig tree which is preserved in Luke xiii. 6 ff. The second view assumes that it records an actual occurrence, but that the episode was an enacted parable. It is difficult to accept the first view—that the story is a development of an original parable—since the point of the parable would be that one cuts down a worthless tree, rather than one should prevent fruit from ever growing on it. The theory of the 'enacted parable' is equally unsatisfactory. Besides being a conjecture unsupported by any word in the text, it is open to the further difficulty that the saying, or moral, of such a 'parable' would have been treasured more than its setting. It is wise in such a situation to confess our inability to discover from the fragmentary evidence what the original facts in the case were. One is tempted to conjecture that a fig tree on the road between Bethany and Jerusalem, from which the disciples and Jesus had several times gathered figs, withered either during the latter days of the ministry or subsequently, and that pious legend supplied the cause. But one guess is as good as another. To Mark, of course, and to the tradition from which he took it, the story was simply another proof of the wonder-working power of Jesus.

xi. 15–19: The Cleansing of the Temple Courts

15 Then they came to Jerusalem, and entering the temple he proceeded to drive out those who were buying and selling inside the temple ; he upset the tables of the money-
16 changers and the stalls of those who sold doves, and would not allow anyone to carry a vessel through the temple ;
17 also he taught them. ' Is it not written,' he asked, ' *My house shall be called a house of prayer for all nations ?* You
18 have made it *a den of robbers.*' This came to the ears of the scribes and high priests, and they tried to have him put to death, for they were afraid of him. But the multitudes
19 were all astounded at his teaching. And when evening came, he went outside the city.

This quite plainly was one of the most important events in the life of Jesus. Here we see Him on the aggressive, defying the constituted authorities and rebuking the public conscience at the shrine of the nation. Quite possibly more than any other single deed it was the one which brought about His death.

The question of chronology must be settled first. As is well known, in John ii. 13 ff. this episode is placed at the beginning of Jesus' ministry. There were scarcely two cleansings of the temple. The details are virtually the same in all accounts, and no Gospel knows of more than one such event. But, as to which of the two datings is more probably correct, different answers have been given. There is no decisive proof one over against the other, but such a rebuke of, and challenge to, the authorities seems to belong more naturally and reasonably to the later stage of Jesus' work than to its beginnings. The stories of the Galilean ministry reveal an attitude of suspicious

CHAPTER XI, VERSES 15-19

interest on the part of the Jerusalem officials, rather than one of implacable opposition such as must have followed this assumption of leadership and authority. It also weakens the evidence of the Fourth Gospel for an early date when one notes that John also states that the episode occurred at the time of Passover (ii. 13). This suggests that perhaps the evangelist was dependent on the Synoptic tradition, which he rearranged to suit his own purposes, rather than on an independent tradition.

The temple of Herod, the national shrine, stood on the site of the ancient temple of Solomon and its successor after the exile, the temple of Zerubbabel. Herod had begun building it in 20 B.C., and work on the colonnades around the outer court was still going on in Jesus' day. It was built of white stone decorated with golden plates, and Josephus describes it as of surpassing beauty and impressiveness. The building itself stood in the midst of four courts. The outermost and largest of all was called the Court of the Gentiles, and this was the location of the stirring scene described in this section. Around this court ran colonnades with magnificent Corinthian columns, and here scribes were wont to teach their disciples grouped about them. In the open pavement were the booths of hucksters and money-changers. The former sold the wine, birds, and possibly larger animals (though there were also markets for these outside the temple enclosures) which were needed for the sacrifices. The money-changers are sometimes described as ordinary business men doing the necessary exchange business for the many pilgrims from many lands. There is no evidence of this business being carried on in the temple, however, and we do know of another sort of money-changer. The annual tax of half a shekel required of every male Israelite for the support of the temple had to be paid in a definite coinage. This was the silver coinage originally put out by the town of Tyre, which had circulated in Palestine for generations and was of so exact a weight and good an alloy as to be preferred to the various coins, mostly copper, which had come from other sources. The work of changing ordinary money to this officially recognized coinage was carried on by special money-changers. This tax was due from all Palestinian Jews by Nisan 1st, which was two weeks before Passover. From the 17th to the 27th of Adar (the month before Nisan) the money-changers set up their 'tables' in all the towns. From the 25th of Adar to Nisan 1st, they set these up in the temple (*Shequalim*, i. 3). Thus we know of money-changers of this sort in the temple a short time before Passover, and, in the absence of evidence of any others, it seems reasonable to identify them with those money-changers whose tables Jesus overturned. This fact yields an important result for the chronology of the last journey to Jerusalem. The cleansing of the temple took place in the week Adar 25th–Nisan 1st. On the assumption that it occurred on the last visit of Jesus to Jerusalem, it is evident that Mark's presentation of one week in the Holy City is inaccurate. If the crucifixion was on the actual eve of Passover, this stay in the city lasted from two to three weeks at a minimum.

The question as to who got the profits from this no doubt lucrative business is not completely clear. As regards the money-changers there is a passage in the Jerusalem Talmud which quotes four rabbinic authorities. But these do not agree, one affirming that the bankers took the profits, the others that they were used for some one of the several activities of the temple. But whatever went with the proceeds, since the tax itself was finally turned over to the temple the collection of it was probably controlled by the priestly group. Some have thought that the money-changers themselves were priests, but this is without proof.

The case is somewhat similar as regards the temple markets. We read of regulations for the purchase of drink offerings by means of a token bought from one official and redeemable from another. Such an arrangement points to an organization in charge of the sales rather than a number of individual tradesmen. This organization would certainly be controlled by the leaders of the priesthood. That the Sadducean-Boethian priesthood profited directly or indirectly from this traffic seems very probable. It is well known that they were powerful and wealthy, hated by the people and rebuked by the scribes for

CHAPTER XI, VERSES 15-19

their avarice and rapacity. The family of Annas, the ex-high-priest who appears in the Gospel story, ran markets for the sale of sacrificial animals somewhere near the temple, and these were destroyed by a popular movement in A.D. 67. There is on record a curse uttered by Abba-Saul, who lived before the destruction of the temple, on the leading priestly families, who were ' themselves high-priests, their sons treasurers, and their sons-in-law temple officials, while their servants beat the people with sticks.' Another Talmudic passage tells how the rabbis taught that the temple court itself cried out, ' Away from here, you sons of Eli, who have dishonoured the temple of the Lord,' a desecration which the succeeding sentences show was not simply by ritual violations, but also through their greed (see *Pesahim*, 57a). Shortly after Jesus' day Simeon ben Gamaliel denounced what he felt to be the exorbitant price of doves, and brought the price down by changing the law concerning these offerings. Jesus' words about the ' den of robbers ' do not sound so extreme in the light of these words of leading scribes.

According to Mark's account Jesus did four things : (1) He drove out **those who were buying and selling** ; (2) **He upset the tables of the money-changers** ; (3) He **would not allow anyone to carry a vessel through the temple,** maintaining, with certain scribes, that the court must not be made a thoroughfare ; and (4) He taught them that the temple should be a **house of prayer.** This is an interesting catalogue. It shows that the object of Jesus' attack was what He felt to be the secularizing of the temple—to use a modern word—and buyers as well as vendors, and townspeople as well as official money-changers were the objects of His wrath. There is no suggestion that He interfered with the regular work of the priests. Nevertheless, His was a bold attack, carried out no doubt with the help of the crowds of pilgrims, on a system which the priestly houses controlled and from which in all probability they derived a not inconsiderable profit.

It is not surprising that from this point on the priests appear in the story as actively plotting the destruction of this rebel who had led the attack on their authority and prestige, if not **on** their income. In verse 18 we read of a plot of **scribes and high priests**. It is also stated that **they were afraid of him**, which is not surprising. The fearless prophet, with the populace at His back and with a proclamation of an imminent judgment of God on all wrongs, was not to be despised. Against Him they had no direct means of attack. The result could have been anticipated. They would make the Romans get rid of Him, if it could be done. Each night Jesus withdrew from the city (verse 19), no doubt for precautionary reasons.

For one brief moment we see Jesus at the height of His power and influence. It is evident that His programme was not merely one of teaching the true interpretation of the law and criticizing the scribes and priests, but also one of reforming and purifying the life of the nation, and so preparing it for the coming reign of God.

xi. 20–25 : Sayings on Faith and Prayer

20 **Now as they passed in the morning, they noticed the fig tree that**
21 **had withered to the root. Then Peter remembered. 'Rabbi,' he said, 'there is the fig tree you cursed, all**
22 **withered!' Jesus answered them, 'Have faith in God! I**
23 **tell you truly, whoever says to this hill, "Take and throw yourself into the sea," and has not a doubt in his mind but**
24 **believes that what he says will happen, he will have it done. So I tell you, whatever you pray for and ask, believe you**
25 **have got it, and you shall have it. Also, whenever you stand up to pray, if you have anything against anybody, forgive him, so that your Father in heaven may forgive you your trespasses.'**

The observation of the withering of the fig tree is used by the evangelist as an occasion for presenting several sayings on the power of faith. It appears that he has such sayings available in some numbers, and presents some of them whenever his text especially suggests it.

The saying in verse 23 is a variant of one in Luke xvii. 6, in which it is said that faith great enough could uproot a sycamore

CHAPTER XI, VERSES 20–25

tree and cast it into the sea. There is no reason to doubt that both were genuine sayings of Jesus. The striking figures would make them remembered. The second saying (verse 24) is similar to the words in Matthew—' Ask and you shall receive, knock and it shall be opened unto you.' Both sayings vividly present Jesus' own faith in God and man, and His endeavour to stimulate this faith in others.

Verse 25 is connected with the previous ones by the mention of prayer. It, too, is a maxim oft-repeated in Jesus' teaching. It is the other side to His teaching of the mercy and love of God—this loving kindness of God demands that we shall act likewise.

xi. 27–33 : THE QUESTION CONCERNING JESUS' AUTHORITY

Once more they came to Jerusalem. And as he was walking 27 within the temple the high priests and scribes and elders came and asked him, 'What authority have you for 28 acting in this way? Who gave you authority to act in 29 this way?' Jesus said to them, 'I am going to ask you a question. Answer this, and I will tell you what authority I have for acting as I do. What about the baptism of John? 30 Was it from heaven or from men?' Now they argued to 31 themselves, 'What are we to say?' If we say, "From 32 heaven," he will ask, "Then why did you not believe him?" No, let us say, From men '—but they were afraid of the multitude, for the people all held that John had been really a prophet. So they replied to Jesus, 'We do not 33 know.' Jesus said to them, 'No more will I tell you what authority I have for acting as I do.'

Up to this point the opponents of Jesus have been consistently the scribes, or the scribes and the Pharisees. Now we have the **high priests and scribes and elders**, representatives, that is, of the three groups who composed the Sanhedrin, the Jewish governing body. We do not know exactly what were the powers of this Sanhedrin under Roman rule—whether they had the power to inflict capital punishment will be discussed later—but it is plain from this passage as well as from other evidence that it exercised considerable authority. The plural **high priests** seems at first sight anomalous, since there was, strictly speaking, only one high priest at a time. The plural, however, is quite true to conditions. Under Herodian and Roman domination the high-priesthood changed so rapidly that there were a number of members of the ruling group who had held the office and whose influence and leadership had not ceased when they had turned over to their successors the robes of office. Josephus uses the same plural in a number of passages.

A delegation of the Sanhedrin came to Jesus in the temple, most likely in the same outer court of the Gentiles which had been the scene of the exciting events previously narrated. They demanded what His authority was. This can only mean that they wanted to ascertain what claims to authority Jesus would make and what His intentions were. It is plain that a situation of open conflict existed, one waged not by physical force, but by moral influence and popular support. Jesus' answer, of course, would be used against Him. Had He claimed the authority of a Jewish king or ruler, had He declared Himself the Expected One, we can readily believe that the Romans would have been asked to take action immediately.

This must be the explanation in part of Jesus' answer. **Answer this, and I will tell you what authority I have for acting as I do. What about the baptism of John ? Was it from heaven or from men ?** The reply is striking both as to what it did not say, and also what it did say. One notes that Jesus did not suggest that His authority was that of the Messiah. He declared that His authority was given Him from heaven. Just as John was sent to be a prophet of God, so Jesus claimed that He was acting under the direct leadership of God. That was His authority and His confidence.

To many readers, particularly to those who believe in Jesus' unique authority, this reply to the delegation of the Sanhedrin seems disappointing. But, in truth, could one want more ? In its simplicity, directness, and confidence in His mission, it presents probably the real Jesus better than more complicated

CHAPTER XI, VERSES 27-33

arguments or greater claims. He affirmed that He, like John, was sent of God, consecrated to the work of declaring to the nation the will of the heavenly Father, and preparing it for the actual establishment of the divine will. What more could be answered to hostile high priests, scribes, and elders?

xii. 1-12 : THE PARABLE OF THE WICKED VINEDRESSERS

xii.
Then he proceeded to address them in parables. *'A man 1 planted a vineyard, fenced it round, dug a trough for the winepress, and built a tower ;* then he leased it to vine- 2 dressers and went abroad. When the season came round, he sent a servant to the vinedressers to collect from the vine- 3 dressers some of the produce of the vineyard, but they took and flogged him and sent him off with nothing. Once more 4 he sent them another servant ; him they knocked on the head and insulted. He sent another, but they killed him. 5 And so they treated many others ; some they flogged and some they killed. He had still one left, a beloved son ; he 6 sent him to them last, saying, " They will respect my son." But these vinedressers said to themselves, " Here 7 is the heir ; come on, let us kill him, and the inheritance will be our own.", So they took and killed him, and threw 8 him outside the vineyard. Now what will the owner of the 9 vineyard do ? He will come and destroy the vinedressers, and he will give the vineyard to others. Have you not even 10 read this scripture ?—

The stone that the builders rejected
is the chief stone now of the corner :
this is the doing of the Lord, 11
and a wonder to our eyes.'

Then they tried to get hold of him, but they were afraid of 12 the multitude. They knew he had meant the parable for them.

This parable, of course, is an allegory. The vineyard is Israel, or perhaps Jerusalem. The owner is God. The wicked vinedressers are the Jewish scribes and priests. The servants are the prophets who have been rejected and persecuted. The son and heir is Jesus. The authenticity of the allegory has been warmly debated. That it was spoken by Jesus has been urged on the ground that it is ' morally certain ' that Jesus anticipated and spoke of His death, and that the parable, if it was a product of Christian reflection, would have contained something about the resurrection. How long before the end Jesus anticipated His death we do not know. The story of the flight of the disciples and of the prayer in Gethsemane suggests that it had not been one of the settled convictions of the band before the closing period. But, granting that Jesus recognized that this would be the final result, it is difficult to think that He would have announced it to the crowds in such a parable as this. For the parable both announces His approaching death and plainly asserts a claim on Jesus' part to a unique position in Israel's history, superior to that of all the ancient prophets. This objection cannot be overruled by suggesting that the parable was delivered privately to the disciples, for its basic point is a warning to the wicked Jewish leaders—that is, it was addressed to outsiders. Verses 10 and 11 are a further difficulty. Previous to the success of the Christian movement they would have had no meaning.

Reference has been made to the absence of any mention of the resurrection. The argument has point, for early Christian theology centred around its apocalyptic Christology, which was built on the belief in the resurrection. A free and original construction of Christian thought would probably have ended in a description of the final triumph and vengeance of the son rather than merely in his death and the punishment of the vinedressers by the owner. Again, it would seem that the tradition is working with some original datum or deposit which it utilizes to express its ideas, rather than constructing a new parable. It might be remarked that the examination of the Gospel thus far has indicated that there are very few passages which should be regarded as free, imaginative constructions.

A suggestion can be made as to this earlier datum. Strack and Billerbeck's commentary lists two parables which are very similar to the one here. In one of them a king leased out a possession to husbandmen from whom he could not secure his share of the fruits. He ejected these tenants and gave the property to their children. These, however, proved as bad as their fathers. So he drove out the wicked tenants and gave the property to his own son. The other parable contains the same basic story of a king taking back a possession for his son, but does not involve the thought of the defrauding of the king by the tenants (vol. i., p. 874).

The fact that this figure of Israel as God's possession or vineyard—which went back originally to Isa. v. 1–7—was current in the teaching of the synagogue suggests two possibilities. Jesus may have used the figure in condemnation of the wicked leaders of Jewish society, emphasizing the number of times the Owner had sent servants in a vain effort to collect the fruits due Him from the possessors of the vineyard, and concluding with the warning that the Owner in such a case would come and destroy the evil tenants and take the vineyard for Himself. The elaboration of the theme will, then, have been the work of the Christian community. The other possibility would be that the entire parable is a Christian re-working of a current parable which, once it had been put into a Christian form, would have been quickly attributed to Jesus Himself.

Between these alternatives the decision is not very important, since we know in any case that Jesus held the ideas here expressed concerning the Jewish leaders. However, if one assumes that the rabbinic parables were told in the first century in the same form in which they have been preserved, the probability would be definitely against the view that Christian scribes were responsible for this parable. For both the rabbinic parables end with the king's son in possession and enjoyment of the property, and it does not seem likely that Christian scribes would have eliminated this point. I thus suggest that we have here in a modified form Jesus' use of Isaiah's figure in a warning to those in possession of God's vineyard, whom He charged with not rendering to the Owner His due return.

xii. 13-17 : JESUS IS ASKED AS TO HIS ATTITUDE TOWARD PAYING TAXES TO CÆSAR

13 So they left him and went away. But they sent some of the Pharisees and Herodians to him for the purpose of catching
14 him with a question. They came up and said to him, 'Teacher, we know you are sincere and fearless ; you do
15 not court human favour, you teach the Way of God honestly. Is it right to pay taxes to Cæsar or not ? Are we to pay, or are we not to pay ? ' But he saw their trick and said to them, ' Why tempt me ? Bring me a shilling.
16 Let me see it.' So they brought one. He said, 'Whose likeness, whose inscription is this ? ' ' Cæsar's,' they
17 said. Jesus said to them, ' Give Cæsar what belongs to Cæsar, give God what belongs to God.' He astonished them.

The mention of the **Pharisees and Herodians** reminds one immediately of iii. 6, where the same combination against Jesus is referred to. As stated in the Introduction, it seems plain that the double mention of these groups is due to the continuation here of the source which Mark used in ii. 1-iii. 6. Apparently when Mark reached in this source the story here recorded, he realized that it called for a Judæan setting. He therefore broke off the use of the document until he reached this point.

The Herodians, as already remarked, were evidently supporters of the Herodian family. In Judæa, where the Herodian line had been superseded by a system of government by Roman procurators, one would naturally think of them as advocates of the former status. ' Those of Herod's party ' whom Josephus once mentions (*Ant*. xiv. 15. 10) were people who wished to put Herod on the throne instead of a Maccabæan descendant. Since the Herodian dynasty was always dependent upon, and careful to cultivate, Roman favour, the Herodians here mentioned would certainly have supported the payment of the tax under discussion.

CHAPTER XII, VERSES 13-17

The tax in question was a head tax, not a property tax or customs duty. It was collected by the Romans from the inhabitants of Judæa, Samaria, and Idumæa. The assessment had begun in A.D. 6, when Archelaus, the son of Herod the Great, was deposed and Roman procurators took over the administration of his territory. A survey of the resources of the country for the purpose of taxation had been undertaken at the time, which aroused intense popular resentment. A revolt broke out. Its leaders declared, according to Josephus, that 'this taxation was nothing but a direct introduction of slavery, and urged the nation to assert its liberty.' The historian goes on to state that this revolt was the beginning of the 'fourth philosophy' of the Jews, namely, an intense nationalism whose representatives asserted 'that God was their only ruler and king.' The revolt was suppressed, but the popular resentment at the tax, and at the Roman rule it symbolized, never ceased. The tax was paid with a silver denarius which, in contrast to the copper coins put out by the procurators of Judæa, bore the name or image of the emperor.

The question of the tax was thus charged with intense popular feeling. To advise its payment meant to many of the crowd a betrayal of the national cause. One who recommended that payment could scarcely continue to have the following of the crowds. To repudiate the payment was tantamount in Roman eyes to inciting a revolt.

The answer of Jesus, **Give Cæsar what belongs to Cæsar, give God what belongs to God,** is one of the most famous sayings in the Gospels. It is worth noting that it seems definitely related to the setting in which it occurs, and that no verbal parallels are to be found in the extant Jewish or Hellenistic literature. There seem no grounds for questioning that this is one of the authentic utterances of Jesus.

The meaning of this famous answer has been variously elucidated, the interpretation usually depending upon the views of the particular commentator as to the proper relation of Church and State. Jewish scholars have tended to regard the reply as primarily an evasion. Even so clear and fair a commentator as Montefiore writes that 'the answer was primarily intended to be non-committal.' This, however, is certainly wrong. The one obvious fact about the answer is that it says that the tax should be paid.

This is the primary meaning of the saying. When one presses further as to the grounds advanced by Jesus, the facts of current ideology make this positive position even clearer. Sovereignty was coterminous with the rights of coinage and the validity of one's money. When Antiochus wrote to Simon Maccabæus soliciting his aid and recognizing him as independently free, he gave him ' leave to coin money for thy country with thine own stamp ' (1 Macc. xv. 6). Many Talmudic passages illustrate the idea. For example David's kingship is once disputed on the ground that the coins of Saul were still money. There is also quoted a divine promise to Abraham of universal sovereignty which is put in the words, ' that thy coins go out through the whole world.' This idea seems to point to the plain meaning of the reply of Jesus. ' Whose money is this ? ' asks Jesus. ' It is Cæsar's.' ' Then Cæsar's authority is here and the tax should be paid.' The Greek word rendered **give** in the translation is in reality much stronger. It means to give back, or to pay an obligation. The translation ' render ' in the King James Version, or simply ' pay,' would express this idea.

So much for the first part of the answer. What is the significance of the addition **give** (or render) **to God what belongs to God**? These words must mean that beside this duty to Cæsar there were other obligations which were due to God. This is to say that one could both pay taxes to Cæsar and render one's debt to God. The point of this unnecessary addition to Jesus' answer must be a reply to the Zealot contention that a Jew could not pay taxes to Cæsar and also regard God as ruler and king.

The position adopted by Jesus in these words is not that of Paul. The latter goes much further and declares that Cæsar and all duly appointed authorities are ordained by God, and are agents of God, so that to resist them is to resist God (Rom. xiii. 1 ff.). Jesus rather takes the position of rabbinic Judaism. Sacrifice for the emperor was offered daily in the temple, and we have from a contemporary of Johanan ben Zakkai the injunction, ' Pray for the peace, of the Roman kingdom.' The position of the Pharisees was quietistic. The Roman power must be accepted—so long as it did not infringe on religious rights and duties—until the day of deliverance which God would give. Jesus was in agreement with this point of view. Cæsar's Court and power would seem to have been matters of indifferent interest to His mind.

There is one point which is usually overlooked in a discussion of this story, namely, that it was necessary to ask Jesus this question in order to know His position on the Roman question. Nothing could better demonstrate His absorption in the religious problem. His message demanded repentance and obedience to God. He seems to have rejected the ardent hopes of a restoration of the kingdom of David. His thought was above the political struggles of the hour, fixed on a vision of obedience in spirit and purpose to the will of God. To all who rendered this obedience salvation would come soon.

xii. 18-27 : THE QUESTION ABOUT THE RESURRECTION

Sadducees, men who hold there is no resurrection, also came 18 up and put a question to him. ' Teacher,' they said, 19 ' Moses has written this law for us, that *if a man's brother dies leaving a wife but no child, his brother is to take the woman and raise offspring for his brother.* **Now there 20 were seven brothers. The first married a wife and died, leaving no offspring : the second took her and died with- 21 out leaving any offspring : so did the third : none of the 22 seven left any offspring. Last of all, the woman died too. At the resurrection, when they rise, whose wife will she 23 be ? She was wife to the seven of them.' Jesus said to 24 them, ' Is this not where you go wrong ?—you understand neither the scriptures nor the power of God. When people 25 rise from the dead, they neither marry nor are married, they are like the angels in heaven. As for the dead being 26 raised, have you not read in the book of Moses, at the passage on the Bush, how God said to him,** *I am the God*

of Abraham and the God of Isaac and the God of Jacob?
27 He is not the God of dead people but of living. You are far wrong.'

This seems, from its similarity to the preceding episode, to come probably from the same collection of 'conflict stories.' In that passage the critics were Pharisees and Herodians; here they are Sadducees. In both stories the issue is presented in the form of a question put to Jesus, and the centre of interest is Jesus' reply. Both stories go back to the earliest tradition.

The Sadducees, mentioned only here in the Gospel, were an aristocratic and conservative party. Its leadership was in the hands of the wealthy priestly families of Jerusalem. They are well known to us from the pages of Josephus. The latter, himself a Pharisee, accuses the Sadducees of believing that the soul dies with the body. More probably they held the older primitive belief of the Hebrews in Sheol, and denied the newer Pharisaic ideas about a resurrection of the body.

The Sadducees were no doubt well aware of Jesus' views on the subject of the resurrection. These would have been quite apparent from His teaching of a New Age in which the righteous would receive their reward. Their effort was to discredit Him by presenting one of the many complications which arise as soon as one thinks of a state or condition which will preserve all of the relationships arising during a time process. Such arguments were evidently common in the period when the two major parties were debating the doctrine. We know of a number of attempts by Pharisaic scribes to prove that the resurrection was taught in all parts of the Scriptures. Probably the Sadducean argument in this case was that the Mosaic law of Levirate marriage was direct scriptural evidence against it. Modern scholars in this instance would say that the Sadducees were right in their assertion that the resurrection was not taught in the law.

The question they brought up involved the Mosaic regulation concerning the Levirate marriage. This law—that a man was obligated to take into his household the childless widow of

CHAPTER XII, VERSES 18-27

his brother, in order to provide children who would carry on his brother's name—had come down from early tribal days. It is generally regarded as a social survival of ideas of ancestor worship. Certainly it indicates the strong sense of family unity and solidarity which was characteristic of primitive society. By the time of the first century, however, the fading of the original motivating ideas, plus economic difficulties in carrying out the regulation, had resulted in a reinterpretation of the law on the subject so that the obligation was greatly limited. That it was still practised occasionally, though perhaps limited to brothers who were unmarried, is shown by the question of the Sadducees in the story here, as well as by several instances of Levirate marriage during the following century which are mentioned in the sources.

Jesus' reply endorses the Pharisaic belief: **You understand neither the scriptures nor the power of God**, hence your denial of the resurrection. As to the question of the woman and her seven husbands, it must be recognized that **when people rise from the dead they neither marry nor are** given in marriage, **they are like the angels in heaven**. Earthly conditions no longer exist. The new life will be a heavenly one. Questions based on earthly conditions are beside the point.

Jewish ideas of the resurrected state were divided. There is a famous saying of Rab, a Babylonian teacher of the third century, which reads as follows: ' The World to Come is not like this world. In the world to come there is no eating and drinking, no begetting of children, no bargaining, no jealousy and hatred and strife; but the righteous shall sit with crowns on their heads enjoying the effulgence of the divine Presence.' Similar in import and earlier in date is the fine passage in the *Apocalypse of Baruch* which declares that in the resurrection the righteous ' shall be made like unto the angels, and be made equal to the stars, and shall be changed into every form they desire ' (li. 10). In Enoch, civ. 6, the righteous are told that they shall become ' companions of the hosts of heaven.' Over against these views was the line of thought which stated the reward of the righteous in terms similar to this earth's experiences. The whole subject was complicated further by the double conception of the future state which was developing—namely, of the 'Days of the Messiah' on this earth, to be followed by the Age to Come. Uniformity of thought, or even consistency of terminology, had not yet been reached.

Jesus' answer to the Sadducees' question is a startling formulation of the more transcendental view of the future reward. Indeed, it goes beyond anything which can be cited for that century or the following one, in the clearness and definiteness of its rejection of the materialistic conceptions which Jewish eschatology had inherited, though this may be merely a matter of wording. Certainly in this respect as in others we see Jesus accepting and carrying forward the noblest elements in the Judaism of His day.

This saying fits in with other indications in the Gospels that Jesus rejected the popular ideas of Israel's reward in terms of the restoration of the ancient glories of the nation. There seems no room in His thought for the 'Days of the Messiah.' The only reward He refers to is one in which the righteous will be like the angels in heaven. The expression about the meek inheriting the earth is only a figure of speech. The more carefully Jesus' sayings are studied, the more clear it becomes that He turned away from the series of political and temporal ideas which the popular religion of the people made so much of. This means that Jesus' idea of the Anointed One whom God would send would necessarily be different, if it remained at all, from popular and conventional ideas.

To this answer in verses 24, 25 is added a proof from the Scriptures that the dead are raised. This consists of an argument from the statement of God to Moses in Exod. iii. 6—**I am the God of Abraham and the God of Isaac and the God of Jacob.** These patriarchs had long since died, and the divine statement would be meaningless unless they were to live again. Only in that case could God say, ' I am their God.' The argument is a verbal, exegetical one, quite in the fashion of, and similar to, a number to be found in various tractates of the Talmud. It appears almost verbally in 4 Macc. vii. 19, and xvi. 25. It has been suggested that the argument is not an original word of Jesus. This is possible. It is an easily separable unit from the rest of the section, and may well be the achievement of an early Christian scribe. In either case, to modern minds the argument itself has no value, but only the faith that produced it.

xii. 28-34 : THE FIRST COMMANDMENT

Then a scribe came up, who had listened to the discussion. Knowing Jesus had given them an apt answer, he put this question to him, ' What is the chief of all the commands ? ' Jesus replied, ' The chief one is : *Hear, O Israel, the Lord our God is one Lord, and you must love the Lord your God with your whole heart, with your whole soul, with your whole mind, and with your whole strength.* The second is this : *You must love your neighbour as yourself.* There is no other command greater than these.' The scribe said to him, ' Right, teacher ! You have truly said, He is One, and there is none else but Him. Also, to love Him with the whole heart, with the whole understanding, and with the whole strength, and to love one's neighbour as oneself—that is far more than all holocausts and sacrifices.' Jesus noted his intelligent answer and said to him, ' You are not far from the Realm of God.' After that no one ventured to put any more questions to him.

Unlike the two preceding ones, this story is not a ' conflict episode,' the scribe being a questioner but not a critic. It may be assumed, therefore, not to have belonged to the same cycle or written collection from which those narratives came. The documentary source which can be dimly envisaged probably breaks off at verse 27.

This is one of the few episodes in the Gospel which is preserved in double form. In Luke x. 25-28 there appears a version which most patently is not derived from the Marcan source. Certain verbal agreements with Matthew's account against the Marcan story indicate that it came to Luke from the ' Q ' material. This version in Luke seems to stand nearer the original event than does Mark's account. The grounds for this judgment are two : Luke's account states that the selection of the two commandments of love to God and to man as the basic ones was done by the scribe, and that Jesus agreed with his selection. Christian tradition would naturally tend to convert Jesus' approval of a noble saying into His utterance of it. In the second place, the Marcan account itself seems to show some recollection that on this occasion the scribe made a striking answer which won Jesus' unqualified approval. For in verses 32–34 the scribe repeats the saying, and the story closes with Jesus' commendation of the scribe. The account in Luke seems to provide the natural explanation of this otherwise curious detail.

Granted, then, that Luke x. 25–28 represents an earlier form of the story, one is able to observe, by comparing them, the tendencies which were at work in the development of the early Christian tradition. Jesus' hearty agreement with the scribe becomes His utterance of the saying. This is, therefore, a case in which Jesus' indebtedness to scribal teaching is plainly before our eyes, and helps to correct the impression of constant opposition which the Gospels make. One notes, also, in comparing the stories that they are differently located in Mark and Luke. Evidently the evangelists had no fixed sequence of events. The presentation of the story by Mark as occurring during the last week in Jerusalem is purely editorial. Lastly, one observes in the residual details of verses 32–34 referred to above the gradual way in which the tradition was modified. Modification took place, but it was gradual and unconscious rather than radical and deliberate. If an authentic tradition lies in greater part behind the Gospel story, there is a scholarly obligation upon students to seek in each case to recover it.

The question which the scribe asked was not a strange one. It is now known that the question of the primary or first commandment was a popular one in scribal circles. By it was meant not which commandment men were most obligated to observe—for the scribal answer was that all the commandments must be obeyed—but, rather, which one was fundamental to, or provided a basic principle for, the rest. Statements of the first or basic commandment are thus summaries

CHAPTER XII, VERSES 28-34

of the content of the Law. A number of these have been preserved, and they embody in clear form the ethical spirit of Judaism. Hillel said, ' What is hateful to thyself, do not to thy neighbour ; this is the whole law, the rest is commentary.' Akiba said : ' Thou shalt love thy neighbour as thyself ; this is the greatest general principle of the Law.' In commenting on this, Ben Azzai said, ' When God created Adam He made him in the likeness of God, this is a greater principle than that.' There is a famous saying of Rabbi Simlai of the third century which sums up the law in various precepts of David, Isaiah, Micah, and Amos, and which closes with the words : ' Habbakuk came and made the law to stand on one fundamental idea, " The righteous man liveth by his faithfulness." ' These sayings bring to clear expression the deepening ethical insight and conviction of rabbinic Judaism. Jesus was nourished in this tradition, and it is evident that He drew from it. He would have differed from the scribes who uttered these summaries only in that He did not associate with the summaries the conviction that nevertheless all the commandments of the law should be obeyed with equal scrupulousness.

In the story before us, in Luke's version, Jesus turned back the question as to the primary or basic commandment to the questioner. The scribe answered by citing two. First he quoted a portion of the ' Shema,' the confession of Judaism, recited twice daily by all adult male Jews. The opening words which affirm the Jewish monotheistic faith are omitted in Luke's account and are probably a natural addition to the citation. The command to **love the Lord your God with your whole heart** was evidently the on the scribe had in mind. This is followed by the precept in Lev. xix. 18—**You must love your neighbour as yourself.** The second of these was the precept which Akiba later was to cite as the chief commandment. The association of love to God and love to men is found three times in the ethical treatise, *The Testament of the XII Patriarchs* (Issachar, v. 2, vii. 5, and Dan. v. 3.). It is evident that the whole saying thus comes out of the heart of Jewish ethical religion. With the scribe's selection Jesus whole-heartedly agreed. 'Do this, and thou shalt live,' is the wording in Luke.

It is the evidence of the Gospels that in His thinking these precepts summed up and largely embodied His conception of righteousness.

This passage thus shows clearly the essential unity of the best ethic of the synagogue and that of Jesus.

xii. 35-37 : THE MESSIAH IS NOT DAVID'S SON BUT DAVID'S LORD

35 And as Jesus taught in the temple, he asked, ' How can the
36 scribes say that the Christ is David's son ? David himself said, inspired by the holy Spirit,
> *The Lord said to my Lord, " Sit at my right hand,*
> *till I make your enemies a footstool for your feet."*

37 David here calls him *Lord*. Then how can he be his son ? Now the mass of the people listened with delight to him.

This is a strange and difficult passage. In contrast to previous episodes no opponents of Jesus are present. The sayings are detached from any setting or framework. Jesus attacks the teaching of the scribes that **the Christ is David's son,** and affirms instead that He is David's **Lord.** But what is denied is exactly what Christians from Paul's day on believed—namely, that Jesus was a descendant of David (see Rom. i. 3, and the genealogies in Matt. and Luke). Furthermore there is no elaboration of the point nor application of the thesis enunciated to any current issue. The sayings remain unexplained and almost cryptic.

The first step in unravelling the puzzle must be to determine the meaning of the saying to the evangelist and his readers. By the time he wrote, belief in the Davidic lineage of Jesus was no doubt current throughout the Christian movement. Mark certainly did not doubt it. Had he done so he would scarcely have placed in the mouth of the blind beggar of Jericho the cry, ' Jesus, son of David, have pity on me,' even granting that the primary meaning of the phrase in that context was ' the Messiah.' No doubt he incorporated the

CHAPTER XII, VERSES 35-37

saying under attention because he found it in one of his sources, but he certainly must have understood it in some sense which did not contradict what he had written elsewhere.

There seems only one answer to the difficulty. Mark must have regarded the passage as affirming not whether or not Jesus was related to David, but how He was related. The emphasis falls on the contrast between **son** and **Lord**, and which of these is the correct predicate to apply to **the Christ**. So understood, the sayings could be preserved by a tradition which also asserted that Jesus was descended from David according to the flesh. A Hebrew idiom made this easier for Jewish readers than for western ones. Hosea's words, ' I desire mercy and not sacrifice,' were read piously by generations which went on with scores of sacrifices daily, because they were familiar with the Hebrew figure of speech which expressed emphatic preference by denial. To them it simply meant, ' I desire mercy more than I do sacrifice.' Other examples of the same idiom might be cited. In accordance with this idiom the expression here would mean simply, the Christ is David's Lord much more than He is his son.

Wherein the superiority of the Messiah to David consisted, which made the latter by prophetic insight call Him **Lord**, is not explained. Certain other Christian documents, however, supply the evidence to support what would otherwise be a natural guess. In Acts ii. 34 the same passage from Ps. cx. is quoted in a speech by Peter. The apostle speaks of how Jesus had been raised from the dead and elevated to God's right hand. David had no such honour or dignity. ' It was not David who ascended to heaven; David [himself] says, The Lord said to my Lord, " Sit at My right hand . . . " ' and there follows the remainder of Ps. cx. 1, which is quoted here. This citation in Acts explicitly states the point of contrast between Jesus and David. The former was elevated after death to God's right hand, and thus became a heavenly being, David was not. Hence the Psalmist called Him **Lord**. The passage is also quoted in part in Heb. 1. 13 and x. 13. Here again it is used with reference to Christ's resurrection to a place at God's right hand, although no comparison to

David is drawn. The passage is also alluded to in 1 Cor. xv. 25, and Eph. i. 20, 21.

Ps. cx. 1 was thus the favourite proof passage of early Christian apologists in maintaining against Jewish critics their quite original doctrine—that the Messiah had appeared as a man, but had been elevated to heaven whence He would return to judge and to rule. While a great deal of freedom existed in views concerning eschatology and the Messianic hope, this Christian belief was so different from the usual view that it must have necessitated a good deal of explanation and defence. We have before us part of such a defence.

Granted that this was the interpretation given to the saying by Christians of the period A.D. 50-90, and that the evangelist included it in his Gospel with these thoughts in mind, the question remains whether the words were ever uttered by Jesus Himself. Various answers to this question have been given. Some have thought that the verses are authentic sayings and represent a defence which Jesus, claiming to be the Messiah, made against the fact that He was not of Davidic lineage. Another possible view is that the saying is genuine but that Jesus was not referring to Himself, but to such a heavenly figure as John the Baptist had in mind. The balance of probability, however, inclines against the words having been uttered by Jesus at all

(1) Ps. cx. 1 is cited, as already remarked, in Acts ii. 34, to prove the same point as it is used here to prove. The citation and argument there is attributed to Peter, not to Jesus. The early chapters of Acts are among the most primitive Christian records which we possess. Similarly, in Heb. x., and in the other passages, there is no hint that a word of the Lord is being quoted.

(2) These words uttered by Jesus without any further explanation or elaboration would have been meaningless.

(3) The saying belongs to the area of Christological debate. The Gospels contain convincing evidence that Jesus avoided this issue in His discussions with His critics. It would have been strange, indeed, had Jesus so constantly refused to say whether He was the Messiah, but yet had gone to such pains

CHAPTER XII, VERSES 35-37

to have proved that He was eligible to that title or office. His methods and habits of mind were much more direct than that.

I conclude, therefore, that we have here a part of early Christian apologetics which was designed to commend to Jewish hearers the concept of a Messiah who had been elevated to God's right hand. From an early Christian citation of the Old Testament it came to be regarded as a word of Jesus. But it is interesting and instructive that it remains without any introductory setting such as some critics believe early Christianity invented in such abundance.

xii. 38-40 : JESUS WARNS AGAINST THE SCRIBES

And in the course of his teaching he said, ' Beware of the 38 scribes ! They like to walk about in long robes, to get saluted in the marketplaces, to secure the front seats in 39 the synagogues and the best places at banquets ; they 40 prey upon the property of widows, and offer long, unreal prayers. All the heavier will their sentence be ! '

The Gospels contain several collections of sayings in which Jesus denounced His opponents. The one preserved here in Mark is the shortest of them all, and gives the impression of being an excerpt from some longer list. Luke takes over these three verses in xx. 45 ff., but preserves from another source a much longer collection in xi. 39 ff. Matthew combines these two groups of sayings with some additional material into a denunciation which forms the whole of chapter xxiii.

The grounds of the conflict between Jesus and the scribes need not be gone into here, since various aspects of the general issue have been touched on in the previous pages. Three points are involved in the criticisms in these verses. The first is the special privileges and honours which the scribes claimed. **They like to walk about in long robes,** is a reference to the outer robe or cloak which, in the case of the scribes, was easily recognisable and was thus a badge of scribal dignity. Special greetings, prefaced by honorific titles, were to be addressed to them. In the synagogues they sat on seats in front of, and facing, the congregation, a custom which Billerbeck thinks was just being established in Jesus' day. The deference which they expected and received resulted in their being given **the best places at banquets**. These claims for special honours were especially objectionable to those Jews whom the scribes were endeavouring to exclude from the full social privileges of Jewish society.

The second charge is more difficult to understand: **They prey upon the property of widows**. Just what is referred to is not known. *Aboth* i. 13, and iv. 5, warns teachers against using the law for their own profit, and there is no indication that the scribes as a class were wealthy. The charge here made cannot have had a very general justification. The words would seem to fit much better an attack on the wealthy, unscrupulous priesthood than one directed against the scribes. One of the lacunæ in the Gospels is the absence of any such criticism of the priestly class.

The third charge is that they were hypocritical in their religious performances. There is a good deal more of this in Matthew, the term 'hypocrite' being applied repeatedly. The basis of this charge was, no doubt, the scribal and Pharisaic insistence on the externals and the minutiæ of the law, to the neglect of its weightier matters.

These attacks on the scribes and Pharisees in the Gospels have been sharpened in the course of their transmission. The persecutions which the Christian believers received from the Jewish authorities have affected the form and tone of these denunciations. There is, however, no doubt that a good deal of this goes back to Jesus. There is, of course, no question of their application to all scribes individually, but rather to the group as a class. That the scribal leaders of Jesus' day were guilty to a greater or less extent of intellectual pride and their followers of a mechanical piety is psychologically likely and historically attested by Jewish documents as well as the Gospels. Such faults are too likely in all religious movements, but they were the special dangers of the type of religion which the scribes represented. They would have been especially evident to Jesus, who was out of sympathy with the spirit of the Pharisaic organizations and was opposed by the scribes' authority.

xii. 41-44 : THE WIDOW'S GIFT TO THE TEMPLE

Sitting down opposite the treasury, he watched the people 41 putting their money into the treasury. A number of the rich were putting in large sums, but a poor widow came up 42 and put in two little coins amounting to a halfpenny. So he called his disciples and said to them, ' I tell you 43 truly, this poor widow has put in more than all who have put their money into the treasury ; for they have all put 44 in a contribution out of their surplus, but she has given out of her neediness all she possessed, her whole living.'

It is a relief to move from the area of conflict to this beautiful story. It calls for little explanation. There has been some uncertainty as to exactly what **the treasury** was. Most likely it was a section or room in one of the porticoes of the Court of the Women where the thirteen trumpet-shaped receptacles for the receipt of money for the temple stood. Each of these receptacles was for a different purpose. Priests were in charge and inquired of the people the purpose of their gift, ascertaining if the amount which they brought was in accordance with the legal requirements for that purpose and was in the right coinage. Through such a conversation one sitting near could easily learn that the poor woman's gift was only two ' lepta,' the smallest coins in circulation, the value of which was less than an English farthing or an American penny. The statement of the Teacher—**I tell you . . . this poor widow has put in more than all**—is in line with His judgment that ' a man's life does not consist in the abundance of his possessions,' and His saying that one could not give a cup of cold water in the right spirit without receiving his reward. It is also quite in line with rabbinic teaching.

Indeed, there are sayings of several rabbis recorded which parallel the thought, and almost the words, of the saying here.

xiii. 1–2: 'THE TEMPLE WILL BE DESTROYED'

xiii.
1 As he went out of the temple one of his disciples said to him, ' Look, teacher, what a size these stones and buildings
2 are ! ' Jesus said to him, ' You see these great buildings ? Not a stone shall be left on another, without being torn down.'

The saying here recorded would have been of special interest to the readers of the Gospel, since only a few years before (on the dating accepted in this volume) Jerusalem had been destroyed by the Romans. Josephus says that after the capture of the city, during the course of which the temple was burned, the emperor had ' ordered the whole city and the temple to be razed to the ground ' (*War*, vii. 1. 1). Nevertheless it is probable that Jesus did prophesy in some form the destruction of the temple. A confused charge against Him to that effect appears in the story of the trial (xiv. 58), and a similar tradition, which has been given a theological interpretation, is preserved in John ii. 19 ff.

Historically there is nothing unlikely in such a prophecy on Jesus' part. He was in close touch with the restless multitudes, and we have seen that He regarded the way of the Zealots as a mistaken one. According to the Talmud, Johanan ben Zakkai, standing within the temple forty years before its destruction, had foretold that this would come to pass (*Joma*, 39b). The dating of this prophecy makes it almost the very year of the utterance of Jesus. This is a curious coincidence, and suggests the possibility that the rabbinic tradition has confused the author of the dire prophecy which came so true. But ' forty years ' is a conventional Jewish term for a long period—compare the citation of the same date for the removal of the right of capital punishment from the Sanhedrin—and it may be that the coincidence is only an apparent one. If accepted as accurate, this tradition would mean that the

CHAPTER XIII, VERSES 1-2

inevitable destruction of the city was clear not only to the leader of an independent religious movement, but to the future leader of the scribal body as well. Jesus, no more than Johanan ben Zakkai, was opposed to the temple and its cultus, and if He made this prophecy it was in the fashion of the older prophets, as a punishment on an unrepentant nation.

The saying, if accepted as authentic, is important not so much as a prophecy which came true, as an indication of a pessimistic attitude toward the nation on Jesus' part. Other sayings confirm this note. There is the contrast between 'the many' who follow the broad way to destruction and 'the few' who find the narrow way to life (Matt. vii. 13). More emphatic still is the lament over Jerusalem in Matt. xxiii. 47, and Luke xiii. 34. With these sayings go the utterances which speak of the judgment on the wicked which the coming of God's Realm brings, parables such as those of the net cast into the sea and the tares sown with the wheat. There is no evidence that Jesus believed that the whole nation would repent and enter the coming Kingdom of God. However, it is unfair to take a prophet with strict literalness in his announcements of approaching doom, as a study of the Old Testament prophecies makes clear. A prophet sees and proclaims the punishment that God will bring unless the people repent, and he declares the certainty of this punishment in the hope of arousing a change of heart on the part of his hearers. Were the latter hope not present, there would be no reason for his preaching at all. Jesus, while proclaiming the certainty of divine judgment on a people, only a few of whom He said would escape, nevertheless was engaged in a struggle to extend the spirit of obedience to God's law, and encouraged His disciples by precept and parable to have faith that the seed sown with apparent futility would in many cases bring forth fruit a hundredfold.

It is, of course, possible that we have before us in this saying—that the temple would be destroyed—the last stage in the development of Jesus' views about His people. He came up to Jerusalem, still hoping, one must believe, for a mass movement of repentance and a manifestation of individual and social righteousness. But within a few weeks He came to see that before this could be achieved His enemies would bring about His death. He would scarcely have been deceived for long as to the extent of His success. The saying about the destruction of the temple may have occurred at this time. Nevertheless, though it fits in with the mood of the last days, it could have been uttered at any time, either as a warning to the Zealot agitation or as a judgment of divine punishment to come on the unrepentant nation, or, more likely, as expressing both convictions.

THE APOCALYPTIC DISCOURSE
(xiii. 3-37)

THE address which appears in this chapter is unique in the Gospel. Mark contains no other such lengthy discourse on a single theme. Isolated from its setting, it makes complete sense—better sense, in fact, than in its present position. For the introductory words refer to the destruction of the temple, whereas the discourse itself says nothing about this but deals with the End of the Age and the coming of the Son of Man. These facts—even apart from the reference to **the reader** in verse 14—indicate that Mark found the discourse ready to hand, though it is likely that he made some changes in it before incorporating it in his Gospel. But, even though it no doubt existed as a unit previous to its appearance here, it contains contradictions and discrepancies which show that it was a composite work rather than a single literary production. Thus in verses 6-8 the false Christs are the beginning of the Woes, in verses 21 ff. they come in the midst of the calamity. Up to verse 31 the discourse purports to reveal the signs of the End and its time of occurrence; verse 32 says that **no one knows anything about that day or hour**. Portions of the discourse are in the second person, other parts in the third.

The section thus appears to have been an apocalyptic prophecy which has been modified in the light of the experiences of the Church. The original was certainly composed before A.D. 70, since, in spite of the interest in Judæa (verse 14), there are no references to the actual events of the fall of Jerusalem. It has also been pointed out that verse 14 contradicts what actually happened, since the Christians fled, **not to the hills,** but to the little town of Pella, in the Jordan valley (Eusebius, *Church History*, III. v. 3). How much before A.D. 70 it was composed one cannot say, but the most likely suggestion relates it to the order of Caligula in A.D. 40 that his statue be set up in the temple in Jerusalem. The order caused great excitement among the Jews everywhere, and a revolt was avoided only by the death of Caligula and the rescinding of the order. The suggestion is that the prospect of the emperor's statue being set up in the Holy of Holies would have revived Jewish, and therefore Jewish-Christian, interest in the prophecy of Dan. ix. 27, which foretold that an 'abomination which makes desolate' would appear in the temple before the last days. Such a threat would, no doubt, have stimulated the appearance of apocalyptic writings, and may have been the occasion of this one. But, if so, the Christian writer regarded the statue of Caligula only as the symbol of a more transcendental evil power, or else in time the thought of the document shifted. For the 'abomination' (**Horror** in Moffatt) in verse 14 is modified by a masculine participle, and evidently means, in its present context, the Antichrist, or 'man of sin,' to whom Paul also refers in 2 Thessalonians. Thus, while the events of A.D. 40 may have stimulated the production of this and other apocalypses, the present document is not stated in terms of that specific event, but rather of the victory of the heavenly Son of Man over the regimented forces of evil.

Certain modifications which the original document had undergone can still be seen. The plainest of these is a revision by which Christian readers were warned that the expected end would be delayed. The opening words of verse 5 strike this note—**Take care that no one misleads you.** In verse 7 it is insisted that, even though there be **wars and rumours of war . . . it is not the end yet.** Clearest of all is the evidence of verses 14-28. In 14 the implication is that the appearance of the great calamity in Judæa is to lead on to the end. The parable of the fig-tree in verses 28-29 impresses this point : **whenever you see this happen, you may be sure He is at hand.** Yet in verse 21, after the horrors that will take place in Judæa have been described, the elect are warned lest false prophets make them think the coming of the Christ would be at that time, while verse 24 goes on to say that the Parousia will be **when that misery is past.** These facts can only mean that the apocalypse has been re-edited in the light of A.D. 70. While

CHAPTER XIII, VERSES 3-37

there has been no attempt to rewrite it, its message has been brought in line with the obvious fact that the End of the Age did not follow immediately the destruction of Jerusalem.

This judgment probably explains a curious wording in verse 14. In Dan. ix. 27 and 1 Macc. i. 54, the only other passages which foretell the coming of 'the abomination which makes desolate,' the phrase reads, 'in the temple,' or 'upon the altar.' In 2 Thess. ii. 4, similarly, the 'man of Lawlessness' sets himself 'in the sanctuary of God.' All the associations of the phrase, therefore, point toward some similar description of the place of appearance of the 'abomination' or **Horror**. The curious phrase, **standing where he has no right to stand**, looks as if it were a vague substitute for an earlier reference to the temple, which at the time Mark wrote was no longer in existence.

We have thus in Mark xiii. an apocalyptic document composed some time earlier than A.D. 70, reflecting conventional apocalyptic beliefs in a Christian form. It may be that genuine sayings of Jesus are to be found in the chapter, but the identification of these in the midst of a document which must be regarded as the product of Christian hope and prophecy is highly conjectural.

xiii. 3-5 : INTRODUCTION TO THE APOCALYPTIC DISCOURSE

And as he sat on the Hill of Olives opposite the temple, Peter 3
and James and John and Andrew asked him in private,
' Tell us, when is this to happen ? What will be the sign 4
for all this to be accomplished ? ' So Jesus began : 5
' Take care that no one misleads you : '

Verses 3 and 4 are obviously editorial, providing a setting for the discourse to follow. The question of the disciples is framed to connect two units of sayings which deal with different themes, the one with the destruction of the temple, the other with the End of the Age. The wording, particularly the phrase **in private**, betrays the editor's hand (see iv. 34, vi.

32, vii. 33, etc.). The discourse itself does not read as if it was addressed to intimate disciples, but rather to Christians generally. Both Matthew and Luke drop the mention of the four disciples in verse 3, and make the discourse one delivered to a larger group. Verse 5, as remarked in the last note, seems clearly to be a retouching of the apocalypse to make it conform to the situation after the destruction of Jerusalem had failed to lead up to the Parousia.

The topographical allusion in verse 3, **the Hill of Olives opposite the temple**, seems so natural and vivid as to suggest that the editor was acquainted with the topography of Jerusalem.

xiii. 6–13 : THE BEGINNING OF THE END

6 '—many will come in my name saying, "I am he," and mislead
7 many. When you hear of wars and rumours of war, do not be alarmed ; *these have to come*, but it is not the end
8 yet. For *nation will rise against nation, and realm against realm* ; there will be earthquakes here and there, and famines too. All that is but the beginning of the trouble.
9 Look to yourselves. Men will hand you over to sanhedrins and you will be flogged in synagogues and brought before
10 governors and kings for my sake, to testify to them. (Ere the end, the gospel must be preached to all nations.)
11 Now when they carry you off to trial, never worry beforehand about what you are to say ; say whatever comes to your lips at the moment, for he who speaks is not you
12 but the Holy Spirit. Brother will betray brother to death, the father will betray his child, *children will rise against their parents* and put them to death, and you will be hated
13 by all men on account of my name ; but he will be saved who holds out to the very end.'

The preliminary signs of the approaching end are said to be the appearance of many who would claim to be the expected Messiah, wars and rumours of war, earthquakes, famines, and

CHAPTER XIII, VERSES 6–13

the persecution of the saints. This is the familiar language of apocalyptic literature. One thinks, for example, of the terrible Four Horsemen of the Apocalypse (Rev. vi.), or of the signs portrayed in 4 Ezra ix. 3 and xiii. 31. The literary roots of these calamities are to be found, for the most part, in the Old Testament prophecies.

To the readers of the Gospel it would seem that all these signs had been fulfilled. Josephus tells of individuals in Palestine who had collected great crowds of followers on the promise of working marvels at the proper moment, and Acts mentions two of these—Judas and Theudas (v. 36 f). There was a famine under Claudius (Acts xi. 28), an earthquake in Phrygia in A.D. 61 and the one in Pompeii in A.D. 63. Of wars one need only recall the campaigns in Britain under Claudius and Nero, the war in Armenia, the constant threat of invasion by the Parthians, the disturbances at the end of Nero's reign, and the revolt in Palestine in A.D. 66–70. The description of the persecutions which the righteous would have to suffer would also seem to have been fulfilled. Paul says he was flogged five times by Jewish authorities (2 Cor. xi. 24), and no doubt there were other Christians who had suffered the same experience. The statement, **you will be ... brought before governors and kings for my sake, to testify to them**, looks like a direct reference to Paul's appearance before Felix, Festus, Herod Agrippa, and the Court of Cæsar. The prophecy of betrayals by members of one's own family, while going back ultimately to the language of Micah vii. 6, and being common in apocalyptic literature, certainly seems to have in mind the martyrdoms of the Christians in Rome at the time of Nero's persecution in A.D. 64. According to Tacitus, those first arrested betrayed others to the authorities.

One detail in this list of persecutions calls for a further word of comment. The saying, **when they carry you off to trial, never worry beforehand about what you are to say; ... for he who speaks is not you but the Holy Spirit**, existed independently before it was incorporated in the apocalyptic document. For it is to be found in a different context in Matt. x. 19, and Luke xii. 11. The saying belonged to the cycle of tradition which dealt with discipleship and the persecutions which the early Church regarded as inevitably going with it. It reveals the extent to which the community believed itself to be guided by the Holy Spirit. The statement here, however, is a theological formulation of a very practical religious attitude—one of confidence that their inadequate efforts would be utilized by God in a way and to a degree which they could not foresee. The responsibility was theirs to hold out to the very end ; the results could be left confidently in the hands of a divine providence.

These things—wars, famine, earthquakes, and persecutions—were the beginning of the trouble. Literally this last would be translated ' the beginning of travail.' This phrase is a technical one in Jewish apocalyptic usage. It means the ' birth-pangs of the new order.' For apocalyptic thought was the child of persecution and hope, and it always described the New Age of happiness and peace as ushered in through calamities and sufferings.

xiii. 14–23 : THE APPEARANCE OF THE ANTICHRIST

14 ' But when you see *the appalling Horror* standing where he has no right to stand (let the reader note this), then let
15 those who are in Judæa fly to the hills ; a man on the housetop must not go down into the house or go inside
16 to fetch anything out of his house, and a man in the field
17 must not turn back to get his coat. Woe to women with
18, child and to women who give suck in those days ! Pray
19 it may not be winter when it comes, for those days will be days of *misery, the like of which has never been from the beginning of God's creation until now* —no and never
20 shall be. Had not the Lord cut short those days, not a soul would be saved alive ; but he has cut them short for the sake of the elect whom he has chosen.
21 If anyone tells you at that time, "Look, here is the Christ,"
22 or, "Look, there he is," do not believe it ; for false Christs and *false prophets will rise* and *perform* signs and

CHAPTER XIII, VERSES 14-23

wonders to mislead the elect, if they can. Now take you 23 care! I am telling you of it all beforehand.'

The translation *appalling Horror* adopted by Moffatt in verse 14 renders only one of two ideas in the Greek phrase. Literally 'the abomination of desolation,' the two words describe an object regarded as foul, disgusting, and hateful, which at the same time desecrates and destroys all that is good. The Greek phrase comes from the Septuagint, or Greek, version of Dan. ix. 27. The original reference was to the altar to Olympic Zeus which Antiochus Epiphanes set up in the temple enclosure in 168 B.C. in connection with his desecration of the temple. It reappears in 1 Macc. i. 54 with reference to the same altar. The Hebrew which the Greek phrase rendered means 'a profanation which is appalling.' By the time of our Gospel, however, the original reference of the passage had been lost sight of, and it was merely a mysterious prophecy which yet was to be fulfilled.

In the context here it is clear that the phrase is used to describe, not an altar nor a statue of Caligula, but a person, for it is modified by a masculine participle. We might translate therefore, 'When you see the Abominable One, who desecrates and destroys, standing where he has no right to stand, then let those in Judæa flee to the hills.' The interpretation of the mysterious words is supplied by the other apocalyptic writings of the New Testament. Paul, in 2 Thess. ii. 3 ff., warns his readers of a figure whom he calls 'the lawless one, the doomed one, the adversary who vaunts himself above and against every so-called God or object of worship, actually sitting himself in the temple of God with the proclamation that he is God.' This description was written in A.D. 52 or 53, long after Caligula's mad intention had been dropped. The reference is clearly to the idea of an Antichrist, or Man of Sin, the opponent of God in the struggle for control of the universe. The ultimate origin of this concept lies to the east in the Babylonian and Iranian mythologies. It came into Christianity through Judaism, and appears three times in the New Testament: in Paul's words quoted above, in the present passage in Mark, and in chapters xii., xix., and xx. of the Apocalypse of John. The other statements of the section are typical apocalyptic utterances and call for no special comment.

xiii. 24–37 : THE PAROUSIA OF THE SON OF MAN

24 ' But when that misery is past, in those days,
    the sun will be darkened
    and the moon will not yield her light,
25   *the stars will drop from heaven*,
    and the orbs of the heavens will be shaken.
26 Then shall be seen *the Son of man coming in the clouds*
27 with great power and glory ; and he will then despatch his angels and *muster* the elect *from the four winds*, from the verge of earth to the verge of heaven.
28 Let the fig tree teach you a parable. As soon as its branches turn soft and put out leaves, you know summer is at hand ;
29 so, whenever you see this happen, you may be sure that he is at hand, at the very door.
30 I tell you truly, the present generation will not pass away till
31 all this happens. Heaven and earth will pass away, but my words never !
32 Now no one knows anything about that day or hour, not even the angels in heaven, not even the Son, but only the
33 Father. Take care, keep awake and pray ; you never
34 know the time. It is like a man leaving his house to go abroad ; he puts his servants in charge, each with his work
35 to do, and he orders the porter to keep watch. Watch then, for you never know when the Lord of the House will come, in the late evening or at midnight or at cock-crow
36 or in the morning. Watch, in case he comes suddenly
37 and finds you asleep. Watch : I say it to you, and I say it to all.'

After the birth-pangs of the New Order comes the Advent of the Messiah. The description here is taken from Old Testament passages. The central event, *the Son of man*

CHAPTER XIII, VERSES 24-37

coming in the clouds, is stated in the language of Dan. vii. 13. Nothing is said here as to the destruction of the 'Abominable One' mentioned above. Apparently that belonged, according to the scheme of this writer, to the period of distress before the Advent. The appearance of the Son of Man is **after that misery.** The elect only are gathered **from the four winds,** there being no mention of the wicked. The judgment scene which one might expect is left out. The writer's interest is not in depicting the complete eschatalogical drama but in insisting on the certainty and nearness of the reward of the righteous. **You may be sure that he is at hand, at the very door.**

The closing verses are contradictory. Verse 30 declares that the Parousia will be within the lifetime of Jesus' generation. That sounds like a late addition, a reassurance to those who had begun to doubt. But verses 32-37 declare emphatically that **no one knows anything about that day or hour ... not even the Son.** Such a statement quite obviously was not a part of the original document. No apocalypse could be written with the assertion that nothing could be known about the time of the Advent. This verse must represent a different stream of Christian tradition, and must have been added to the original document by a later hand.

That Jesus made some statement denying His knowledge of the exact time of the coming of the divine Realm seems probable. Schmiedel made it one of his ' foundation stones ' —that is, sayings which for reasons of reverence would never have been put into the mouth of Jesus by His followers, and, therefore, must have been original. Burkitt more recently has taken the verse as representing Jesus' final position. He had come to Jerusalem expecting the Kingdom to appear. Nothing happened, and it became more and more clear that He would be delivered over to His opponents to be put to death. A new conviction, therefore, formed itself. The End was not so near after all. Man must be patient and wait. This view, however, while attractive, is extremely speculative. No such dependence can be put on the chronological arrangement of the Gospel as to warrant a reconstruction of the story on the basis of the present order of Jesus' sayings. But had Jesus not given some intimation that He did not know the time and the hour, it seems that no such tradition as this one would ever have been formed. There is also other evidence of such an attitude on Jesus' part, namely, His answer to the Pharisees who wished to know when the Kingdom of God would come (Luke xvii. 20). Jesus refused to answer the question, but reminded them of the rule of God within. This is not to deny that Jesus regarded the Age to Come as near at hand. Even though He did read the signs of His day as indicating that affairs were coming to their great crisis, He may very well have declared Himself ignorant of the exact day.

The final parable carries on the thought of verse 32. **You never know the time.... Watch, in case he comes suddenly and finds you asleep.** The parable which ended the original document was the one of the fig-tree in verse 28 f. The parable of verses 34 ff, was added apparently at the same time as the saying in verse 32.

V. THE DEATH AND RESURRECTION OF JESUS
(xiv. 1–xvi. 8)

AT this point the account of the Passion begins. After the opening sentences one cannot help noticing that the story becomes more circumstantial and possesses a unity which the earlier chapters plainly lacked. This has been attributed to the fact that Mark lived in Jerusalem, or even that he himself was an actor in some of the scenes recorded in this section. The explanation is probably to be sought in another direction. The death and resurrection of Jesus were subjects of permanent interest to the early Church. How came the Christ to have been executed by the Romans? This was a question which would have had to have been answered over and over again. Nor could it be answered by a single story; it involved a series of events. The enemies who plotted against Him, how they arrested Him at night, their false charges at the trial, the part played by the Roman or Jewish officials respectively, the execution with its last word, the proofs of an actual burial, and finally the victory over death—all were involved as necessary elements in any account. This was true not only in Palestine, but also in Gentile lands. 'O foolish Galatians,' says Paul, '... before whose eyes Jesus Christ was depicted as crucified.' Although the Church's tradition on other periods of Jesus' life may have been rather general and vague, on these final events it tended to be more detailed and exact.

But the very interest and importance of these events made them the objects of reflection, interpretation, and hence, inevitably, development. It was essential to show that the death of Christ was prophesied in the Scriptures, and in the effort at demonstration, proof-text and event were made to meet as closely as possible. The apologetic necessity of showing that the Leader had not been a rebel against Rome, although executed by Roman soldiers, and the antagonism which the Church felt toward the Jewish authorities, both affected the story of the trial. Theological interpretations of the death of Christ can also be seen to have influenced the story at points. The result is that while there is greater circumstantiality and continuity, the interpretative elements are the more easily recognizable, particularly by comparing the several Gospels. The remarkable feature about the narrative of the Passion, however, is not the influences which have coloured it at recognizable points, but the fact that so detailed an account of the original events has been preserved. Mark's story is not dependable at all points, as we shall see, but it does provide an intelligible picture of the general course of the last events.

xiv. 1–2: Priests and Scribes Plot to Secure Jesus' Execution before the Feast

xiv.
1 **The passover and the festival of unleavened bread fell two days later ; so the high priests and scribes were trying how to get hold of him by craft and have him put to death.**
2 **'Only,' they said, 'it must not be during the festival ; that would mean a popular riot.'**

The story of the Passion opens with a reference to the coming Passover and the seven-day feast of unleavened bread which immediately followed it. The Passover lamb was slain on the afternoon of Nisan 14th—the first full moon after the vernal equinox—and the celebration of the feast continued until midnight. This would be midnight of Nisan 15th, since the Jewish day began at sundown. The feast of unleavened bread was from Nisan 15th to 21st.

Verse 1 is apparently a sort of introduction or heading to this section. With this statement the evangelist picks up again the narrative, and also binds together the several threads of the story he has to tell. He probably does not mean that the determination to put Jesus to death was made only two days before the Passover. This decision was referred to in iii. 6, and implied in xii. 8. The mention of the plot is only to set the stage for what is to follow.

CHAPTER XIV, VERSES 1-2

According to the chronology of this Gospel, the crucifixion took place on Friday, Nisan 15th, and the Passover itself was on the previous Thursday evening. This would make the point designated by verse 1 as Wednesday. This suggests that perhaps the evangelist had a special motive in giving this virtually unconnected note of time. The events of this day are, apparently, the dinner in Bethany and the betrayal by Judas. Somewhat later in Christian literature one finds the statement that the reason why the Church fasted on Fridays and Wednesdays instead of on the regular Jewish fast days was because these days were the days of the crucifixion and the betrayal by Judas (see *The Apostolic Constitutions*, vii. 23). The explanation is fairly late, but these days, as fast days, go back into the first century. It may be that, in the Christian circle for which Mark wrote, the Wednesday and Friday fasts were being practised, and Mark gave this statement of the day of the week to explain its significance in Christian history. Otherwise there seems no clear reason for the fixing of the date.

Verse 2 is both important and strange. The leaders feared a **popular riot**. Then it is clear that Jesus was a popular leader or hero. The hierarchy, of course, could not know that His aims and those of the multitude which delighted in Him were far apart. But the statement that the execution **must not be during the festival** is most surprising, for this is exactly what Mark proceeds to tell us the leaders did do, and this without any statement of a change of purpose. Verse 2 thus contradicts a good deal of what follows. It is evident that Mark here is not composing freely, but is following some source or tradition which had a different dating from that which the evangelist adopted for his Gospel. We shall return to this point when we come to the discussion of the Passover meal.

xiv. 3-9 : THE ANOINTING IN BETHANY

When he was at Bethany in the house of Simon the 3 leper, lying at table, a woman came up with an alabaster

flask of pure nard perfume, which had cost a great sum; the flask she broke and poured the perfume over his head. 4 This angered some of those present. 'What was the use 5 of wasting perfume like this? This perfume might have been sold for over three hundred shillings, and the poor 6 might have got that.' So they upbraided her. But Jesus said, 'Let her alone. Why are you annoying her? 7 She has done a beautiful thing to me. The poor you always have beside you, and you can be kind to them whenever 8 you want; but you will not always have me. She has done all she could—she has anticipated the perfuming 9 of my body for burial. I tell you truly, wherever the gospel is preached all over the world, men will speak of what she has done in memory of her.'

An account of an anointing of Jesus by a woman with costly ointment at a dinner, and a criticism of her act by those present with Jesus' reply, is told by all four Gospels. Matthew takes his story from Mark, with virtually no changes. Luke's account, in vii. 36 ff., however, varies on practically all points. Jesus is at dinner in the house of a Pharisee. The woman who performs the act is a notorious sinner. The criticism which is made is that if Jesus were a prophet He would know the character of the woman and refuse to have anything to do with her. Jesus replies, 'Her sins which are many are forgiven; therefore, she loves much.' This is almost a completely different story from the one above. The only important points of similarity are the act of anointing and the fact that in Jesus' remarks to His Pharisaic host He addresses him as 'Simon.'

The account in the Fourth Gospel follows the main lines of the Marcan one, the most important differences being that the house is said to be that of Lazarus in Bethany, and the woman, who in Mark is unnamed, is identified as Mary, the sister of Lazarus and Martha.

These similarities and diversities have produced many theories and suggestions as to the relationship of the stories.

CHAPTER XIV, VERSES 3-9

The real question, of course, is the relation of Luke's account and Mark's. One solution is to maintain that the two are variants of the same story: the Lucan form usually being taken as the more nearly authentic report, and the Marcan one being regarded as an adaptation to the Passion story. But, apart from the woman's act of devotion, these stories have no connection and cannot have developed one from the other. The reappearance of the name Simon in Luke vii. 40 —after its conspicuous absence in the introduction to his story—is best explained as due to the influence of Mark's account. After all, we do know that Luke had read Mark before he wrote.

In other words, we have here two early stories which are independent of each other. I see no reason for not thinking that this sort of episode may have happened twice. There are illustrations in abundance of the fact that an act of appreciation or homage to a popular hero suggests to others the same gesture. Certainly it is no good attempting to interpret Mark's story by Luke's or vice versa. Whether the Fourth Gospel's change of location from the house of Simon the leper to that of Lazarus and the designation of the woman as Mary have any claim to acceptance may be doubted. John has a fondness for supplying the names of anonymous figures in the narratives of Mark and Luke.

The use of unguents in the Near East, both in ancient and modern times, is well known. Anointing the body, or parts of it, with olive or other vegetable oils was a routine made necessary by the climate. We know also of the use of oil as a medicant and as a cosmetic. It was the custom at fashionable dinners, as the guests arrived, to have servants bathe their feet and anoint the hair of the head and beard, and oft-times their feet, with fragrant oils. Such expensive standards of entertainment were scarcely practised among the working and middle classes with whom Jesus was for the most part in contact. The criticism of the woman's act, in which the entire flask of an especially expensive perfume was used, as 'needless waste,' is an entirely characteristic remark in such circumstances.

How much of the reply to this criticism can be accepted as genuine? Here the newer methods of the 'Form Criticism' seem to be especially helpful. Through these studies we have learned that oral traditions usually preserve a simple striking saying as the conclusion to an episode rather than several disconnected ones. In this case the response which fits the criticism expressed are the words, '**Let her alone.** . . . **The poor you always have** among you.' That the further statements are additions or amplifications of the saying in the light of subsequent events is suggested also by their content. That the body of Jesus would not be perfumed in the regular way (see xv. 46 and xvi. 1) was not known at the time. The reference to the preaching of the gospel all over the world is certainly a later Christian wording.

The kernel of the story, the historicity of which there is no reason to doubt, seems thus to have been an episode which reveals both the devotion which He inspired in those who listened to Him so gladly (xii. 37) and the kindness and graciousness of His nature. One who criticized Mary for being concerned with so many things for dinner and insisted that only one thing was needed, or who contrasted the greatness of John with those who wore soft raiment and dwelt in king's houses, would scarcely have delighted in perfumed unguents. But He did honour the woman's devotion and resented a criticism which would shame her for her loving deed.

Jesus' body was not anointed for burial in the proper manner, and this fact was distressing to His intimate friends and followers. One need only note the plans of the women narrated in Mark xvi. 1, and also how the Fourth Gospel remedied the situation by His statement, plainly unhistorical, in xix. 40. This is no doubt the reason why this story has become a part of the Passion narrative. An anointing by a woman whose name had been forgotten very early was seen to be anticipatory, either because of a remark by Jesus at the time that He would not always be with them, or because the episode happened, or was believed to have happened, only a short while before His death.

CHAPTER XIV, VERSES 10-11

xiv. 10-11 : Judas Turns Traitor

Then Judas Iscariot, one of the twelve, went to the high priests 10 to betray him to them. They were delighted to hear it, 11 and promised to pay him for it. Meantime he sought a good opportunity for betraying him.

It was one of the firmly fixed facts of the tradition that Jesus at the last was betrayed to His enemies by one of His intimate disciples. There are no grounds for doubting the fact, as difficult as it is to explain it. A member of the Twelve, Judas, had been a loyal disciple. Why he turned against Jesus, and was willing to assist in bringing about His death, we probably shall never know. The deed can scarcely be put down to cupidity, as was done in early Christian circles (see Matt. xxvi. 15, and John xii, 6). The explanation that Judas was disappointed at Jesus' failure to appear in the role of Messianic deliverer is put forward in many recent books. If this was the case, there must have been other factors also. One who had been chosen as a member of the Twelve would hardly have taken the step he did unless he had come to feel, not only that he had been disappointed in Jesus, but that He actually was a dangerous figure, a deceiver and false prophet. In other words, Judas must have gone over to the Pharisaic and Sadducean attitude toward Jesus. What forces and influences, personal and otherwise, may have led him to such a change of view, we do not know. But the stark fact of a betrayal at the end by a member of the Twelve serves to remind one that Jesus was one of those figures toward whom one could with difficulty adopt an indifferent attitude. His demands and objectives were so radical and complete that it was inevitable that He should be regarded either as the saviour of His people or as a dangerous and destructive individual.

The verse which follows, while it does not say so explicitly, suggests that the betrayal was entirely on Judas' own initiative. One notes that it is the **high priests** here to whom he goes. Although **scribes** were mentioned, in verse 1, as also in the plot, it is apparent that it is the priestly group who are the prime—if not the sole—agents in bringing about the execution. The statement that **meanwhile he sought a good opportunity for betraying him** is very strange on the basis of the Marcan chronology of the Passion story, according to which the arrest took place the following night. It seems plain that the events were not compressed into the short compass of two days as xiv. 1 states.

Just as we do not know the influences which led Judas to his decision to betray Jesus, neither can we be sure what it was that he betrayed. The view has frequently been expressed that the chief priests could easily have found out through their own agents where Jesus could be found at night, and that Judas' betrayal must have been something further—namely, that Jesus claimed to be the Messiah. But, interesting as this is, the Gospels give no indication of it. Judas does not appear in connection with the trial in any way. The Gospels agree that he betrayed information as to a secluded spot in which Jesus could be found, and that he identified Him to the arresting body. It is better to accept this as fact than to speculate on other possibilities against the actual evidence. There is a corollary which must be drawn from the fact. If Judas informed the authorities as to where Jesus could be found at night outside the city, the latter, in spite of their desire to get rid of Jesus, had been unable to get this information. This means that, to an extent which we cannot now determine, Jesus was in hiding. Had He withdrawn from active work in Jerusalem to await some occasion or event—perhaps the great day of the festival—to reappear in the city, or did He merely conceal His whereabouts when He left the city each day? The question is of the greatest interest, but unfortunately we have no information on which to base an answer.

The figure of Judas very early became the subject of speculation and legend. In accordance with Zechariah xi. 12 it was concluded that the price paid for Jesus' betrayal was thirty pieces of silver (note that this is mentioned in Matthew only).

CHAPTER XIV, VERSES 10–11

Two versions of his death are preserved in the New Testament, one that he hung himself (Matt. xxvii. 3 ff.), the other that he burst asunder (Acts i. 18 f.). The vague suggestions of avarice as the motive, and that ' Satan entered into him ' (John xiii. 27), coupled with the absence of any clear-cut explanation of Judas' act, show that it was not understood by the early Church. They were content to fall back on the explanation that the deed was foretold in the Scriptures.

xiv. 12 : WAS THE LAST SUPPER THE PASSOVER MEAL ?

On the first day of unleavened bread (the day when the paschal 12 lamb was sacrificed), his disciples said to him, ' Where do you want us to go and prepare for you to eat the passover ?

This statement is clear and definite. True, it has been pointed out that the statement, **the first day of unleavened bread (the day when the paschal lamb was sacrificed)**, is, strictly speaking, incorrect. For the Passover lamb was sacrificed on the afternoon of Nisan 14th, the meal being eaten that night, while Nisan 15th was the first of the seven days of unleavened bread. In strict parlance the Passover was not part of, but preceded, the latter feast, and this distinction is clearly preserved in Jewish writings. Josephus, however, in *Ant*. II. xv. 1, writes, ' We celebrate for eight days the feast called that of unleavened bread,' and there are other indications that the two were sometimes reckoned together to make one festival of eight days. Mark's wording is in line with this tendency, which the sentence from Josephus illustrates. In any case, there is no doubt of Mark's meaning. Verse 16 repeats that it was the Passover which the disciples prepared.

This fixed date regulates the rest of the chronology of the Passion story in Mark. The arrest occurred during the night between Nisan 14th and 15th (Nisan 15th by Jewish reckoning), the crucifixion on Nisan 15th, the first day of the feast of unleavened bread, the burial that afternoon. Mark xv. 42 declares that this afternoon was the preparation, the day before the Sabbath, which gives the day of the week—namely, Friday. On the Sabbath the body lay in the tomb. On Sunday, the first day of the week, the women came to the tomb and found that Jesus had risen (xvi. 1).

Now it is common knowledge that the Fourth Gospel has a different chronology. That evangelist goes out of his way to insist that this last meal of Jesus with His disciples was not the Passover (see John xiii. 1). On the morning of the trial before Pilate the Jews do not enter the Prætorium, ' in order that they may not defile themselves but eat the Passover ' (xviii. 28). In xix. 14 it is said that this was the eve of the Passover. Thus, according to John, the crucifixion took place on Nisan 14th, the Last Supper being the evening after Nisan 13th. Now xix. 31 says that this day of the crucifixion was also the preparation of the Sabbath—i.e. that the Passover fell that year on the Sabbath. Thus John and Mark agree that the crucifixion was on Friday, but disagree as to whether this was Nisan 14th, the day when the paschal lamb was slain, or Nisan 15th, the first great day of the feast of unleavened bread, the day which followed the Passover meal.

The solution of the problem created by this contradictory evidence not only involves the question of the date of the crucifixion, but has bearing also on the movements of Jesus during the last days of His life. Scholars have been sharply divided over which chronology is the correct one. To the present writer the evidence strongly supports the Johannine presentation that Jesus was crucified before the Passover feast began. The reasons for this conclusion are the following :

(1) As already pointed out, Mark's dating is not consistent. In xiv. 2 it is stated that the authorities determined to put Jesus out of the way before the festival, and no change of purpose or circumstance is mentioned subsequently. Mark seems to have combined portions of two different traditions.

(2) A number of the episodes of the Passion narrative seem most unlikely on the night of the Passover and the first day of unleavened bread. This argument has been overdone, as Dalman and Billerbeck have shown. Thus the rule that celebrants of the Passover must remain in the house until

CHAPTER XIV, VERSE 12

morning was not always observed at this time. The journey to Gethsemane would not have exceeded the Sabbath day's journey permitted on a feast-day. The law against carrying arms on feast-days would not have applied to the police who probably composed the arresting party, while the two swords of the disciples might easily have been hidden weapons in violation of scribal law. The expression about ' Simon coming from the fields ' does not mean that he had been at work. Nevertheless, the entire account, without any reference to the feast in connection with these episodes, implies strongly that the source Mark has used did not think of the night and day as Nisan 15th. This applies particularly to the story of the examination before the Jewish authorities. No matter what happened originally, the source describes this as a formal trial. Even if it was merely an examination, it would have involved difficulties on the Passover night.

(3) The evidence of Paul is not conclusive, but supports the Johannine dating : 1 Corinthians was written some time near the Passover season, and shows very strongly the influence of the ideas of the feast. In v. 6-8 Paul writes that Christ ' our paschal lamb has been sacrificed.' This could imply merely that Jesus' death occurred at the Passover season, but becomes more pointed if Paul believed that the crucifixion took place on exactly the day on which the paschal lambs were slain, as John affirms. One is struck also by the absence of any reference to the Passover in Paul's description of the Lords' Supper in xi. 23. The dating of the Supper is very general : ' The Lord Jesus in the night in which He was betrayed took bread,' etc. Had Paul understood that the meal was on the Passover night, one would expect him to have said so.

(4) The eucharistic meal was celebrated weekly, if not more often, in the early Church. If this meal had been the Passover celebration, one would have expected an annual repetition of the rite by the first followers of Jesus.

(5) The Talmud (*Sanh.* 43*a*) states that Jesus was hanged on the eve of the Passover. The passage rests on no direct knowledge of the event, but it does suggest that the Christians with whom the orthodox Jewish leaders were in conflict believed

that the execution was on the eve of, rather than after, Passover.

(6) The Quartodeciman controversy during the second century shows that a large body of the Church believe that the crucifixion was on Nisan 14th. The Churches of Asia Minor, which maintained the practice of celebrating their redemption on that date, claimed that their custom in this respect was sanctioned by such authorities as Philip (no doubt the one mentioned in Acts) and his daughters, and ' John who . . . reclined upon the bosom of the Lord,' Polycarp, and others. ' We observe,' says Polycrates, the exponent and defender of the Quartodeciman practice, ' the exact day ' (Eusebius, *Church History*, v. 24). The primary contention of the other Churches was not that this was wrong, but rather that the celebration should be held on the Sunday of the resurrection. In other words, over against the Quartodeciman practice of celebrating the Passover as the day of Christ's death, there was no other date insisted upon. The Roman practice was to hold the annual celebration on the resurrection Sunday, no matter what day of the month it fell on.

(7) These considerations have not touched upon the question whether the details of the meal itself resemble those of the Passover celebration. This is a question which has been warmly debated, for the reason that the Gospel evidence does not all point the same way.

Certain features of the account which are often cited as proving that the meal was the Passover were also characteristic of ordinary Jewish meals when guests were present—notably the breaking of bread and its distribution, and the blessing of the cup of wine after the meal. That the meal was at night accords with the Passover ritual, but guest meals also continued into the night. Definitely against the Passover interpretation is the fact that the distinctive, indeed the definitive, features of that celebration, the lamb, the bitter herbs, and the unleavened bread, are not mentioned in any of the accounts. That Mark speaks of *artos*, the word for ordinary bread, instead of *azuma*, unleavened bread, almost rules out the thought of the Passover. Nor is there any indication that

CHAPTER XIV, VERSE 12

the meal lasted until midnight, as the Passover ritual required. In fact, it is difficult to think that the other events of the night could have all taken place, if it had done so.

Two features do suggest the paschal meal—namely, that it is described as being held within the precincts of Jerusalem by special arrangement with one of the city's householders, and that the singing of a hymn is mentioned at the close of the repast. The Passover had to be eaten within the city limits, and residents were enjoined to provide quarters for pilgrims for the purpose. The hymn would be the Hallel, Psalms cxiii.–cxviii., the last part of which closed the Passover meal. There may have been other reasons, however, for holding the meal in Jerusalem, accepting the location as correct, and one will be suggested in the commentary. The hymn would have to be regarded as the evangelist's addition made on the assumption that this was the paschal celebration, or else be thought of as a hymn sung together before the group broke up, quite apart from any legal requirement. We know that singing often closed the entertainment of guests. On the whole these two details alone do not seem sufficient to identify the meal as the Passover in view of the strong evidence against the identification.

The records thus seem to compel one to accept the Johannine view that Jesus died before the Passover meal. If, in the light of this conclusion, one re-examines the Marcan chronology, one is struck by the fact that only one of the chronological references requires a different dating than the Johannine one—namely, xiv. 12, with perhaps also the editorial introduction in xiv. 1. It seems clear that Mark's basic narrative of the Passion assumed that Christ died before the Passover, and that this has been modified by the insertion, quite probably by the evangelist, of an account of the Last Supper which described it as a Passover meal.

But why should the early Church or any part of it have wished to identify the meal at which the Eucharist was instituted with the Jewish Passover ? When one reflects upon the conditions in early Christianity, the answer does not seem so difficult to find. The first Christians were mostly Jews, or

Gentiles with Jewish leaders, and there is an abundance of evidence that the Jewish Passover still remained in their minds one of the dominant occasions of the annual calendar. 1 Corinthians v. 6–8 illustrates this excellently. The primary ideas of the Passover were those of the memorial of Israel's deliverance and the thought of the future reward which the first deliverance suggested. These were also the primary ideas of the Christian Eucharist—a memorial of the deliverance of God's people through Christ's death and the promise of the salvation to come. It would be natural, therefore, for the Christian Eucharistic meal to be thought of as a Christian substitute for the Jewish Passover, even though it was celebrated many times per year. The impulse behind this substitution would not be a Jewish leaning, but opposition to Judaism and its rites. The idea would be supported by the general Christian knowledge that the institution of the Eucharist and the death of Christ occurred at the Passover season. Of course, a more exact knowledge of the Passion story which kept in mind the fact that Christ died before that Passover would have prevented this development. In such circles the Passover might be observed as the day of Christ's death—i.e. by the Quartodecimans of Asia Minor. But where the actual day of the death was unknown or forgotten, due to the emphasis on the resurrection Sunday as the day of celebration, the identification of Passover with the Last Supper could easily occur and would have been particularly valuable. In Rome, where Mark's Gospel probably originated, the conditions here described seem to have obtained.

Before leaving this complicated subject, there is one further point which should be mentioned. Most of the above arguments have only shown that the Last Supper was not a Passover meal, and hence that the crucifixion and burial were not on the first day of the festival. But is there any reason for accepting the Johannine dating that the crucifixion and burial were during the day just before the paschal meal ? May not these events have occurred several days before the feast ? This is suggested by the wording of Mark xiv. 2—' not during the feast lest there be an uproar.' Would not that day have been almost as dangerous as the following ones as regards the presence of pilgrims in Jerusalem ? Furthermore, it is rather striking that once one concludes that the Last Supper was not the Passover, there is virtually nothing in the Passion story which points to the Passover. The chief point is the fact that the day after the crucifixion is said to have been a legal rest day, but this may have been merely the Sabbath, which all the Gospels assert it was.

On this point it appears that one cannot be positive. It may be that the early Christian tradition remembered that these events took place shortly before the Passover and that just as Mark has mistakenly identified the final meal as the Passover, so John may have mistakenly identified the next day after the tragedy as the Passover and first day of the festival. Over against this possibility stand chiefly three considerations : the Quartodeciman practice—'We observe the exact day, neither adding nor taking away'; Paul's interpretation of Christ as the Christian Passover sacrifice, and His resurrection as the Christian 'first fruits'; and the statements in the Fourth Gospel. These show that the thought of the death of Jesus on the Passover day was deeply imprinted on early Christian thought and practice. The error, if it be one, occurred in the earliest days of the Church.

xiv. 13–16 : THE PREPARATIONS FOR THE LAST MEAL OF JESUS
WITH HIS DISCIPLES

So he despatched two of his disciples, telling them, 'Go into 13 the city and you will meet a man carrying a water-jar ; follow him, and whatever house he goes into, tell the 14 owner that the Teacher says, "Where is my room, that I may eat the passover there with my disciples ? " He 15 will show you a large room upstairs, with couches spread, all ready ; prepare the passover for us there.' The dis- 16 ciples went away into the city and found it was as he had told them.

If this meal were a Passover, these preparations for a meal in Jerusalem would be quite understandable. If, however, we are compelled to reject the presentation of Mark on this point, what is one to make of the story of these arrangements? Burkitt thought that Jesus, realizing His imminent arrest, arranged a paschal meal in advance of the proper date. But while postponements of the meal were permitted under certain circumstances, anticipations were not. If the regulations concerning the sacrifice of the lamb in the temple at the proper time were not obeyed, there would have been little point in endeavouring to keep other rules of the feast. Other scholars have suggested that the meal really was in Bethany and was transferred to Jerusalem under the influence of the Passover theory.

Certain aspects of the story cause one to reflect on the question of Jesus' movements during these last days. He is outside Jerusalem; He sends His disciples into the city, not knowing their destination, but to meet an individual whom they will recognize by a certain sign, who will guide them to the house. This suggests secrecy. Is there anything else in the Passion narratives which carries the same suggestion?

One thinks immediately of the statements that although Jesus taught in the temple by day He withdrew to Bethany each night (see xi. 11 and xi. 19; cf. xiv. 3). Matthew repeats this tradition (xxi. 17). Luke states that Jesus spent His nights on the Mount of Olives (xxi. 37). There is no mention of any secrecy in connection with these movements. Luke, in part, says that what Judas sought was an opportunity to deliver Him up 'apart from the crowd' (xxii. 6). But the Fourth Gospel preserves two notes which suggest a different situation. In xi. 55 f. it is said that the crowd which came up to Jerusalem for the Passover did not find Jesus there, and wondered if He would come. This may be an editorial touch to heighten the dramatic effect, but in xii. 36*b* is a statement which is quite specific and rather surprising in a Christian document: 'With these words Jesus went away and hid from them.' Except for a few verses of typical Johannine discourse, this statement immediately precedes the account of the final supper with the disciples. This certainly agrees with the evidence of the betrayal of Judas. The authorities apparently did not know where Jesus was to be found until Judas gave them the information.

Thus there is more than one indication that Jesus took precautions at the last not to fall into the hands of His enemies. We cannot reconstruct the events in detail. Some two or three weeks before the Passover He cleanses the temple and is teaching publicly. As the animus of the authorities became more and more evident, we may assume that He began to take precautions. Certainly He planned to appeal to the crowds at the time of the festival. To be sure of this, He may have had to withdraw during the days immediately preceding. The authorities plainly did not wish to arrest Him publicly during the feast days, for fear of trouble with the people. It was this situation which provided Judas with his opportunity. He knew the secluded spot where Jesus gathered with His disciples on the outskirts of the city. There He could be seized without difficulty and despatched before the great day of the festival ever arrived.

If some such reconstruction as this is sound, then this meal in Jerusalem may have been planned that Jesus might meet with some of His followers in the city. By this time He probably knew or strongly suspected Judas' treachery, and, though ignorant of how or when the blow would fall, surmised that it was imminent. The large room upstairs, which a follower would be glad to make available, would accommodate those whom He wished and at the same time be safe from interruption.

xiv. 17–21 : ANNOUNCEMENT OF JUDAS' BETRAYAL

So they prepared the passover, and when evening fell he 17 arrived along with the twelve. As they were at table eating, 18 Jesus said, ' Truly I tell you, one of you is going to betray me, one who is eating with me.' They were distressed at 19 this, and said to him one after another, ' Surely it is not me ? ' ' Surely it is not me ? ' ' One of the twelve,' he 20 told them, ' one who is dipping into the same dish as I am. The Son of man goes the road that the scripture has 21

described for him, but woe to the man by whom the Son of man is betrayed! Better for that man had he never been born!'

According to Mark and Matthew those present on this memorable occasion were **the twelve**. Luke says ' the apostles,' which probably means the same thing (see Luke vi. 13). A few statements in early Christian writings state or imply that others were present. According to Jerome, the *Gospel According to the Hebrews* referred to James as having been present. The *Apostolic Constitutions* says that Mary and Martha were present. Justin Martyr, in his *Apology* (66), says that the Lord gave the elements to the apostles ' only,' which implies that others were present.

The statement that Jesus foretold during the meal that one of those eating with Him would betray Him is surprisingly reticent. If the story had been an assumption based on belief in the Lord's foreknowledge, one would expect to have the traitor called by name. This is done only in the Fourth Gospel (xiii. 26), where the general designation, ' **One who is dipping into the same dish as I am**,' is changed to the very definite, ' The one to whom I give this piece of bread.' This fact suggests that we have here a genuine reminiscence. There is nothing unreasonable in the story. Jesus may have had definite information, through some of His friends and supporters, of visits Judas had made to the authorities. Or He may have become convinced by Judas' bearing, or by words of anger, that he had cast his lot with the priests and scribes.

The **dipping into the dish** refers to the table custom of the time according to which the guests, reclining on couches or cushions, used pieces of flat bread to dip the food from the main dishes on the table.

xiv. 22–25 : THE LAST SUPPER

22 **As they were eating, he took a loaf, and after the blessing he broke and gave it to them, saying, ' Take this, it means
23 my body.'** He also took a cup and after thanking God he gave it to them, and they all drank of it ; he said to

CHAPTER XIV, VERSES 22-25

them, ' This means my *covenant-blood* which is shed for many; truly I tell you, I will never drink the produce of the vine again, till the day I drink it new within the Realm of God.'

In the previous discussions it has been concluded that this meal was not, as Mark describes it, a celebration of the Passover feast. The special features of the meal—the blessing, breaking and distributing of bread, and the blessing and giving of wine—call, however, for some explanation, and other Jewish rites have been examined in search of the pattern which Jesus followed. One does not need to enter upon this search, for a natural explanation of the particular acts of the supper is to be found in the ordinary rules of Jewish social etiquette.

The entertainment of guests in Jewish homes at this period was done in accordance with certain well-defined rules of procedure. Servants received the guests, bathed their feet and anointed the head, beard, and clothing with perfumes. Sometimes garlands were placed on their heads. They then assembled in a room where preliminary relishes or *hors d'œuvres*, perhaps with wine, were served. When all the guests had arrived, the party transferred to the dining-room, where they reclined on couches around the table, the order of arrangement being based on the respective dignity or rank of the various guests. The host took bread, pronounced for the entire group a blessing over it, broke it, and gave pieces to each guest, and with this act the regular meal began. There were other benedictions also, but the most important one was after the meal. A cup of wine was brought, and the host, or someone he honoured with the request to take his place, pronounced over it a blessing, in which thanks were given for God's gifts of food and of ' the land,' with quite possibly a prayer for the establishment of God's rule and the restoration of the House of David. This benediction having been pronounced, each guest drank of the wine. While the later custom was for each to have his own cup, Dalman has shown that there are reasons for thinking that, earlier, the cup of the one speaking the blessing may have been passed around. After this blessing, dessert and wine might be served. The dinner often ended with singing.

The points of contact which are evident between the procedures of Jewish social meals and the account of the Last Supper suggests that it is along this line that we should reconstruct the story of this last night of Jesus' life. He and His disciples scarcely followed these formalities in their everyday association. Nor would wine have been a regular item at their meals. It would appear that He wished this meal to be a more formal one, a dinner to which His most intimate followers were invited. This would not mean necessarily that all of the above formalities were carried out. The servants to bathe the feet and the perfumed ointments were no doubt lacking. Probably also one would be wrong in assuming an elaborate menu. But the tradition seems plainly to preserve the recollection of a special meal on the last night of Jesus' life. If we are right in concluding that during a short period before the festival Jesus had withdrawn from public activity and was in hiding, what would have been the purpose of this meal? It seems necessary to choose between two possibilities. Either this was a gathering of His most intimate and trusted disciples to make the final plans for the great effort at the time of the festival, or we must assume that He had learned of Judas' treachery and suspected or knew that the end was only a matter of a few hours. The indications point toward the latter alternative.

Any attempt to understand what took place at this last meal must take into account the fact that there are two different traditions concerning it in early Christian writings. One of these is the one which Mark and Paul follow, for, while the account here and the one in 1 Cor. xi. 23 ff. exhibit important differences, they rest on the same stream of tradition. Matthew's account, taken directly from Mark, belongs to this group of writings also. The second tradition is represented in the passage Luke xxii. 15–19a (the words in 19b and 20 being in all probability a harmonizing addition to the text), and in the account of the Eucharist in the second-century Church

CHAPTER XIV, VERSES 22-25

manual, the *Didache*. The difference between these two types is, first, in form : in Luke and the *Didache* the breaking of bread comes after the wine cup, and is the central act of the rite ; and, secondly, in thought : in Luke and the *Didache* the interest is dominantly eschatological, while in Mark and Paul it is in the idea of a new covenant in the sacrificial blood of Christ.

A ritual celebration of the type which Luke and the *Didache* represent can be seen in the practice of the early Church. Acts ii. 42 tells of the ' breaking of bread ' of the earliest brotherhood, as it continued ' in the apostles' teaching and fellowship.' Reference to this practice is frequent in the Acts. In later works we read of a Eucharist in which the elements were bread and water (*Acts of Peter* 2 and 5, *Acts of John* 110). In the *Acts of Thomas*, bread is accompanied by water, oil, and wine. Justin Martyr refers to bread, water, and wine. In all of these cases it is plain that the central element in the rite was the bread. Acts adds another detail about this ' breaking of bread '—the tone of the gathering was one of ' gladness.' This suggests that the dominant note was the eschatological hope, rather than the recollection of the death of Christ.

The origin of this type of Eucharist can be simply and reasonably explained as the continuation by the disciples of the daily meals which they had eaten together while the Lord was still with them. Just as Jesus had always broken the bread after pronouncing the prayer of praise and thanksgiving —a prayer in which we may believe that the petition ' Thy Kingdom come ' appeared in some form—so they continued the practice. Water would have been the usual drink rather than wine. The meal was a glad anticipation of the coming reunion in the Kingdom of God. The *Didache* ritual describes just such a meal, the prayer at the breaking of the bread reading, ' As this wheat was scattered upon the mountains and being gathered became one, so may Thy Church be gathered together from the ends of the earth into Thy Kingdom.' The wine cup which has been added to this liturgy is only of secondary importance.

But, besides this common meal partaken of with gladness, there was another rite in which the bread represented Christ's body, and the wine, now the central element, represented his blood. The latter is said to be *covenant-blood*, the reference being to the sacrificial blood with which Moses sealed the covenant of the law (Exod. xxiv. 8 ; cf. Heb. ix. 14 ff.). This covenant Christian readers would recognize to be the new covenant of Jer. xxxi. 31 (cf. Gal. iv. 24 ; 2 Cor. iii. 6, 14 ; Heb. vii. 22, ix. 15). Whence came this rite which is described here in Mark ?

Many have concluded that it developed from the ' breaking of bread,' the sacramental features being due to the religious ideas of the Græco-Roman world. This is the simplest view. But there are two objections to it. The first is that it is difficult to see how the ritual as described by Paul could have been derived from the ideas preserved, for example, in the *Didache*. The words, ' This means my body,' seem far removed from the figure of the wheat scattered upon the mountains and brought together in one loaf. In the second place, this rite claimed a quite different origin from what seems the reasonable explanation of the common meals of the early Christians, namely, in an episode which took place on the last night of Jesus' life. ' In the night in which he was betrayed,' says Paul, ' Jesus took bread and broke it, and said, " This is my body." ' This evidence is all the stronger since Paul is quoting a single episode detached from any setting. Not only do we seem to have a totally different set of ideas from ' the breaking of bread with gladness,' but also a practice which the Church believed to have originated in some special deed or words of Jesus on the last night of His life.

In the light of these facts it seems that one should not simply give up the problem, and attribute the Marcan and Pauline ritual to a Hellenistic development of the simpler, normal breaking of bread together. But it is difficult to form any clear idea of what the original incidents could have been which gave rise to this form of the Eucharist.

Perhaps it will be easier to work backward. A later development is certainly to be seen in the words about the *covenant-*

blood. The grounds for this statement are several. In the first place, the drinking of wine which had just been declared to be Jesus' own blood would have been abhorrent to a Palestinian Jew. Furthermore, wherein lay the point of the comparison ? If it was that Jesus' blood was to be shed, one would expect some reference to this aspect. One would have thought also that the wine would have been poured out on the floor rather than distributed. One notes, furthermore, that the wine cup in the text of Mark has two meanings, one sacramental and the other eschatological, and the latter idea is to be found also at the close of Paul's account (verse 26). It seems likely that the figure of the wine cup, originally referring to the Messianic banquet, has been assimilated, under the influence of the tendency of all liturgies toward parallelism, to the figure of the bread just before it. Finally, there is the evidence of the benedictions which were customarily pronounced over the wine cup. Four of these have come down to us, two of them from before A.D. 70. These give thanks to God for His gifts of food, for the land, for deliverance from Egypt and the gift of the law, and for His love for Israel. The suggestion of such words would be in the direction of the hope for the future reward, of which God's love and care were the guarantee. These facts, taken together with the absence of any other teachings of Jesus with reference to a new covenant in His blood, make it evident that those words are the result of later reflection.

This leaves as the historical kernel of the account the words, ' **This is my body,** ' uttered in connection with the bread, and the reference to the Messianic banquet in connection with the wine. The only point of comparison between the bread and Jesus' body would seem to be in the breaking. Against this is the objection already mentioned that one would not expect the bread in that case to be distributed to be eaten. This is not so serious as in the case of drinking the blood, but it is a real difficulty. To avoid it one might assume that Jesus broke a loaf of bread to make vivid His figure, but did not distribute these pieces as food ; or, again, that His figure was a simile, which referred explicitly to the breaking of the bread, rather than a general metaphor which left the point of the comparison unstated. Under the influence of Hellenistic religious practices such a saying would immediately be given the fuller meaning which it has in its present context. This, of course, is to reconstruct the evidence, but this seems less radical than to reject it entirely.

Thus, as best one can recover the earlier tradition of that night's gathering—and one must remember that there were many witnesses—Jesus summoned His disciples to a final meal, knowing that the end was near. Either at the meal, or before it, He announced to them that He had been betrayed. Like John the Baptist, He would suffer martyrdom for God's Kingdom. Taking the bread, He broke it and gave pieces to all present to begin the repast. The breaking suggested the figure—His body would be broken like that bread. After the supper, taking the cup, He raised it as prescribed by custom and rule, and pronounced the benediction of thanks. With the coming tragedy in the minds of all present, He added to the benediction His faith that the separation would be but temporary. In that day when 'grace had come and this world passed away,' He and they would drink again of the fruits of the vine at the great banquet which God would give. In this reconstruction the basic elements are the announcement by Jesus of His approaching death at the time of a last meal with His disciples, and the promise of a renewal of their fellowship in God's Kingdom. If this was the first occasion when Jesus had made to His disciples such a definite statement, one can understand how the memory of the meal would have so impressed itself on the minds of the disciples that it would have become the starting-point of the later sacramental developments.

xiv. 26–31 : JESUS FORETELLS THE DISCIPLES' DESERTION OF HIS CAUSE AND HIS RESURRECTION APPEARANCE IN GALILEE

26 After the hymn of praise they went out to the Hill of Olives.
27   Jesus said to them, ' You will all be disconcerted, for it is written : *I will strike at the shepherd, and the sheep will be*

scattered. But after my rising I will precede you to Galilee.' 28 Peter said to him, ' Though all are disconcerted, I will not 29 be.' Jesus said to him. ' I tell you truly, to-day you will 30 disown me three times, this very night, before the cock crows twice.' But he persisted, ' Though I have to die with 31 you, I will never disown you.' And they all said the same.

Mark regards the meal which has ended as a Passover, and the mention of the hymn may be due to his knowledge that the Passover ritual ended with the Hallel. If authentic, one would assume that the singing was of some one or more of the Psalms which expressed that faith in God in the midst of dangers of which Jesus had spoken. Such singing would be entirely appropriate as the conclusion of a social gathering.

The citation of Zech. xiii. 7 has all the appearance of being a product of early Christian scriptural study. To their Jewish neighbours they wished to prove that the sufferings and death of the Messiah were prophesied in the law and the prophets. The demonstration seemed also to answer the questions of the faithful. It was known that the disciples had fled from Jerusalem. Why had they deserted at that time of crisis ? The answer is given that this also was foretold in the Scriptures. The quotation varies slightly from the regular text, and probably is taken from some early Christian collection of proof-texts.

But while this appears to be true of the quotation of this passage, it is entirely possible that Jesus may have surmised that His disciples would flee when it became clear that the authorities were ready to use force, and may have warned them in general terms of the danger of deserting their cause. Such a possibility seems confirmed by the story of the warning to Peter. The source of this unit of the tradition will certainly have been the apostle himself. While the exact number of denials and the statement of the time may be later accretions, one can scarcely do otherwise than accept Peter's word that the Lord had warned him of his approaching denial. No doubt such a warning would have included the others also.

Verse 28 is important. It is a clear indication of the way in which the Gospel ended, or was intended to end. The verse is omitted from the Fayoum papyrus fragment, now in Vienna, but this fragment is of uncertain date, and may not be from a copy of the Gospel. The other manuscript evidence does not suggest its omission.

The evidence seems to point toward the omission of the word **twice** in verse 30. It is lacking in a number of manuscripts both here and in verse 72, and appears in neither Matthew nor Luke. ' **Cock crow** ' was a popular designation of an early hour before dawn (see xiii. 35). Another suggestion which has been made makes it refer to the signal *gallicinium* (i.e. ' cock-crow '), blown on a bugle when the Roman guard of the castle Antonia, overlooking the temple, was changed in the early morning hours. Mark, however, takes the expression literally, as verse 72 shows.

xiv. 32–42 : GETHSEMANE

32 Then they came to a place called Gethsemane, and he told
33 his disciples, ' Sit here till I pray.' But he took Peter and James and John along with him ; and as he began
34 to feel appalled and agitated, he said to them, ' *My heart*
35 *is sad*, sad even to death ; stay here and watch.' Then he went forward a little and fell to the earth, praying that the hour might pass away from him, if possible.
36 ' Abba, Father,' he said, ' Thou canst do anything. Take this cup away from me. Yet, not what I will but what
37 thou wilt.' Then he came and found them asleep ; so he said to Peter, ' Are you sleeping, Simon ? Could you
38 not watch for a single hour ? Watch and pray, all of you, so that you may not slip into temptation. The spirit is
39 eager, but the flesh is weak.' Again he went away and
40 prayed in the same words as before ; then he returned and found them once more asleep, for their eyes were
41 heavy. They did not know what to say to him. Then he came for the third time and said to them, ' Still asleep ? still resting ? No more of that ! The hour has come, here is the Son of man betrayed into the hands of sinners.
42 Come, rise, here is my betrayer close at hand.'

CHAPTER XIV, VERSES 32-42

From verse 26 it is clear that the **place called Gethsemane** was somewhere on the Mount of Olives. Luke xxii. 39, together with xxi. 37, shows that this evangelist understood that the place of the arrest was the one in which Jesus and His disciples spent the nights regularly. John xviii. 1 states that it was ' across Kedron,' the stream-bed which divided the Mount of Olives from the city ridges, and that there was a ' garden ' there. Gethsemane probably meant olive-press, and one would more naturally think of an olive-grove rather than a garden of some other type.

The mounting tragedy of the story comes to its climax in the scene which is here presented. The account bears the marks of the dramatic and religious instincts of the early Christian community, but to deny its essential historicity is arbitrary and unwarranted. That Jesus was arrested at night in a secluded spot called Gethsemane, and that His disciples were with Him at the time, is unquestioned. The source of the account, therefore, was one or more of the disciples. The picture of Jesus **appalled and agitated** is in striking contrast to the attitude of complete foreknowledge and calm which is ascribed to Him in the Gospels. According to Mark elsewhere, He explained to the disciples even before leaving Galilee exactly what was to take place, and was aware not only of His death but also that a resurrection triumph would follow. In the stories of the arrest, trial, and execution He is always described as maintaining an attitude of calm serenity. This tradition of a period of anguish and inner struggle before He was able to accept the impending tragedy as the will of God can scarcely be due to anything other than a recollection by certain of the disciples to this effect. Incidentally, the same tradition is referred to in Heb. v. 7. The explanation that the story is a product of Old Testament passages which deal with the righteous man surrounded by his enemies, such as Ps. xl.–xlii., has little to support it. True, the phrase, *My heart is sad*, appears twice in Ps. xlii. 6–11, and no doubt comes from that source. But it does not seem likely that the general idea of Jesus' attitude during these last moments can be set down as a Christian invention.

One would not, however, wish to insist on the verbal accuracy of the words of the prayer. The recollection of the disciples is summed up in verse 35. Jesus' words, while no doubt true to His general attitude, are probably an elaboration by the Church of a tradition that was too meagre for its fullest religious use. As stated by the Gospel, the disciples were at a distance, and, after a while at least, asleep. Certain phrases of the prayer no doubt come from the Psalms, as, for example, the opening words from Ps. xxii. 1.

The rest of the story is no doubt to be viewed in the same way. That the disciples fell asleep in the night hours—if Luke be right, this was their regular place to rest and sleep—and were aroused by Jesus, must rest on their own testimony. But the repetition of the experience three times, and the words of general exhortation, are more probably not to be taken strictly. The point of the story to the early Christians was that those exposed to temptation must **watch and pray**. One could not take one's courage for granted ; **the spirit is eager but the flesh is weak**. Thrice Peter and the others fell asleep and thrice Peter denied his Lord. An almost liturgical rhythm has been given to the narrative.

xiv. 43-52 : The Arrest

43 At that very moment, while He was still speaking, Judas Iscariot, one of the twelve, came up accompanied by a mob with swords and cudgels, who had come from the
44 high priests and scribes and elders. Now his betrayer had given them a signal ; he said, ' Whoever I kiss, that is
45 the man. Seize him and get him safely away.' So when
46 he arrived he at once went up to Him and said, ' Rabbi,
47 rabbi !' and kissed him. Then they laid hands on him and seized him, but one of the bystanders drew his sword and struck the servant of the high priest, cutting off his
48 ear. Jesus turned on them, saying, ' Have you sallied out to arrest me like a robber, with swords and cudgels ?
49 Day after day I was beside you in the temple teaching,

CHAPTER XIV, VERSES 43-52

and you never seized me. However, it is to let the scriptures be fulfilled.'
Then they left him and fled, all of them; one young man did follow him, with only a linen sheet thrown round his body, but when the other youths seized him he fled away naked, leaving the sheet behind him. 50, 51 52

According to Mark, the arresting party consisted of a band or throng (not a mob—there is no disorder at the arrest) sent out by the Sanhedrin. The Fourth Gospel states that the party was composed in part of Roman soldiers under the command of an officer. This latter may be authentic, since we shall see that it is likely that the Jewish officials had a clear understanding with Pilate before they proceded to the arrest, and the latter may have placed a detachment of troops at their disposal. The view that the arrest was solely the work of the Romans, and on their own initiative, is, however, scarcely worth debating.

Judas is said to have identified Jesus by giving Him a kiss. Some form of identification would probably have been necessary since the arrest took place in a dim light at best, and a mistake could easily have happened. The recent account of the assassination of a relative of Premier Okada of Japan, in place of the statesman himself, by a party at night illustrates this possibility. A kiss was the normal greeting of affection between a teacher and a scholar. It would have been given on the head rather than on the face.

The arresting party was well armed. It is plain that they feared resistance on the part of the followers of the Galilean teacher and prophet. That these fears were not entirely without ground is shown by the sequel—at least one sword was drawn, and one member of the arresting party was wounded. The clash was only for a moment. **Then they left him and fled.** According to Mark, Jesus rebuked the soldiers for coming out to arrest Him as though He were a robber, when He had taught daily in the temple. But the words probably are part of the Christian elaboration of the story. It was not a time for speech-making. Again one notes the apologetic touch: this humiliating experience was **to let the scriptures be fulfilled.**

Verses 51 and 52 are a curious addendum to the story of the arrest. They have led to endless speculation as to who the **young man** was. A frequent guess has been that it was John Mark himself. Once this is accepted the way is cleared for a number of further conjectures. The house of the Last Supper was that of Mark's mother, mentioned in Acts xii. 12, and Mark had been in bed during the Supper. Judas brought the arresting party there, but arrived after Jesus and the disciples left. The traitor then led them to Gethsemane. Mark dashed from the house just as he was in order to warn Jesus, but arrived too late. All of this is interesting but entirely speculative. There are, for example, no grounds for thinking that the house where the Last Supper was eaten was the one mentioned in Acts xii. 12.

Two facts suggest that the **young man** was not the evangelist. One is that the sentence structure indicates that the writer of the Gospel is here following a written source, rather than drawing upon his recollection. The Greek text reads, ' And a certain young man followed,' which does not fit with the previous statement that all of His followers fled. (The elimination of this contradiction in a small group of manuscripts, ' But a young man did follow,' etc., is scarcely the original wording.) That looks as if Mark is drawing on a written narrative which did not fit smoothly with his primary account. The second reason for rejecting the hypothesis that the person was Mark is the absence of any further details. Had the writer been the person in the story he surely would have given us some further statement as to how he came to be present, and the condition of his clothing.

As a matter of fact, if we recognize that Mark is here drawing on a written source which he cannot interrogate further, but must take as he finds it, it is quite problematical whether the **young man** in question has not been the victim of an unintentional linguistic libel. The word translated **sheet** is used twice in the Greek Old Testament to mean simply a linen garment. (See, for example, the wager which Samson made in Judges

CHAPTER XIV, VERSES 43-52

xiv. 12.) Billerbeck has shown that **naked** in Talmudic literature could be used of one without his outer garment—that is, clad simply in underwear. Thus the story in its original Aramaic form may well have been one of a young man who, when seized, fled in his undergarment, leaving his linen tunic in the hands of his would-be captors. In favour of this possibility are the facts that an undergarment was indispensable among the Jews, both rich and poor (see Krauss, *Talmudische Archæologie*, I, p. 161), and that the point of the story would then be the loyalty of the disciple and his presence as a witness, rather than the state of nudity in which he fled.

It is a difficult question in any case why the story was preserved. The Passion narrative, as it was transmitted, became more and more elevated in content and feeling. The early Christians were not interested in a good story, merely for its own sake, at this crucial moment in the sacred narrative. One can only guess that the young man was one of the witnesses and narrators of the story of the arrest, and his experience was thus both known and remembered. His name, however, meant nothing, and the story itself seems to have dropped out of Mark's primary account. Matthew and Luke both omit it.

xiv. 53-54 : JESUS IS DELIVERED TO THE JEWISH AUTHORITIES

They took Jesus away to the high priest, and all the high 53 priests and scribes and elders met there with him. Peter 54 followed him at a distance till he got inside the courtyard of the high priest, where he sat down with the attendants to warm himself at the fire.

According to Mark, Jesus was led immediately before the supreme court of the Jewish people, the Sanhedrin. Before proceeding further with the story of the trial and execution, it will be well to ask, What were the powers of this Sanhedrin at this time ? Did they have the right on their own authority to try capital cases and pronounce sentence ? Or had this right been taken away from them by the Romans ?

Up until recently this last question has been usually answered in the affirmative, the basis for the answer being the statement in John xviii. 31 f. that it was not lawful for the Jews to put anyone to death, together with a statement, which occurs twice in the Talmud, that forty years before the destruction of the temple the right of capital punishment was taken away from the Jews. But this view has been seriously challenged by the French scholar, Juster, who maintains that the evidence shows that the Sanhedrin still had the right of capital punishment in Jesus' day. If so, the question why they did not exercise it instead of sending Jesus to Pilate immediately arises.

Unfortunately the data concerning the powers of the Sanhedrin during this period are extremely meagre, and a positive decision is difficult to make. Most of the evidence is inconclusive, and some of it is conflicting. The chief facts we have to go on are the following:

Before the Romans took direct control of the country the Sanhedrin was the supreme body, and no one could be put to death 'unless he had first been sentenced to death by the Sanhedrin' (*Ant.* XIV. ix. 3). Herod and Archelaus had repeatedly usurped the rights of the body. When the Jews protested to Augustus against the rule of the latter he was banished. It would seem likely that this would be followed by the re-establishment of the Sanhedrin's rights, and this is borne out by Josephus' statement that 'the government became an aristocracy and the high priests were intrusted with dominion over the nation' (*Ant.* XX. x. 5). At the same time the procurators were put in charge of the country, and Josephus also says that the first one was sent out 'with full powers, including the infliction of capital punishment' (*War*, ii. 8. 1). These statements taken together would seem to mean that the Sanhedrin exercised its control of the normal life of the people, but that the procurators handled directly cases which most concerned the Roman power—namely, cases of sedition. There is no instance in Josephus of the procurators executing individuals for any other offence.

The control of the country by procurators was broken once

CHAPTER XIV, VERSES 53-54

by the reign of Agrippa. After his death Claudius 'again reduced the kingdom to a province and sent as procurator Cuspius Fadus and then Tiberius Alexander, who by abstaining from all interference with the customs of the country kept the nation at peace' (*War*, ii. 11. 6). This implies that under the procurators the Sanhedrin certainly was not prohibited from its usual judicial functions in connection with Jewish laws. There is one probable reference to the exercise of such function in Josephus' writings: in *War*, vi. 2. 4, we have a speech which Titus is said to have made to the Jews in protest against their desecration of their temple. He refers to the barriers put up before the sanctuary, and adds, 'Did we not permit you to put to death any who passed it, even were he a Roman?' It is possible that the Romans permitted such executions on the spot, but unlikely.

Only once in Josephus is there a clear instance of a trial by the Sanhedrin of a capital case between A.D. 6 and A.D. 70. That is the story of the death of James, the brother of Jesus. Ananus, the high priest in the interval between the death of Festus and the arrival of Albinus, the new procurator, assembled the Sanhedrin, accused James and others of breaking the law, and delivered them to be stoned. A group of Jews, 'uneasy over this break of the laws,' met Albinus on his way to Jerusalem and 'informed him that it was not lawful for Ananus to assemble a Sanhedrin without his consent.' Albinus then threatened Ananus with punishment. This story is plain enough up to a certain point. It shows that in some way the procurators controlled the Sanhedrin in capital cases. But the illegal act of Ananus is not said to have been the execution of James and the others, but convening the Sanhedrin. This suggests that the procurator either had to approve the assembling of the Sanhedrin or its consideration of special cases, or perhaps had to approve its decisions.

Josephus' evidence thus points toward a continuation of the Sanhedrin under the procurators as the official legislative and judicial body of the Jews. To the positive evidence must be added the negative fact that nowhere does he tell of any cancellation of the Sanhedrin's right to try capital cases. Nor could the Romans have well done without some such native court or body to interpret and enforce the peculiar laws of the Jewish people. The analogy of their attitude toward Jews in Hellenistic countries, and their treatment of other conquered peoples, points in the same direction.

This impression left by a reading of Josephus is contradicted by the statement in the Talmudic writings which has been referred to—that ' forty years before the destruction of the temple the right of capital punishment was taken away from the Jews ' (*pal. Sanh.* I. 1). The date would take us back to the time of the death of Jesus, but the date here is not so important as the question of fact. There is a parallel to this passage in *Sanh.*, 41a, which states that ' forty years before the destruction of the temple the Sanhedrin moved from the Hall of Hewn Stones and took up residence elsewhere, whereupon R. Isaac ben Abudimi [end of the third century] said, " This is to teach that they did not try cases of *Kenas* [punishment by fines]. Say rather, they did not try capital charges." ' There is still a third passage which is pertinent. In *Ab Zara*, 8b, one reads, ' R. Ismael ben Jose [end of the second century] said that his father said that forty years before the destruction of the temple the Sanhedrin moved from the Hall of Hewn Stones.' Now it is a striking fact that this tradition of the cancellation of the Sanhedrin's right of capital punishment disappears as one goes backward in time. The first passage quoted affirms it flatly; the second (end of the third century) deduces it from the removal of the Sanhedrin ; while the earliest tradition, which goes back to the middle of the second century, only knows of the removal of the Sanhedrin.

Apart from this passage, the Talmudic evidence is in line with that in Josephus : *Sanh.* VII. 2 states that R. Eleazar ben Zadok, who died in A.D. 130, told that in his youth he had seen a priest's daughter burned for adultery. This was the penalty which the Jewish law required. Elsewhere the Talmud seems to assume that the Sanhedrin did have the power of enforcing the Jewish laws. But one cannot tell whether its decisions had to have Roman approval before being carried into effect.

CHAPTER XIV, VERSES 53-54

The evidence of the New Testament is clear only up to a certain point. Acts iv. and v. show the Sanhedrin acting in criminal cases; they arrest and scourge and warn the apostles. In the case of Stephen it is too uncertain whether his death was an execution or an act of mob violence to use it as evidence. The story of the trial of Jesus does not help, since, as will be pointed out, there was no legal trial by the Sanhedrin.

The conclusion which these various pieces of evidence leaves is that the Sanhedrin certainly remained the judicial body of the Jews, as Acts shows. They seem also to have sentenced people to death, as in the case of the priest's daughter, the case of James, and probably the case of Gentiles who invaded the temple enclosure. But the story of the death of James and its consequences shows plainly that the Sanhedrin was limited in some way when it came to capital cases. What this limitation was, we do not know exactly—whether an approval by the procurator of the consideration of the case or its confirmation. Such an interpretation best explains the data at our disposal, and would provide the basis for the late Talmudic view that the Sanhedrin lost this privilege when it removed from the Hall of Hewn Stones. The statement in the Fourth Gospel, ' It is not lawful for us to put to death anyone,' is perhaps to be viewed as an exaggeration of the facts in the case, in order to remove all blame from Pilate for considering the case at all.

It thus appears that the Sanhedrin were able to have tried Jesus. It is, however, quite certain that they did not do so. As will be noted below, the alleged Jewish trial violates practically every rule which governed the procedure of the Sanhedrin. Nor is there any evidence that the Roman trial was a review of the Jewish one. Jesus was apparently tried by the Romans for sedition, and executed in the Roman fashion. The appearance of Jesus before the Sanhedrin which Mark records, if historical at all, must have been something other than a formal legal trial. But if the Sanhedrin could have dealt with His case, why did they not do so?

There are three answers which might be given to this question:

(1) Some writers have thought that the entire story of Jewish participation in the death of Jesus is due to early Christian anti-Semitism, that the Jewish authorities had neither the intention nor desire to bring about His death, and that it was Pilate who from the beginning took the initiative, arrested Jesus, and executed Him lest He cause a popular disturbance. In favour of such a view is cited the statement in John xviii. 12, that Roman soldiers took part in the arrest, the well-known harshness of Pilate's rule, and the increasing exoneration of the Romans in the process of the Gospel formation. But against this is the unanimous testimony of Christian literature that the Jewish leaders were responsible for Jesus' death, not only in all of the Gospels, but in the writings of Paul (1 Thess. ii. 14 ff.), and in the early chapters in Acts (iii. 13, iv. 10, v. 30). The record of Jesus' activity earlier is, furthermore, a series of continuous conflicts with these authorities. This explanation may, therefore, be rejected.

(2) A second explanation is that the Jewish authorities had no grounds for a capital charge against Jesus under the Jewish law ; He is, therefore, turned over to the Romans as a dangerous leader who was inciting the people to overthrow the established order. There is much to commend this interpretation of the facts, since Jesus was certainly guilty of no serious offences. Yet the analogy of the case of James is convincing. Ananus ' assembled the Sanhedrin and brought before them . . . James and some others ; and when he had found an accusation against them as breakers of the law, he delivered them to be stoned.' If the Sanhedrin could find grounds for executing James as a law-breaker, it would have been easy to have done the same as regards Jesus.

(3) This leaves only a third explanation, which is the one offered in the Gospels—' They feared the people,' or, to put it differently, Roman action was surer and safer. Jesus was held in the highest favour by the people. A Jewish trial and execution no doubt could have been carried through, but the risk of an uproar and an investigation of the case was great. The obvious answer was to let the Romans handle the case

CHAPTER XIV, VERSES 53-54

from the beginning on the grounds of sedition. Incidentally, the case of James offers here a second analogy. The high priest lost his office as a result of the episode, though in that case it is probable that the victim had more support among the leading Jewish citizens than had Jesus.

xiv. 55-64: THE EXAMINATION BEFORE THE HIGH PRIEST

Now the high priests and the whole of the Sanhedrin tried to 55 secure evidence against Jesus, in order to have him put to death; but they could find none, for while many bore false 56 witness against him, their evidence did not agree. Some 57 got up and bore false witness against him, saying, ' We heard him say, " I will destroy this temple made by hands, 58 and in three days I will build another temple, not made by hands." ' But even so the evidence did not agree. So the 59 high priest rose in their midst and asked Jesus, ' Have you 60 no reply to make? What about this evidence against you? ' He said nothing, he made no answer. Again the 61 high priest put a question to him. ' Are you the Christ? ' he said, ' the Son of the Blessed? ' Jesus said, ' I am. 62 And, what is more, you will all see *the Son of man sitting at the right hand* of the Power and *coming with the clouds of heaven.*' Then the high priest tore his clothes and cried, 63 ' What more evidence do we want? You have heard his 64 blasphemy for yourselves. What is your mind? ' They condemned him, all of them, to the doom of death;

Mark presents this scene as a final trial by the whole of the Sanhedrin. But there are any number of considerations which indicate that there was no such trial. In the first place, practically every rule of procedure which, according to the Talmud, governed the Sanhedrin in its criminal procedure is violated in this case. The requirements in the Mishna that trials on capital charges could take place only by day, that there had to be a second session on the following day before conviction, that no trial, therefore, could be begun on the day before the Sabbath or a feast-day, that the less impartial judges expressed their judgment first, that blasphemy required mention of the divine name—these and a number of other regulations are violated. The answer that these rules come from the later Talmudic period is not quite sufficient, since the theoretical development of criminal procedure which the scribes might well have accomplished would at least have been on the basis of the earlier practice and tradition. Furthermore, when Jesus is examined by Pilate, there is no suggestion of a review of a Jewish trial nor any reference to a previous one. The charge is not blasphemy, but, apparently, sedition, and the penalty is not the Jewish one of stoning required in cases of blasphemy, but the Roman one of crucifixion. It is also to the point to note than in the Fourth Gospel there is no reference to a trial by the Jewish Sanhedrin, but only of an examination, first by Annas and then by Caiaphas. Thus it appears from every standpoint likely that what we have in Mark is merely a popular Christian version of what took place between the arrest and the trial by Pilate.

The conclusion which some have drawn that this story, therefore, is entirely unhistorical has already been rejected. Jewish participation in the series of events can scarcely be eliminated, and, if the initiative lay with the Jewish authorities rather than with the Roman ones, it is probable that the tradition of Jesus being taken before the leaders immediately upon His arrest is based on fact. But this will not have been a session of **the whole of the Sanhedrin,** nor a formal trial in accordance with the requirement of Jewish law. The prisoner is to stand before a Roman court, and the examination by the high priest and his advisers, here described, would have been with a view to preparing themselves for the final proceedings on the morrow.

It follows that a good deal of what is presented here is unhistorical, and is due to the assumption in the Christian tradition that a trial took place before the Jewish authorities. The *false witnesses* who do not appear in the trial the next day, the charge of *blasphemy*, which is dropped as soon as the conviction is secured, and the final *condemnation*, are in all

CHAPTER XIV, VERSES 55-64

probability developments of the tradition. The tearing of his garments by the high priest is subordinate to the charge of blasphemy. Other details like the silence of Jesus (verse 61) seem due to the influence of the second story of the trial before Pilate.

What happened behind the closed doors of the high priest's house, in the dead of night when no follower of Jesus was present, we can never be sure. True, it is quite possible that some information may have leaked out later, after the crucifixion, but at best it would have been information of the most second-hand or uncertain character. Had some member of the high priest's council been converted to the Christian movement later and have told the story, one would expect some mention of his name and a much more circumstantial account. But, though what transpired must be only a matter of conjecture, two points in the account have the appearance of verisimilitude.

The first is the reference to a saying about the destruction of the temple (verses 57 f.). Jesus quite evidently made a statement about a future destruction of the temple. It is recorded in xiii. 2, and a reference to it reappears in xv. 29, and in Acts vi. 14. Apparently it was a source of embarrassment to the earliest Christian groups, for both in Acts and here it is said that they were false witnesses who charged that Jesus had said that He would destroy the temple. In John ii. 19 the same saying is given an allegorical turn. Even here in Mark the phrases, **made *by* hands,** and **not made *by* hands,** are added to the **false** accusation to guard it still further from misunderstanding. The belief that Jesus had said this, particularly in the light of the cleansing of the temple, would have given particular offence to the Jewish aristocracy. It would also probably have been a proof of Jesus' revolutionary intent.

The same is true of the question as to Jesus' claim to Messiahship. Since this was evidently the basis of the charge which was pressed before Pilate (see xv. 2), it is more than likely that the question was addressed to Jesus during the examination. His answer, if the question was asked directly, was certainly not a denial, though He may have kept silent. This is assured by the absence of any such denial during the trial before Pilate, as well as by the faith of the disciples. But there are no grounds on which one can argue that the wording of the reply in verse 62 is authentic and exact. The reply is a composite of Ps. cx. 1 and Dan. vii. 13, and formulates the early Christian belief in Jesus as the apocalyptic Son of Man.

That these two points in the story thus have the appearance of historical probability suggests the possibility that the Christian groups may have secured some information concerning what transpired in the house of Caiaphas. But while this cannot be denied, it seems even more likely that the account has been developed from a knowledge of the accusations made by the Jewish leaders before Pilate, and from the criticism of Jesus made by orthodox Jews subsequently. The 'appearance of historical probability' means only that these elements appear in the trial before Pilate, and involve issues which the Jewish authorities are likely to have raised.

xiv. 65: Mockery and Blows from the High Priest's Attendants

65 and some of them started to spit on him and to blindfold him and buffet him, asking him, 'Prophesy.' The attendants treated him to cuffs and slaps.

After the examination there came the wait until morning. The authorities of the Sanhedrin retired to their beds for rest, and the prisoner was turned over probably to the band which had made the arrest. According to the account, the members of this band passed their time by making sport of the prophet. The text above suggests that those who engaged in this mockery were the members of the Sanhedrin themselves, but this is not likely. The end of the verse mentions the **attendants,** and the aristocracy would scarcely have mingled with their servants in such indignities. The episode duplicates the account of the mockery by the Roman soldiers after the sentence by Pilate, except for the difference that in xv. 16 Jesus is mocked as the King of the Jews, while here it is His powers as a prophet which the attendants wish Him to demonstrate. While the episode may merely have been carried over from the brutal treatment by the Roman soldiers, there is nothing impossible or unlikely in the account.

xiv. 66–72 : THE DENIAL OF PETER

Now as Peter was downstairs in the courtyard, a maidservant 66 of the high priest came along, and when she noticed Peter 67 warming himself she looked at him and said, ' You were 68 with the Nazarene too, with Jesus !' He denied it. ' I don't understand,' he said, ' I don't see—what do you mean?' Then he went outside into the passage. The cock crowed. Again the maidservant who noticed him began to tell the 69 bystanders, ' That fellow is one of them.' But he denied 70 it again. After a little the bystanders once more said to Peter, ' To be sure, you are one of them. Why, you are a Galilean !'* But he broke out cursing and swearing, ' I 71 don't know the man you mean.' At that moment the 72 cock crowed for the second time. Then Peter remembered how Jesus had told him, ' Before the cock crows twice, you will disown me thrice ' ; and he burst into tears.

* Omitting καὶ ἡ λαλιά σου ὁμοιάζει.

Goguel, the distinguished French Protestant scholar, has recently concluded that this story of Peter's denial has no historical value. His chief arguments are that Peter's place of leadership in the earliest days of the Church would have been impossible, had he been guilty of such a serious defection as the one described. It is also argued that Paul would certainly have alluded to the defection in his rebuke of Peter at Antioch. The historical kernel of the story is conjectured to have been only a saying by Jesus rebuking Peter's bold assertion of loyalty in verse 30, and warning him against an hour of weakness. But this is to create a difficulty, rather than to solve one. The assertion that Peter, the leading apostle, who was active in missionary work as late as Paul's letter to the Corinthians, and who probably lived and worked until the Neronian persecution in A.D. 64, had denied Jesus with cursing at the crucial hour of His Lord's Passion, would, if it had no foundation in fact, have been vehemently rejected by Peter and all his friends. There are traces that part of the original narrative of the Passion goes back to the testimony of Peter, and that must have been the case with this incident. The shame of his denial was wiped out by an appearance of Jesus to Peter alone (see Luke xxiv. 34, 1 Cor. xv. 5; cf. Mark xvi. 7), quite probably to him first of all. There is no reason why Paul should have mentioned Peter's denial in his rebuke at Antioch, for his criticism of Peter is on grounds of general principles.

The scene takes place in the court of the high priest's house. Mark says 'below,' which seems to mean that he thinks of the examination of Jesus as happening upstairs. Luke states that after the third denial the Lord 'turned and looked at Peter,' which indicates that he thinks of Jesus as being held somewhere adjacent to the group around the fire. These references are all vague and uninformative. The maidservant who first recognized Peter had no doubt seen him with Jesus during His public activity. After the first denial, we are to understand that he moves away from the fire into the open vestibule where he is again recognized. A third time he is charged with being one of Jesus' group, and the point is made that he is obviously a Galilean. Matthew adds, 'for his speech betrays him,' but this is the evident meaning of Mark as well.

A number of important manuscripts omit the mention of the cock-crowing in verse 68, and the words **for the second time** in verse 72. According to this version, there was only one crowing of the cock. As remarked in the note on xiv. 30, this was a popular expression for early morning, and it is unnecessary to think of the blowing of the bugle in the Roman castle at the early-morning changing of the guard. Mark, however, takes the reference to be to an actual bird, whose crowing called back to Peter's mind Jesus' words of warning.

CHAPTER XIV, VERSES 66–72

The last words of verse 72 are of uncertain meaning. The verb which Moffatt translates **burst into** means, literally, to throw or cast upon. Thus the sentence has been variously translated : ' When he thought thereon (i.e. put his mind on it) he wept ' ; or, ' Rushing outside, he wept.' One translator renders it, ' Throwing something over his head, he wept.' Although the first of these seems preferable, a commentator has the advantage of a translator, in that he can remark that the evidence is insufficient for a positive decision and leave the choice to his readers.

xv. 1–5 : THE TRIAL BEFORE PILATE

xv.
Immediately morning came, the high priests held a consulta- 1 tion* with the elders and scribes and all the Sanhedrin, and after binding Jesus they led him off and handed him over to Pilate. Pilate asked him, ' Are you the king of 2 the Jews ? ' He replied, ' Certainly.' Then the high 3 priest brought many accusations against him, and once more Pilate asked him, ' Have you no reply to make ? 4 Look at all their charges against you.' But, to the 5 astonishment of Pilate, Jesus answered no more.

* Reading ποιήσαντες instead of ἑτοιμάσαντες.

The meaning of verse 1 seems to be that the Sanhedrin met again in the morning and agreed upon the charge which they would make against Jesus before Pilate. Luke, who has no mention of a trial by the Sanhedrin in the night, has transferred the Marcan account of that examination to the morning hour. John, as has been remarked, refers to no such trial at any time, but only to a questioning by Annas and Caiaphas during the night. Mark's statements, which are very general, may be simply an inference based on the presence of the Jewish officials in Pilate's court. Certainly, in view of the uncertain testimony of the Gospels concerning the activities of the Sanhedrin, little reliance can be placed on the detailed moves which are recorded.

But whereas the Jewish trial was held behind closed doors, and with no one present except a few officials, the trial before

CHAPTER XV, VERSES 1-5

be questioned. The fact of the execution of their leader and founder by the Roman Government was an embarrassment to the Christian cause which it was one of the functions of the Passion narrative to mitigate as much as possible, and the Church would never have invented a political charge of this sort as the grounds for the execution.

This charge in the circumstances of the case could only have meant that the chief priests accused Jesus of claiming to be the Messiah of popular hopes. The political features of this popular expectation would, in Pilate's mind, have justified the charge, provided the claims could be established. How could this have been done? What evidence could be cited? No doubt the accusers would insist that He had disturbed the people, as Luke—obviously elaborating the tradition—makes them do in xxiii. 2, but there is a considerable step from this to the specific charge that the prisoner claimed to be a king. Quite possibly, also, some popular expressions of hope that the Galilean prophet would prove to be the nation's deliverer could be cited, though the Gospels give little evidence that the populace regarded Him as more than a prophet. But such evidence, even if it could be produced, in the absence of anything more direct would have little weight in the face of the prisoner's denial of any such belief or claim. With all possible allowance for Pilate's indifference to justice, we must still assume that the chief priests would not have brought Jesus before the Roman court on a charge on which they had no evidence. The only satisfactory answer seems to be the assumption that the leaders of the Sanhedrin knew that Jesus had accepted the designation of Messiah and would not deny it when questioned by the procurator. The most obvious source of this information would have been Judas, who no doubt discussed the whole matter with the authorities when he made his agreement to guide the high priest's soldiers to Jesus' place of concealment.

Did Jesus deny it? It is one of the strange facts of biblical study that at this one moment when Jesus stood before the Roman court, in the full light of public knowledge, and was asked, '**Are you the king of the Jews?**' His answer is in words

CHAPTER XV, VERSES 1-5

to the Jews, ' What shall I do with Him whom you call the king of the Jews ? ' The procurator's insistence on the innocence of the prisoner, furthermore, would be absent had the latter already confessed Himself guilty of the charge against Him. In the parallel passages in Matthew and Luke the facts are the same.

These are the Gospel passages. Of the Talmudic instances the most important one is the story of *pal. Kilaim*, ix. 32, of the report of the death of Judah, the patriarch. The people had declared that they would kill whoever brought the tidings of his death. Bar Kappara appeared before them in the garb of mourning and implied in a parable that Judah was deceased. ' Is Rabbi dead ? ' the people asked ; whereupon Bar Kappara replied ' You have said.' The point of this reply is that Bar Kappara insisted that the people had made the statement themselves, he had not said it. This is made explicit in the Babylonian version, which reads, ' Ye have said it, I have not said it.' The second rabbinic passage, *Tos. Kelim*, I. i. 6, is ambiguous and can be read either as an affirmation or a denial.

A survey of the evidence thus shows that in the particular passage, Mark xv. 2, and its parallels in Matthew and Luke, ' Thou hast said ' is not a definite affirmation, but is non-committal. Other instances of its use bear this out, indicating that its meaning was simply, ' That is your statement.' Only in Luke xxii. 70 does this interpretation seem strained, and even there is still possible. To view the phrase as an affirmation, or even concession, makes shipwreck of the sense of the rest of the story of the trial before Pilate.

I conclude, then, that when the Roman Government asked Jesus, ' **Are you the king of the Jews ?** ' He gave a non-committal reply. The Christian tradition preserved the recollection that Jesus kept silent at the trial. ' **Have you no reply to make ?** ' asked Pilate. ' **Look at all their charges against you.**' But, to the astonishment of Pilate, Jesus answered no more.

If one asks the reason for this non-committal answer, the simplest explanation is that the question was not one which Jesus could answer. No more than Joan of Arc would deny her 'voices,' would Jesus deny His divine mission. But to accept His enemies' definition of His task and purpose was equally impossible. In this silence before His accusers, early Christians saw another fulfilment of prophecy : ' He was oppressed, yet when He was afflicted, He opened not His mouth.' Some would regard the prophecy as responsible for the tradition that Jesus made no defence. In view of the speeches of defence which are recorded of Stephen and Paul, this does not seem very likely.

xv. 6–15 : ' Jesus or Barabbas '

6 At festival time he used to release for them some prisoner
7 whom they begged from him. (There was a man called Bar-Abbas in prison, among the rioters who had committed
8 murder during the insurrection.) So the crowd pressed up
9 and started to ask him for his usual boon. Pilate replied, 'Would you like me to release the king of the Jews for you ? '
10 (For he knew the high priests had handed him over out of
11 envy.) But the high priests stirred up the crowd to get him
12 to release Bar-Abbas for them instead. Pilate asked them again, ' And what am I to do with your so-called king of
13 the Jews ? ' Whereupon they shouted again, ' Crucify
14 him.' ' Why,' said Pilate, ' what has he done wrong ? ' But they shouted more fiercely than ever, ' Crucify him ! '
15 So, as Pilate wanted to satisfy the crowd, he released Bar-Abbas for them ; Jesus he handed over to be crucified, after he had scourged him.

There are two difficulties in connection with this story. In the first place nothing is known of any such custom as is here described. That at the feast of the Passover the Roman procurators regularly released one prisoner, and that the crowds named the individual no matter what his offence had been, is not only without any attestation whatsoever, but also contrary to what we know of the spirit and manner of the Roman rule over Palestine. In the second place, Pilate is said to have found no wrong in Jesus, but the choice of Barabbas by the multitude forced him to put Jesus to death. This

CHAPTER XV, VERSES 6-15

unbelievable explanation looks definitely like the familiar tendency in the Passion narratives to exonerate the procurator and to throw the blame for Jesus' death on the Jews. In the third place, the crowds up to this point have been in favour of Jesus, so much so that the priests feared that an action against Jesus would cause an uproar. Here the crowd demands Barabbas' release and Jesus' death, though it is added rather lamely that the high priests stirred up the crowd.

Besides these difficulties there is a curious but important fact of the textual evidence to consider. In Matt. xxvii. 16-17 a body of manuscripts, which represents the reading of one of the earliest families, gives the name of the insurrectionist as, ' Jesus called Barabbas.' Origen also is a witness for this reading, which he regarded as having been inserted by heretics. His attitude is typical. Orthodox Christians would never have supplied the revered name Jesus as that of a criminal. Yet Jesus was one of the commonest Jewish names of the first century, as the text of Josephus abundantly shows. Evidently Jesus called (surnamed) Barabbas was the original text of Matthew. But this conclusion carries a further consequence : Jesus Barabbas was probably the form of the name in Mark's text also, the first name having dropped out. This would explain the curious reading of our text of Mark : ' And there was the one called Barabbas.' Some name has evidently dropped out.

The best explanation of the difficulties mentioned above seems to be that this identity of name has brought about an addition to the original narrative of how Pilate, having examined Jesus and having found Him innocent of any wrongdoing, nevertheless condemned Him to the cross. The Barabbas story is certainly not sheer invention, for, if so, the criminal would have borne a different name. It seems likely that a story of how the populace saved by its entreaties a prisoner named Jesus Barabbas was well known. That the crowd had urged the release of Jesus, the murderer, and let Jesus, the Messiah, go to His death, was a fact which invited Christian midrashic developments. The Barabbas story has coalesced in Christian tradition with the story of the trial of

THE GOSPEL OF MARK

Jesus. The polemical interest which it served is obvious. The Jews—the people, as well as the priests—were to blame for Jesus' death. Pilate, it is implied, did his best, but had to yield to the choice which the multitude made. Luke xxiii. 24-25 makes this thought especially clear.

Pilate's verdict of condemnation is not recorded. The sequel shows it to have been pronounced. **Jesus he handed over**, not to the Jews, but to his soldiers, **to be crucified**. This was **after he had scourged him**, the regular Roman custom in such executions.

xv. 16-20 : Mockery by Roman Soldiers

16 The soldiers took him inside the courtyard (that is, the
17 prætorium) and got all the regiment together ; they dressed him in purple, put on his head a crown of thorns
18 which they had plaited, and began to salute him with,
19 ' Hail, O king of the Jews ! ' They struck him on the head with a stick and spat upon him and bent their knees to
20 him in homage. Then, after making fun of him, they stripped off the purple, put on his own clothes, and took him away to crucify him.

From verse 16 it is clear that the trial took place at the **prætorium**, or residence of the procurator, and that the Via Dolorosa began at that point. Opinions are divided as to where the prætorium was. Popular tradition identifies the paved place in front of the prætorium mentioned in John xix. 13 with a piece of pavement which has been uncovered near the site of the Castle of Antonia. In support of this, it is argued that Pilate would have stayed in the fortress during the festival when the populace was so restless. But the evidence of Josephus is different. In *War*, ii. 14. 8, we are told that Florus, coming to Jerusalem at a time of turmoil, lodged in Herod's palace, which was in the south-west part of the city. After a riot which Florus' troops provoked, a number of Jews were arrested. On the following day ' he had a tribunal placed in front of the building and took his seat.' Before this tribunal were brought a number of citizens, who were first scourged and then crucified. This suggests that Herod's palace was the regular residence and tribunal of the procurators while in Jerusalem. Philo also states that it was in the palace of Herod that Pilate hung up the golden shields which brought him into trouble with the Jews (*Leg. ad Caium*, 31). These passages point to the palace rather than to the Fortress Antonia as the site of the condemnation, scourging, and mocking.

The mockery of the soldiers is similar to that which is said to have taken place in the house of Caiaphas. The charge on which He was condemned—that He claimed to be the King of the Jews—is made the subject of ridicule and brutal horseplay. The **purple** in which Jesus was dressed may have been the scarlet cloak of the Roman soldiers. The crown of thorns would most naturally be regarded as a wreath of some thorny substance plaited to imitate the laurel wreath of the Roman conquerors. There is nothing impossible or unlikely in the scene. But between the lines of the account one also seems to hear the solemn phrases of Isaiah's description of the suffering and humiliation of the Servant of Jehovah : ' I gave My back to the smiters . . . I hid not My face from shame and spitting. . . . He was despised and rejected of men ; a man of sorrow and acquainted with grief.' Certainly the episode was closely associated in Christian minds with those prophecies. That they have influenced the details of the scene is not unlikely.

xv. 21–32 : The Crucifixion

They forced Simon a Cyrenian, who was passing on his way 21 from the country (the father of Alexander and Rufus), to carry His cross, and they led him to the place called 22 Golgotha (which means the place of a skull). They offered 23 him wine flavoured with myrrh, but he would not take it. Then they crucified him and *distributed his clothes among* 24 *themselves, drawing lots for them* **to decide each man's share. It was nine in the morning when they crucified him. The 25 inscription bearing his charge was :** 26

THE KING OF THE JEWS

THE GOSPEL OF MARK

27 They also crucified two robbers along with him, one at his
29 right and one at his left.* Those who passed by scoffed at
him, nodding at him in derision and calling, ' Ha ! You
were to destroy the temple and build it in three days !
30 Come down from the cross and save yourself ! ' So, too,
the high priests made fun of him to themselves with the
31 scribes ; 'He saved others,' they said, 'but he cannot save
32 himself ! Let "the Christ," "the king of Israel " come
down now from the cross ! Let us see that and we'll
believe ! ' Those who were crucified with him also
denounced him.

* Von Soden retains ver. 28 (cp. Luke xxii. 37): 'So the scripture was fulfilled which says, *He was classed among criminals.*'

Crucifixion was a form of execution which the Romans from the days of the Punic War had used for slaves and criminals of the lowest grade. Their military officials employed it frequently in Palestine, particularly in the days before, and during, the revolt of A.D. 69–70. The method of its employment varied in details. While a single stake might be used, the usual form was to fix the victim to a cross. The cross-bar went either on top of or across the upright. The condemned individual was always scourged first, and made to carry the heavy crosspiece to the place of execution, which was always in as public a place as possible. Here he was stripped of his clothing, his hands fixed to the cross-piece either with nails or thongs, and his feet to the vertical beam. Death, which came from exhaustion, might be postponed even for days. Few more terrible means of execution could be devised. Pain, thirst, the torture of insects, exposure to brutal spectators, the horror of rigid fixation, all continuing interminably, combined to make it a supreme humiliation and torture.

John xix. 17 states that Jesus carried His own cross, but Mark tells of how a certain **Simon a Cyrenian** was forced to carry it. The latter is described as **the father of Alexander and Rufus**, who, not being designated in any way, evidently were well-known people. Why Jesus was relieved of the burden we are not told. It certainly was not from pity.

CHAPTER XV, VERSES 21-32

Later legend declared that He fell beneath the weight, and Simon was impressed to complete the journey. This explanation may be the correct one, and is supported somewhat by the fact of the death after three hours. Simon, of course, was a Jew, one of the Diaspora, but whether he was in Jerusalem permanently or merely on a pilgrimage is not told. Paul, in Rom. xvi. 13, sends his salutations 'to Rufus, the elect in the Lord, and to his mother,' and this may be one of the sons of Simon. The commonness of the name, however, apart from the uncertainty as to the original destination of that part of Romans, makes any dependence on this identification precarious.

They led him to the place called Golgotha (which means the place of a skull). The painful journey, beginning most probably at the palace of Herod, seems to have led outside the city walls. If it were known exactly where the northern wall ran at this time, the general limits of Golgotha's location could be specified. But, since this is not known, we have little to guide us. The tradition which located both Golgotha and the tomb at the site of the present Church of the Holy Sepulchre goes back to A.D. 327, when, under Constantine's direction, a number of holy spots were discovered, including the cave of the nativity in Bethlehem. The tradition cannot be traced earlier, and is open to considerable question. We do not know where Golgotha was located. All that can be said is that it was no doubt near one of the gates to the city on the northern or western side, and that it was near the public road. This last is shown by the reference in verse 29 to **those who passed by.** Apparently it was an open space with a rocky projection which gave some resemblance to a skull.

The drink which is referred to in verse 23 was an opiate. From Mark it would appear that this was given by the Roman soldiers. Billerbeck, however, has shown from the rabbinic writings that it was the custom of the Jewish women of the city to prepare this drink and send it to condemned men. The giving of the drink was thus a humane act. Jesus is said to have refused it. Mark means simply that He endured His sufferings to the end. The reason for the refusal, if authentic, must have been a desire to keep His mind clear until the last moment.

Then they crucified him. The restraint of the narrative is very noticeable. There is no effort to harrow the feelings of the reader. In Jesus' case nails seem to have been used, at least for the hands (see John xx. 25-27). But this last passage, plus the fact that the use of nails in the feet seems to be a somewhat later custom, suggests that the feet were bound. If so, the phraseology of Luke xxiv. 39 would be attributed to the influence of Ps. xxii. 16—'They pierced My hands and My feet.'

The division of the clothes among the executioners was a familiar detail. In Christian circles it was seen to be a fulfilment of Ps. xxii. 18, and the passage is quoted by Mark. By the time of the Fourth Gospel it was noticed that the psalm spoke of casting lots for the clothing. A distinction was, therefore, made. The garments were divided except the tunic; for this they cast lots.

It was customary in Roman executions for a placard, stating the charges, to be carried before the condemned person and affixed to the cross. According to Mark this read, **The King of the Jews.** The Fourth Gospel makes much of this inscription, declaring that it was in the three languages—Latin, Greek, and Hebrew. In this one sees a curious development, one analogous to that which took place as regards the fact of crucifixion. The cross at first was a stumbling-block and offence, but, having been accepted, the fact was embraced and made the centre of preaching and faith. So, also, as regards the charge on which Jesus was condemned. That it was as a political disturber must have been an embarrassment for Christian preachers. But the fact could not be denied, and as the Christian story took form, instead of minimizing or obscuring the charge, it is repeated, emphasized, and presented as an unintended witness to Jesus' lordship and rightful claims. But the charge cannot have been invented by Christian faith in the first place, any more than the fact of crucifixion.

With Jesus two robbers were crucified. Verse 28 adds, ' and so the Scripture was fulfilled which says, And He was numbered with the transgressors ' (Isa. liii. 12). The verse, however, is scarcely original. Not only is it omitted by the majority of the important manuscript authorities, but it does not appear in the parallel passages in either Matthew or Luke. The latter, however, has the quotation in another context in which Jesus speaks in general terms of His approaching humiliation and death (Luke xxii. 37). In other words, Isa. liii. 12 appears first with reference to the general fact of Jesus' death as a criminal, rather than in connection with the execution of the two robbers. This would seem to answer the suggestion that the latter detail is unhistorical and due to the prophetic passage. The crucifixion of a number of individuals at one time and place can be amply illustrated from Josephus.

To this scene, with its several realistic details, there is added a description of further insults and mockery. This is the third of these scenes, the first being placed in the high priests' house, and the second in the prætorium of the procurator. The emphasis on this element in the Passion story is due certainly to such Old Testament passages as Isa. liii. (' He was despised and rejected of men ') and Ps. xxii. The present scene is lacking in realism, and seems to be constructed out of materials with which we are already familiar, plus certain phrases from Ps. xxii. The references to the destruction of the temple and to Jesus as ' **the king of Israel** ' repeat the charges presented in connection with the trials. That the priests **made fun of him,** nodding their heads in derision, and that they and the passers-by called on Him to **save himself,** echo the statements and even part of the wording of Ps. xxii. 7-8. Nor can one imagine the aristocratic leaders of Jerusalem joining in a public mockery of a dying man who had been a popular idol. In the light of these facts, it is difficult to resist the impression that this account is a secondary development in the history of the Passion, a filling in of details of the crucifixion by those who had sat many times and heard the words of Ps. xxii. and Isa. liii. read as prophetic of the experiences of their Lord.

xv. 33-39: THE DEATH OF JESUS

When twelve o'clock came, darkness covered the whole land 33 till three o'clock, and at three o'clock Jesus gave a 34

THE GOSPEL OF MARK

35, 36 loud cry, '*Elôi, Elôi, lema sabachthanei*' (which means, My God, My God, why forsake me?) On hearing this some of the bystanders said, 'Look, he is calling for Elijah.' One man ran off, soaked a sponge in vinegar, and put it on the end of a stick to give him a drink, saying, 'Come on, let us see if Elijah does come to take him down!' But Jesus gave a loud cry and expired. And the curtain of the temple was torn in two, from top to bottom. Now when the army-captain who stood facing him saw that he expired in this way, he said, 'This man was certainly a son of God!'

37, 38

39

The crucifixion began, according to verse 25, at nine in the morning. At twelve we are told a darkness descended on the land, covering it over until the ordeal was finished. Luke explains this as an eclipse of the sun (xxiii. 44), but some of the early Christian Fathers recognized that at the time of the full moon of Passover, this was out of the question. Other natural phenomena have been suggested. Dalman, for example, speaks of a 'sirocco vapour which became so thick that it blotted out the sunlight' which he witnessed in April 1913 at the Sea of Tiberias. It is not necessary, however, to appeal to some such accidental natural occurrence, for darkness upon the land was the natural accompaniment of tragic events to ancient writers, both Jewish and Greek. It indicated the judgment of heaven on the event occurring. The darkness at the hour of Jesus' death parallels the angelic songs in the heavens which proclaimed the Saviour's birth. The thought of this darkness upon the earth during the hours of the crucifixion was rooted first of all in the Christian conviction that this was the world's supreme tragedy. There was a more specific influence which probably was at work also. In Amos viii. 9 they read the words, 'In that day, saith the Lord Jehovah, I will cause the sun to go down at noon, and I will darken the earth in the clear day.' This passage probably accounts for the tradition that the darkness began at noon rather than at nine in the morning, when the crucifixion took place.

CHAPTER XV, VERSES 33-39

The tradition related that it was about three o'clock that Jesus died. He gave a loud cry and expired. This was the last act. Mark and Matthew preface this with another cry, which they give, Mark entirely in Aramaic and Matthew with a change of the first words of address to Hebrew. This cry, *Elôi, Elôi, lema sabachthanei* (My God, My God, why forsake me?), has caused an endless amount of discussion. It is a quotation of the opening words of Ps. xxii.

In the first place, there is a linguistic or textual puzzle in connection with the words which is difficult to unravel. The Marcan form as printed above is Aramaic throughout. But the misunderstanding of the opening words as a call for Elijah (Eli'a) points to the Hebrew form, Eli, rather than the Aramaic, Elôi or Elahi. Matthew has made this change in the address, though he retains the rest of the cry in Aramaic. In Mark there is some manuscript support for the Hebrew, but it is not very strong. Nevertheless, it is clear that at some point in the tradition earlier than Mark the Hebrew words were quoted either in whole or in part; otherwise the detail about the call for Elijah would have been almost meaningless.

The real question, however, is the significance of these words. On the surface it would seem to be a cry of utter despair. One notes that Luke feels the inappropriateness of these as the last words of Jesus, and changes the cry to, ' Father, into Thy hands I commit My spirit ' (xxiii. 46). John substitutes the simple statement, ' It is finished.' But, in spite of this evidence, it is not certain that in Palestinian circles these words were regarded as expressive of despair. Dalman in *Jesus-Joshua* (p. 206) quotes a Midrash on the passage in Ps. xxii : ' When Esther instituted for herself her three-day fast, she prayed on the first day " My God." On the second day again she prayed " My God." On the third day she prayed, " Why hast Thou forsaken me ? " But when at last she prayed with a loud voice, " My God, my God, why hast Thou forsaken me ? " her prayer was answered at once.' This certainly suggests that in Jewish interpretation these words of the psalm were not regarded as an expression of despair, but as a prayer of the righteous in the midst of adversity. Certainly that is the way in which Mark regards the quotation on Jesus' lips. Had he considered it otherwise, he would doubtless have regarded it as a mistaken tradition, and left it out.

Thus, even if the words be historic, it is by no means certain that they indicate that Jesus died in a spiritual agony of believing Himself abandoned by God, as even so excellent a writer as Goguel suggests. But there are a number of considerations which make this premise rather dubious.

The fact which weighs most heavily against the authenticity of these particular words is that Ps. xxii. parallels the Passion story at so many points. Jesus was mocked with wagging heads and taunting words as in verses 6–8. Verses 14–15 describe the dissolution which comes with approaching death. Verse 15 mentions particularly the sufferings of thirst. Verse 16 mentions the piercing of hands and feet. Verse 18 states that the garments of the righteous one are divided among His enemies. The psalm was thus almost a portrayal of the Passion.

Now Mark xv. 37 tells of a loud cry from the cross, and the desire to fill in the content of the cry would have been very strong. With Ps. xxii. in the minds of those who preserved and transmitted the story, it is easy to believe that its opening words may have supplied the wording recorded. Regarded in the light of the faith of the psalm as a whole, and quite probably also in the light of the traditional scribal exegesis, these words would have seemed particularly appropriate. Furthermore, there are the linguistic data mentioned above. Although the first impression which is made by Mark's Aramaic is that it represents the original words uttered, we have seen that at an earlier stage the quotation was probably in Hebrew—at least in its words of address. Jesus spoke Aramaic in everday life. It does not seem very likely that the last cry would have been in the classical language of the scribes, even granting that Jesus knew Hebrew. At least it does not seem as likely as that the quotation was supplied by Christian readers of the Old Testament, and particularly of Ps. xxii.

CHAPTER XV, VERSES 33-39

The same problem of determining whether or not an episode in the account is due to an Old Testament passage applies also to the incident of the drink. Ps. lxix. 21 reads, ' In My thirst they gave Me vinegar to drink.' Is the story due to Psalms or not ? John xix. 28 says definitely that this was to fulfil the Scripture, but Mark does not have the quotation. On the whole, one is inclined to regard the giving of a drink as historic, and the motive, **let us see if Elijah does come to take him down,** as part of the early Christian elaboration of the story. In any case, there is nothing Messianic in the reference to Elijah. The latter was, in Jewish folklore, a valiant helper and defender of the righteous.

With the loud cry Jesus expired. His death at about three in the afternoon was unexpectedly soon. What caused it is not known. An internal breakage or collapse is often conjectured. Mark declares that **the curtain** which stood before the inner sanctuary of the temple **was torn in two.** The *Gospel to the Hebrews* said that a lintel of the temple of enormous size broke of itself. Matthew adds that an earthquake split the rocks and opened the tombs. These portents are not unlike some which are mentioned in the rabbinic writings as having occurred at the death of certain rabbis. The tearing of the curtain of the temple was probably understood in Christian circles to be a prophecy of its coming destruction.

The remark of the Roman officer need mean nothing more than that Jesus was a righteous individual and not a criminal. But Mark's readers probably took it as a confession of faith, the first one due to the power of the cross. It is not surprising that later tradition supplies further details concerning this officer. According to one tradition, his name was Longinus and he became a martyr, though this name is also given to the soldier who thrust the spear into Jesus' side. In the *Gospel of Peter* the officer is said to have been named Petronius.

XV. 40-41 : THE WOMEN WATCH FROM A DISTANCE

There were some women also watching at a distance, among 40 them Mary of Magdala, Mary the mother of James the

41 younger and of Joses, and Salomê, women who had followed him when he was in Galilee and waited on him, besides a number of other women who had accompanied him to Jerusalem.

This is a very striking conclusion to the account. In spite of much scepticism which has been expressed concerning it, it arouses considerable confidence. Had these witnesses been fabricated, as has been suggested, one would expect to be told that they were at the cross and both ministered to Jesus and received His last instructions. Furthermore, a purely imaginative creation would not have asserted that the only followers who witnessed the last events were women. But these arguments are really unnecessary. The Gospel nowhere shows any consciousness of needing to cite witnesses of the events recorded. Such a need might have been felt as regards the resurrection appearances, but scarcely concerning the crucifixion.

The mention of these women who did not desert their beloved Lord, yet feared to come within the circle of the brutal soldiers and so watched from a distance, may thus be accepted as a valuable historical reminiscence. If so, it is probable that the Christian account of the crucifixion goes back to their testimony. If one regards the taunts of verse 29 and the wording of the cry from the cross as later developments, the facts which Mark records are all such as could be observed from a distance.

The Fourth Gospel states that several women, including Jesus' mother, were present at the foot of the cross. Mark knows nothing of this, and the tradition which he incorporates practically disproves the Johannine account. Had friends or followers been present at the cross, the story of their courage and loyalty and the facts which they reported would have been one of the primary elements in the tradition of the Passion. This would have made meaningless and useless a tradition that a group of women watched from a distance. One is compelled, therefore, to regard the Johannine story at this point as a later conjecture, which in all probability was without foundation.

CHAPTER XV, VERSES 40-41

Mark mentions three of the women by name, **Mary of Magdala, Mary the mother of James the younger and of Joses, and Salomê.** Besides these there were others who had followed Jesus from Galilee to Jerusalem. The name of **Mary of Magdala** is a fixed point in the tradition. All of the Gospels agree that she was present at the cross. Luke mentions this Mary in viii. 1-3, in speaking of several women who followed Jesus in Galilee and contributed to His support, and describes her as one from whom seven devils had been driven out. The Latin tradition that she had been a notorious sinner, the one mentioned in Luke vii. 37, rests on no valid evidence, and is an unjustifiable blot on Mary's name. The second name in Mark's list cannot be identified, since we do not know which James is referred to. Matthew substitutes for Salomê, the third name, the designation, 'the mother of the sons of Zebedee.' Since Matthew is following Mark closely at this point, this identification has usually been accepted.

xv. 42-47 : The Burial

By this time it was evening, and as it was the day of Preparation 42 **(that is, the day before the sabbath) Joseph of Arimathæa,** 43 **a councillor of good position who himself was on the outlook for the Reign of God, ventured to go to Pilate and ask for the body of Jesus. Pilate was surprised that he was** 44 **dead already ; he summoned the captain and asked if he had been dead some time, and on ascertaining this from** 45 **the captain he bestowed the corpse on Joseph. He, after** 46 **buying a linen sheet, took him down and swathed Him in the linen, laying him in a tomb which had been cut out of the rock and rolling a boulder up against the opening of the tomb. Now Mary of Magdala and Mary the mother** 47 **of Joses noted where he was laid.**

According to Jewish law and custom, the dead were buried, if possible, on the day of death. If there were no relatives or friends to care for a body, it was a most meritorious deed for some individual to see that it received proper burial. There were also charitable societies whose particular work it was to assist at funerals and to provide a proper burial for those dying unattended, though these may have arisen somewhat later. Illustrations of this general attitude could be cited in abundance, but one which is particularly pertinent is sufficient. ' The Jews are so careful about funeral rites,' says Josephus, ' that even malefactors who have been sentenced to crucifixion are taken down and buried before sunset ' (*War*, iv. 5. 2). This was in accordance with Deut. xxi. 23, which required the burial before nightfall of one who had been hanged, since his body left upon the tree would defile the land.

Jesus died in the mid-afternoon. A burial before night in the light of this custom requires no special explanation. John xix. 31 implies that it was a special offence for the bodies to remain on the cross on the Sabbath. What is strange is the person who attended to the burial. **Joseph of Arimathæa** has not been mentioned previously, nor is there any further reference to him in the subsequent stories of the empty tomb nor the beginnings of the Church. Mark describes him as a **councillor of good position,** which is usually taken to mean that he was a member of the Sanhedrin, a conclusion which finds some support in Luke's wording in xxiii. 51. But Mark's phrase need not necessarily mean this, and, had Joseph been a member of the supreme council of the land, one would expect Mark to have said so. It is more likely that he was a member of one of the smaller courts which administered the affairs of the Jewish communities, but nevertheless a man of some importance and distinction. As to his attitude toward Jesus, we are told simply that he also was **on the outlook for the Reign of God.** The phrase reminds one of the similar description of Simeon, who blessed the infant Jesus in the temple at Jerusalem (Luke ii. 25), and would seem to indicate a devout Jew who was not, however, a recognized disciple of Jesus. That none of the disciples or the women take part in the burial —that the latter, indeed, knew the location of the tomb only because they **noted where he was laid,** and finally that Joseph does not appear in the subsequent Christian story, in spite of this connection with the central event, suggests that he was

CHAPTER XV, VERSES 42-47

not one of Jesus' recognized followers. Confirmation of this conclusion is found in a striking passage in Acts which is usually overlooked. In Paul's speech at Antioch it is declared that 'the inhabitants of Jerusalem and their rulers,' having secured Jesus' execution, 'took Him down from the tree and laid Him in the tomb' (xiii. 29). No doubt Joseph was interested in Jesus, and sympathetic toward Him, but his act would have had quite sufficient justification in the scribal teaching that it was in all cases a charitable and praiseworthy deed to provide burial for the dead. It was natural that the early Church in time came to view Joseph as a disciple. Even as early as the writing of Matthew the general phraseology of Mark is changed to give that effect. Certainty in the matter is probably impossible, but the facts point toward the conclusion that Jesus was placed in the tomb by one whose act was dictated primarily by the ethical teachings of Pharisaism.

The Jews did not bury their dead in cemeteries but in family tombs. These were by preference cut in the rock, though natural openings were utilized when possible. They had to be outside the city walls. There were several types of these, the general pattern being a chamber, in the walls of which were recesses to receive the bodies. Bodies could also be placed on shelves or slabs in the chamber. The entrance was closed with a rectangular-shaped block like a door, sometimes placed on hinges, or with a round flat stone fitted in a groove, which could be rolled back from the entrance, but which was too heavy to admit easy entrance. It was in a tomb of the latter sort that Joseph placed the body of Jesus. According to John xix. 41, the tomb was very close to the place called Golgotha. Mark does not say that the tomb had not been used before, as do the other Gospels, and one might regard this detail as an inference from the story of the empty tomb, except for a further fact. It was forbidden to bury in the tomb with one's fathers one who had been executed (*Sanh.* 46-7). It is probable, therefore, that Jesus was not placed in a tomb in which others had been buried. The empty new tomb was not a gesture of honour ; even in death, shame and humiliation were not escaped.

There are no details preserved as to the burial. Evidently none of Jesus' disciples was present. Mark states that Joseph bought the **linen sheet** in which the body would be wrapped. While this no doubt could be done on the afternoon of the First Day of Unleavened Bread, the text here seems unaware of any chronology which would make necessary a word of explanation in connection with the purchase. At this period expensive clothing was used for burial, so much so that a half-century later Rabbi Gamaliel directed that he be buried in simple linen clothing as a protest against the high funeral costs. There is no indication of any such extravagance in this case. The burial was certainly hurried, since sundown hastened, and one would naturally assume the simplest possible arrangements.

This account of the burial was important in early Christian circles for two reasons. In the first place, it emphasized and proved the death of Jesus, and thus established the resurrection. When Paul reminds the Corinthians of the gospel in which they have been instructed, the first phrases are that Christ died, that He was buried, and that He rose on the third day (1 Cor. xi. 3). This interest was quite apart from any tradition concerning the empty tomb. But from the standpoint of the latter it was necessary to mention the burial and to make it clear that the women who later were to visit the tomb had accurate information concerning it. Thus Mark names as the witnesses of the burial two of the women who in his account discovered the empty tomb.

There is no good reason to doubt the historical accuracy of this tradition that Jesus was buried by Joseph of Arimathæa in a rock tomb somewhere near the scene of the execution. The vagueness and generality of the account on all except the essential facts indicate that we have to do with a kernel of historical reminiscence and not a product of early Christian speculation.

xvi. 1–8: 'He Has Risen; He Is not Here'

xvi.
1 **And when the sabbath had passed, Mary of Magdala, Mary the mother of James, and Salomê bought some spices in**

CHAPTER XVI, VERSES 1-8

order to go and anoint him ; then very early on the first 2 day of the week they went to the tomb, after sunrise. They said to themselves, 'Who will roll away the boulder 3 for us at the opening of the tomb?' (for it was a very large boulder).* But when they looked they saw the boulder 4 had been rolled to one side, and on entering the tomb they 5 saw a youth sitting on the right, dressed in a white robe. They were bewildered, but he said to them, 'Do not be 6 bewildered. You are looking for Jesus of Nazaret, who was crucified? He has risen, he is not here. There is the place where he was laid. Go and tell his disciples 7 and Peter, "He precedes you to Galilee, as he told you —you shall see him there."' But they fled out of the 8 tomb, for they were seized with terror and beside themselves. They said nothing to anyone, for they were afraid of——

* Transposing the second clause of ver. 4 to the end of ver. 3.

The central proclamation of Christian preaching was that the story of Jesus did not end with His crucifixion by the Roman soldiers and His burial in a rock tomb near the place of execution. 'This Jesus did God raise up ; whereof we are all witnesses.' It was this event which gave meaning and significance to all that had preceded and transformed the life of Jesus from a tragedy to a triumph. That this was true for the second evangelist, as for the other writers of the New Testament, is abundantly evident, in spite of the loss of the conclusion of the work. The story which is now to be told is therefore the climax of the narrative.

The account under consideration is an introduction to this concluding section. It does not record an appearance of Jesus 'alive after His Passion,' but tells an impressive introductory story of how some devoted women went to the tomb, found it empty, and received the announcement from an angelic visitor that Jesus had risen.

Mark's account of the empty tomb differs from the accounts in the other Gospels on a number of points. But the comparisons bring out the greater simplicity and evident priority of the Marcan form of the story. Thus Mark knows nothing of a guard at the tomb such as Matthew records; the women fear only that they would not be able to roll away the stone. The story of the guard is evidently an addition which sprang up in answer to the Jewish explanation that the disciples stole the body of Jesus. Again, Mark has one angel who is seen within the tomb. Matthew tells of an earthquake, the guard falling to the ground, and the angel sitting on the great stone before the tomb. Luke and John both tell of two angels. Furthermore, Mark, in the text which has survived, tells only of the women finding the tomb empty and seeing the angel, while Matthew and John record appearances of Jesus at the tomb to one or more of the women. Finally it is probable on other grounds that the first resurrection appearances took place in Galilee rather than in Jerusalem, and Mark's account rests upon that form of the tradition. From various standpoints thus it appears that we have in Mark the account of the discovery of the empty tomb which stands closest to the original version.

The reason which Mark gives for the visit to the tomb **early on the first day of the week** is surprising. Burial rites among the Jews called for washing and anointing the body with fragrant spices. As there were no undertakers, this was done by relatives or friends. The women may have been aware that the burial took place hurriedly without these attentions, but that they should have had in mind caring for the body in this manner two days later seems strange. However, it must be admitted that those who first collected the Christian tradition were more familiar with Jewish burial customs and attitudes than we are, and in the absence of further data the Gospel statements, made without any apparent reluctance, that this was the purpose of the women's visit must be taken as evidence that this motive was possible. The Fourth Gospel, to be sure, has eliminated the detail, but only because it describes Joseph and Nicodemus as having already anointed the body. This last was not the earliest Christian belief, as can easily be shown. But if the purpose of the visit as here given seems difficult of credence, quite understandable motives were in

CHAPTER XVI, VERSES 1-8

any case present. It was customary for relatives to visit the tomb of their deceased for three days after burial. The motives for this were no doubt the normal, ever-present sentiments of affection and grief which are always operative, but also in Palestine prudential ones. Burial on the day of death always ran the risk of entombing a living person, and visits to the tomb guarded against this possibility. At least one case is on record in which an individual was saved by this means, and lived twenty-five years after his burial. The visiting of the tomb for three days would thus in any case have been a normal procedure.

On reaching the tomb the women found the heavy round stone which closed the entrance already rolled back. We are told that they entered and saw a figure whom Mark certainly regards as an angel. That angels were conventionally described as young men may be illustrated from 2 Macc. iii. 26, 33 and *Ant.* V. viii. 2, and that they wore white robes from Rev. vii. 13 f. The angel announced to them: (*a*) that Jesus had risen, (*b*) that they should tell His disciples and Peter that He had preceded them to Galilee, and (*c*) that they would see Him there. But they **fled out of the tomb and said nothing to anyone, for they were afraid.** And then, probably in the middle of a sentence, the Gospel breaks off.

Into many of the questions which have been raised in connection with this Easter story it is not possible to go in this volume. But there are three main ones which demand an answer.

(1) What was the conclusion which Mark wrote, or intended to write? The answer here is obvious. Already in viii. 31, ix. 31, and x. 34 Jesus had announced that after His death He would rise again, and in xiv. 28 He had declared, in words identical with the angelic announcement, that He would precede them into Galilee. There can be no doubt that Mark recorded, or intended to record, as the climax and conclusion of the story the appearance of Jesus to the disciples in their native district. Furthermore, it is extremely probable, from the special mention of Peter's name, that an appearance to Peter alone was recorded in the conclusion. Paul mentions

that it was to Peter that the Lord first appeared (1 Cor. xv. 8), and Luke xxiv. 34 refers to the same appearance. This appearance to Peter is also implied in the story of Peter's betrayal. One has difficulty in believing that the evangelist intended to close his work leaving the chief apostle of the circumcision in the status of one who denied his Lord with curses. Besides these appearances it is plain that something further was said about the silence of the women. But the difficulties in connection with this topic call for separate treatment.

(2) What is the significance of the statement that the women said nothing to anyone? Or, to put the same question differently, what caused the women to tell of their experiences?

Here there are two possibilities. The answer usually given is that, in the conclusion of Mark, Jesus appeared to the women and transformed their fear into joy. Such an appearance is recorded, of course, in Matthew and in John. But the words of the angel to the women certainly do not seem to anticipate any such encounter. The women are told that Jesus goes ahead to Galilee and that there He would be seen by His disciples. An appearance in Jerusalem seems definitely excluded, and one to the women in Galilee does not seem to be anticipated. True enough, in Matthew the same words of the angel are followed by the statement that Jesus soon afterwards appeared to the women in Jerusalem, and, in the light of this parallel, one cannot deny the possibility of the same inconsistencies in Mark. Matthew is plainly combining two traditions. Perhaps Mark had already done the same. But, in view of the double statement in Mark that Jesus would precede the disciples into Galilee (xiv. 28 and xvi. 7), it seems more likely that Mark's tradition contained only the Galilean appearances, and that these were to the apostles.

The fact that Paul's list in 1 Cor. xv. 3 ff. contains appearances to Peter and to the disciples as a group—all more probably in Galilee—but knows of no appearances to the women, strongly supports this view of Mark's conclusion. For clearly the Marcan tradition and the Pauline one are related to each other.

If for these reasons the suggestion of an appearance to the

CHAPTER XVI, VERSES 1-8

women in the lost conclusion of the Gospel be given up, there remains only one other explanation of the puzzling sentence with which the story breaks off. The author states that for a period the women remained silent concerning their experience at the tomb. Now it can be abundantly established from the Acts of the Apostles and the letters of Paul that Christian faith in the resurrection was based on the appearances of Jesus to His followers and not on the discovery of the empty tomb. The basic assertion of the early Church is clearly stated in the opening words of Acts that Jesus ' showed Himself alive after His Passion by many proofs, appearing unto them [the apostles] by the space of forty days and speaking to them the things of the Kingdom of God' (i. 3). That Paul does not mention the discovery of the empty tomb in his citation of the Christian proofs of the resurrection has been referred to. In other words, the experiences of the women at the tomb were either unknown or disregarded until after a belief in His resurrection had become established on other grounds. If the early Church was aware that this story played no part in the earlier stages of the movement, and was only brought to light later, some explanation would be necessary. Mark's final sentence gives this explanation—at first the women said nothing of those matters because they were afraid. After the disciples declared that Jesus had appeared unto them, they came forward with their story. In time we can see this part of the account developing. Not only do the women discover the tomb to be empty, but Jesus also appears to them (Matt. xxviii. 9 and John xx. 14), and they become the first witnesses of the resurrection. But this development was after Paul's day. He quite possibly knew of the women's story in the form in which Mark records it, and dated the resurrection as having taken place on the third day because of it. But to Paul's trained mind an empty tomb was not proof of the resurrection, and he rests his case on firmer ground.

(3) With this verse the Gospel ends. The arrangement of the Greek words makes it probable that it breaks off in the middle of a sentence, though a number of parallels have been cited recently to show that the writer may have meant a period

to be placed after **afraid**. But these parallels are not the normal form of expression. In any case, it is certain that the Gospel did not or was not intended to end here. In view of the importance of the Gospel of Mark in the history of civilization, it may fairly be said that this sudden unexpected conclusion is the greatest of all literary mysteries.

On further investigation the problem becomes more puzzling. Matthew and Luke evidently knew Mark only in the incomplete form in which it is known to us. The Lucan resurrection appearances are all in and around Jerusalem instead of in Galilee. Some have thought that Matthew's story of the appearance of Jesus to the disciples in Galilee is taken from Mark. But there is nothing in Matthew about an appearance to Peter, and Matthew's presentation that the women told the disciples and the latter proceeded to follow in a body (see xxviii. 8 and 16) is decidely different from the silence of the women and the scattered flight of the despairing disciples which Mark's narrative preserves. Nor can it be shown that the ending of Mark has survived anywhere else.

The explanation has been advanced that Mark's account differed from the other Gospels, and therefore it was deliberately suppressed. This hypothesis takes two forms. One makes the point of objection the location of the Marcan appearances in Galilee rather than in Jerusalem. The other view suggests that Mark's conclusion described the appearances of Jesus as spirit, not as flesh and blood, and that this was destroyed because of the encouragement it gave to the Docetic errors. The weakness of both forms of this explanation is plain. As regards the first one, it is obvious that the Gospel of Matthew, which places the only appearance to the disciples on a mountain in Galilee, was not destroyed. The second ignores the fact that Mark includes the story of the empty tomb, the point of which was that the actual body of Jesus had been resurrected. Against both it must be remembered that the early Christian habit seems to have been to neglect or to rewrite accounts which they might dislike, rather than to attempt to destroy them.

Thus we seem to be left with two possibilities: either

CHAPTER XVI, VERSES 1-8

the Gospel was never finished, which would explain why the ending has survived nowhere, or it was accidentally mutilated shortly after its completion and before copies were made of it. The latter hypothesis would seem to necessitate the supplementary assumption that the author died or left Rome shortly after completing the book, and before its mutilation, otherwise he surely would have repaired the damage.

Between these several possibilities there are no grounds for a decision. They all presume some accidental happening, either to the author or to the roll on which he wrote. On the whole, one inclines against the hypothesis that the author reached this crucial sentence and stopped in the midst of it, never to resume. The combination of chances which this view requires seems too great. True, the short-story writer O. Henry is known to have been seized while writing at his desk by an illness which proved fatal within a few days, but even in that case he was at the beginning of a story, not at its climax. In the days when writing was on fragile papyrus, an accident to the completed work, which we may presume was kept by an official of the Church at Rome, is more likely. If this be the explanation, the accident, which may have been due to a very trivial cause, was nevertheless, as E. F. Scott has described it, the greatest disaster in the history of the New Testament.

xvi. 9-20: THE ENDINGS WHICH HAVE BEEN ADDED*

(a)

Now after he rose early on the first day of the week, he appeared 9 first to Mary of Magdala out of whom he had cast seven dæmons. She went and reported it to those who had been 10 with him, as they mourned and wept; but although they 11 heard that he was alive and had been seen by her, they would not believe it. After this he appeared in another 12 form to two of them as they walked on their way to the

---

* The following appendix represents a couple of second-century attempts to complete the gospel. The passage within brackets in the first of these epilogues originally belonged to it, but was excised for some reason at an early date. Jerome quoted part of it, but the full text has only been discovered quite recently in codex W, the Freer uncial of the gospels.

THE GOSPEL OF MARK

13 country. They too went and reported it to the rest, but
14 they would not believe them either. Afterwards he appeared at table to the eleven themselves and reproached them for their unbelief and dulness of mind, because they had not believed those who saw him risen from the dead. [But they excused themselves, saying, ' This age of lawlessness and unbelief lies under the sway of Satan, who will not allow what lies under the unclean spirits* to understand the truth and power of God ; therefore,' they said to Christ, ' reveal your righteousness now.' Christ answered them, ' The term of years for Satan's power has now expired, but other terrors are at hand. I was delivered to death on behalf of sinners,† that they might return to the truth and sin no more, that they might inherit that glory of righteousness which is spiritual and imperishable in
15 heaven.'] And he said to them, ' Go to all the world and preach the gospel to every creature :
16 he who believes and is baptized shall be saved, but he who will not believe shall be condemned.
17 And for those who believe, these miracles will follow ; they will cast out dæmons in my name, they will talk in foreign tongues,
18 they will handle serpents, and if they drink any deadly poison, it will not hurt them ; they will lay hands on the sick and make them well.'
19 Then, after speaking to them, the Lord Jesus was taken up to
20 heaven and *sat down at the right hand of God*, while they went out and preached everywhere, the Lord working with them and confirming the word by the miracles that endorsed it.

* Or, the unclean things that lie under the control of spirits.
† The Greek is obscure at this point.

The above conclusion to the Gospel, with the exception of the bracketed portion, appears in the majority of manuscripts of Mark which have been preserved. That it is not the original ending, however, is plain from three considerations : (*a*) it is lacking in a number of the most important and

CHAPTER XVI, VERSES 9–20

dependable manuscripts, and some others have the different ending which is given below. (*b*) Eusebius, the most widely read Christian scholar of antiquity, states that in the oldest and best manuscripts known to him Mark ended with the words, ' for they were afraid.' (*c*) There is an obvious break in thought and style between verses 8 and 9. One manuscript of the tenth century states that the ending was written by Aristion, one of the early disciples of the Lord, whom Papias mentions. This late and unsupported testimony, however, is of dubious value.

Irenæus, about A.D. 180, quotes xvi. 19 expressly as from the ending of Mark, and the section was in the text of Mark which Tatian accepted for his *Diatessaron*. These citations show that the ending had been added long enough before this date for these writers to accept the passage without question. But the internal evidence does not suggest a date earlier than about the beginning of the second century. For the appearances enumerated represent a synthesis of the accounts in the canonical gospels. The appearance to Mary of Magdala is given in John and Matthew. The doubt of the disciples with reference to the women's report of the empty tomb is stated in Luke xxiv. 11. The appearance to **two of them as they walked on their way to the country** is the one which Luke records as taking place on the way to Emmaus. An appearance to the Eleven is given in Luke, and also in John. The saying, **Go to all the world and preach the Gospel to every creature**, is related to the final command given by the risen Christ in Matthew. The Ascension comes from Acts. Similarly, the miracles, listed in verse 17, which will follow those who believe are all illustrated in Acts, with the exception of the drinking of the deadly poison. This last detail may be related to the story which Eusebius says Papias told of a certain Justus, who ' drank a deadly poison, and yet, by the grace of the Lord, suffered no harm ' (*History*, iii. 39). The contents of the section thus suggest a sort of compendium of the proofs and promises of the resurrected Lord, made up some time after the beginning of the second century.

In some respects the section does not fit the Marcan text

which it completes. In the first place, nothing is said about appearances in Galilee. This may be attributed to the influence of the Lucan writings. More surprising still is the absence of any reference to the silence and fear of the women. One would expect a writer undertaking to supply a conclusion to a work to take up the narrative at the point where the document breaks off. The fact suggests that possibly this compendium was not composed as a conclusion to Mark, but that it was originally an independent document. In an age when the demand for Christian reading materials far outran the supply, and when, furthermore, no one of the documents in circulation gave all of the appearances of the risen Jesus, the production of such a document for catechetical or other purposes is entirely understandable. Such an explanation of the document makes it an early and brief illustration of the process which is seen later on the grand scale in Tatian's *Diatessaron*.

The section printed in brackets in verse 14 appears in a fifth-century manuscript. Jerome also quotes a part of it as in some manuscripts with which he was acquainted. Moffatt regards it as part of the original conclusion which was excised at an early date. The alternative would be to regard it as a later addition.

(b)

But they gave Peter and his companions a brief account of all these injunctions. And, after that, Jesus himself sent out by means of them from east to west the sacred and imperishable message of eternal salvation.

This ending is found in a few Greek manuscripts and versions. It was written obviously to complete Mark's account. The author's view is that the statement in verse 8, **they said nothing to anyone, for they were afraid**, meant that they made no public announcement of what they had seen and heard, but hastened to give the message which the angel had sent to Peter and the disciples. The phrasing of the second sentence suggests that the ending was added after the Christian message had spread over a large part of the Roman world.